COURTAULDS AND THE
HOSIERY AND KNITWEAR INDUSTRY

COURTAULDS

and the

HOSIERY & KNITWEAR INDUSTRY

a study of

ACQUISITION, MERGER & DECLINE

Bramwell G. Rudd

Courtaulds and the Hosiery and Knitwear Industry

Copyright © Bramwell G. Rudd, 2014

The moral rights of the author have been asserted by him
in accordance with the Copyright, Designs and Patents Act 1988

First edition

Published in 2014 by Crucible Books
an imprint of Carnegie Publishing Ltd
Chatsworth Road,
Lancaster LA1 4SL
www.carnegiepublishing.com

All rights reserved
Unauthorised duplication contravenes existing laws

British Library Cataloguing-in-Publication data
A catalogue record for this book is available from the British Library

ISBN (softback) 978-1-905472-06-2
ISBN (hardback) 978-1-905472-18-5

Designed, typeset and originated by Carnegie Publishing
Printed and bound by in the UK by Short Run Press

Contents

Abbreviations	xv
Preface	xvii
Glossary of terms	xix
Introduction	1
Background	2
Courtaulds' problems	2
Diversification	3
The business faces trouble	3
Problems for Kearton's successors	5
Chain stores and multiples	5
The power of Marks & Spencer	6
Corporate and organisation structure	6
Decline and irresistible price pressure	7
1 Origins: Courtaulds – The Hosiery and Knitwear Industry	9
Courtaulds *c*.1685–1963	9
Samuel Courtauld	10
Crisis in the crape industry	12
Tetley's high risk strategy	13
Samuel Courtauld IV	15
The rayon production boom and the impact of war	16
After the war – rayon under threat	17
Problems loom close	18
Frank Kearton	19
The Hosiery and Knitwear Industry *c*.1580–1960	19
World War One	21
The interwar years	22
Fashion and technology	23
World War Two	23
The period after World War Two	23
Liberalisation of trade and global trading	24
The structure of the hosiery and knitwear industry	24

2   Kearton widens the conglomerate   25

Background to the 1960s diversification   25
Diversification   26
The continued importance of rayon   26
Momentous times – The ICI takeover bid   28
Capital-intensive plants and the Lancashire spinning and textile industry   30
The failure of the 'Northern Plan'   30
Success under Kearton   31
Vertical trading   32
Kearton expands into hosiery and knitwear   33
A captive market for Celon   33
Proprietary yarn brands   34
Problems in the hosiery and knitwear industry   35
Kearton presses ahead   35
A management misfit   36
Strategy   37
Perspectives   38

3   The History of the Hosiery and Knitwear Acquisitions   39

In rise and decline   39
Background to the Hosiery and Knitwear Acquisitions   41
Fully-fashioned styles lose favour   42
Aristoc Ltd   46
The interwar years   46
The effects of World War Two   46
Courtaulds acquired Aristoc   47
Bairnswear Ltd   49
Bairnswear after World War Two   49
Courtaulds acquired Bairnswear   51
Ballito Hosiery Mills Ltd   52
Post World War Two   52
Ballito responds to decline   53
Ballito reorganisation hits trouble   53
Courtaulds acquired Ballito   54
George Brettle & Co. Ltd   55
Absentee management   56
The return of owner management   57
Post World War Two   57
Courtaulds acquired Brettles   59
College Hosiery Ltd   60
Courtaulds acquired College's capacity   60

Contour Hosiery Ltd	61
Intercontinental Fibres acquired Sellors and becomes Contour	61
Post World War Two	62
Machine building – a misfit	62
Further expansion	62
Courtaulds acquired Contour	63
Cook & Watts Ltd – West Riding Hosiery	63
Stockings unprofitable	64
Courtaulds acquired (Holts) West Riding Hosiery	64
Corah Sock Division (N. Corah & Sons)	64
Better times for Corah	64
St Margaret and Marks & Spencer in the interwar years	65
World War Two	66
Corah develops the M&S connection and ethos	66
Corah split up	66
Courtaulds acquired Corah Sock Division	67
Derby and Midland Mills – Blount & Co. Ltd	69
Impact of war	69
Change of ownership	69
Stockings prices under pressure in the 1960s	70
Favourable prospects for Blounts	70
Derby & Midland acquired by Courtaulds	71
Foister, Clay & Ward Ltd	71
F,C&W – three sites in Leicester	72
F,C&W – Kegworth	72
F,C&W – Derby	73
F,C&W – Middlesbrough	73
F,C&W – three factories at Mansfield	73
F,C&W – Irvine, Ayrshire	74
Courtaulds acquired Foister, Clay & Ward	74
Hendry & Spiers Ltd	75
Courtaulds acquired Hendry & Spiers	76
Highfield Productions Ltd	76
Courtaulds acquired Highfield Productions	77
Irvine Knitters Ltd	77
Courtaulds acquired Irvine Knitters	78
Kayser Bondor Ltd	78
Kayser Bondor – a famous brand name	79
Expansion after World War Two and the M&S connection	80
KB profits in decline	80
KB diversifies	81
KB takes action	81

Courtaulds acquired KB	82
Kilsyth Hosiery Co. Ltd	82
Courtaulds acquired Kilsyth Hosiery	83
Meridian Limited	84
Labour shortages in Nottingham after World War Two	86
Courtaulds acquired Meridian	86
Declining brand sales	86
A major acquisition	87
I. & R. Morley Ltd	87
Samuel Morley – outstanding entrepreneur	88
Expansion under Samuel Morley	88
Samuel Morley's successors	89
Morley in trouble after World War Two	89
Disastrous losses	90
Morley reorganises	91
Courtaulds acquired Morley	91
Percy Taylor Ltd	94
Courtaulds acquired Percy Taylor	94
Prew-Smith (Harry) Ltd	94
Courtaulds acquired Prew-Smith	95
R. Rowley & Co. Ltd	96
The interwar years	96
Rowley – A multi-product firm	97
Management change	98
Change in the supply chain	98
Rowley abandons stockings manufacturing	99
Rowley in decline	99
Courtaulds acquired Rowley	100
Skolnick Ltd (P. Beasley & Co. Ltd)	100
Courtaulds acquired Skolnick	101
Stewarton Hosiery Co. Ltd	101
Courtaulds acquired Stewarton	102
(Wolsey Ltd) Lyle & Scott	102
The Interwar Years – difficult times for Lyle & Scott	102
Lyle & Scott and 'Y front'	103
Success after World War Two	104
Lyle & Scott acquired by Wolsey	104
Wolsey Ltd	104
Successful policy in the interwar years	104
Challenges after World War Two	105
Wolsey supplies chain stores	106
Wolsey – Corah merger talks fail	106

	Courtaulds acquired Wolsey (Including Lyle & Scott)	106
	Moving towards Kearton's departure	107
4	**Kearton's Legacy**	**110**
	Complex and fragmented	110
	Mixed success	111
	Structure under Kearton	112
	Courtaulds' main board changes	112
	Financial reporting channels	113
	Company structure	113
	Management reporting – non-financial	114
	Kearton in personal control	115
	Integration and decline of the fine-gauge hosiery businesses	116
	The importance of nylon in the supply chain	117
	The factories were subservient	117
	Celon – a problem yarn, creates culture problems	117
	The decline of the fully-fashioned stockings trade	118
	The acquisitions	118
	Rationalisation	119
	A new use for the Brettle's Belper site	120
	Fine-gauge hosiery – a basic commodity product	121
	Total integration for fine-gauge hosiery	122
	Courtaulds narrows the hosiery brand offer	122
	Expansion in the 1960s – but Courtaulds fine-gauge hosiery loses its way	123
	Courtaulds fails to benefit from the improving market	123
	Hosiery business re-development project	123
	Excess capacity in hosiery	124
	Low-cost imports	125
	Italian high quality tights	125
	Contraction	126
	Deeper cuts	126
	Integration and decline of the knitwear businesses	126
	Courtaulds' three major knitwear acquisitions	127
	Medium sized knitwear enterprises	127
	Satellite acquisitions	128
	Morley – a mixed wholesaling and manufacturing company	128
	Rowley, a mixed product – multi-site general manufacturer	128
	Knitwear reorganisation commences quickly – F,C&W is split up	128
	Wolsey fully-fashioned knitting closed	130
	Further coordination	130
	Client portfolios introduced	130

Selling prices	130
Fully-fashioned knitwear in rapid decline	131
The brand business	131
Retrenchment	131
Technology – Shaped garment panels	132
Further retrenchment	132
Wolsey factories weakened	134
The non-M&S business	134
Rowley struggles on	135
Lyle & Scott and Jockey brands	135
Courtaulds sells Lyle & Scott	136
Further decline	136
Low-cost imports	136
Integration and decline of the knitted underwear businesses	137
The early shakeout	138
Price competition	139
Meridian and Meridian Prew-Smith Division	139
Courtaulds centralises underwear knitting	140
The Underwear Product Group	140
Children's underwear – non-M&S	142
The Mothercare chain	142
Offshore processing – children's underwear	143
Globalisation of trade – M&S	143
Technology	144
Central Underwear Knitting closed	145
Wolsey Brand	145
Management buyout for Wolsey brand name	146
Lyle & Scott 'Y' Front and Jockey	146
Wholesale	146
Closure	146
The integration and decline of the sock businesses	147
Foister, Clay & Ward	147
More sock factories	148
Rowley absorbs Contour	149
Rowley – the advantage of a multi-product range	149
Meridian – the minor brands	150
Wolsey – the major player	150
Courtaulds Sock Division	151
Decline in children's socks	152
Courtaulds Sock Division – a failed concept	152
Philosophy and culture	153
Consolidation	153

	Sock division disbanded	153
	Courtaulds and Marks & Spencer	154
	Courtaulds disposes of Wolsey brand	154
	Children's socks centralised at Queen St Leicester	155
	Courtaulds Sock Division (second version)	155
	Globalisation of trade	156
	Rowley closes	156
	Kearton's legacy in retrospect	156
	The contribution of the acquisitions to the product sectors	157
5	**Change under Kearton's Successors: Devolution and Demerger**	**159**
	Devolution of control	159
	Economies of scale	160
	Courtaulds' structure	163
	Knight's response	163
	Chairman of Courtaulds Textiles plc 1990–93 and 1993–1995	164
	Weakening trading conditions	164
	The breakdown of vertical trading	165
	Multidivisional control	165
	Main board retains vital powers but devolution proceeds	166
	Central aspects of control	167
	Specific circumstances in textiles	168
	Courtaulds Textiles formed 1985	168
	Courtaulds recognises the global threat	169
	Courtaulds, M&S and CTG 2000	170
	Demerger	171
	Results under Kearton's successors	172
	Perspectives	173
6	**Employment, Labour and Industrial Relations**	**174**
	Background	174
	Early trade unions	174
	Trade unionism in the factories	175
	Between the World Wars	175
	The rise and fall of trade unionism from the 1960s	176
	Decline looms	176
	Flexibility, new technology and strikes	177
	Rise and decline in employment	178
	NUHKW merges to become KFAT	180
	Occupations and gender specific work	182
	The NUHKW and gender	188
	Systems of piecework and rate setting	188

Traditional negotiated piecerates		188
Straight proportional measured work		189
Measured day-work		190
Gender and payment		191
Teamwork and quick response		193
Rate fixing problems		195
Benefits and working conditions		197
Physical working conditions		198
The impact of health and safety legislation		199
Courtaulds' employer representation and wage bargaining		200
Staff salaries		202
Staff and worker relations		202
Recruitment and training		203
Sweatshops and low-wage competition		205
Outworkers and part timers		206
Management and technical staff		208
Courtaulds' management void		208
Background of the chairmen		211
Continuity of top management		211
The value of effective middle management		213
Professional staff		214
Technical training		214
Designers		214
Human resources management		215
Career progress		216
Notes to Chapter 6		217
7	**Changing Markets**	**220**
	Courtaulds in the supply chain	220
	The wholesale trade	221
	Courtaulds and the wholesale distributors	222
	Wholesaling – a problem for Courtaulds	223
	Direct to retail	224
	The relationship with Marks & Spencer	224
	Decline by sector	225
	Fine-gauge hosiery manufacturing in decline	226
	Knitwear manufacturing in decline	229
	Knitted underwear manufacturing in decline	232
	Sock manufacturing in decline	234

8	**The Changing Supply Chain**	**237**
	Government policy and labour shortages	237
	The Geography of Courtaulds' hosiery and knitwear factories in the UK	238
	Courtaulds did not influence the geographic spread	240
	The industry manages decline	241
	Small firms, multi-location firms and conglomerates	241
	Employment in the regions	242
	Liberalisation of world trade and globalisation	243
	The Multi-Fibre Arrangement	243
	Low-cost competition	244
	The industry's response	247
	UK brand operator direct to retail	247
	UK based multinational contract supplier	247
	Supply chains	248
	Traditional supply chain	248
	The UK brand operator 'direct to retail'	249
	The UK based multinational contract supplier	249
	Cluster groupings	250
	UK cluster chart	251
	Knitting machine industry	251
	Clear advantage on the demand side	252
	Upstream industries	253
	Specialist suppliers	254
	Dyeing and finishing	254
	High Street and multiple retail outlets cluster	255
	Warehousing and distribution	255
	Perspectives	255
9	**Courtaulds Textiles plc 1990–2000**	**256**
	Problems from the 1980s	256
	The prospects for the industry	258
	Confidence in M&S	258
	Demerger 1990	260
	Management – The main board	262
	Structure of Courtaulds Textiles plc	263
	Continuing decline	263
	Noel Jervis as chief executive under Christopher Hogg	264
	The final decline	266
	European mainland expansion	267
	Colin Dyer as Chief Executive	269
	Claremont	270

	Courtaulds Textiles plc in disarray	271
	Takeover bid	271
	Sara Lee gains control	272
	Post script	273
	New Policy under Brenda C. Barnes	274
10	**Epilogue**	**275**
	Leadership and Corporate Governance	276
	Organisation and Structure	280
	Organisation under Kearton's successors	281
	Scale and Scope	282
	Wholesaling in Courtaulds' supply chain	284
	Globalisation and the supply chain	284
	Changing fashions	286
	Technology	287
	Courtaulds and Marks & Spencer	288
	Management Education	290
	Industrial relations and gender	291
	Courtaulds Textiles plc loses its corporate identity	293
	Perspectives	294
	Decline of the UK hosiery and knitwear industry	294
	Corporate decline of Courtaulds Textiles plc	295

APPENDICES

Appendix 1		**297**
	The Mansfield Hosiery strike	297
Appendix 2		**299**
	Trade organisations, Directories etc.	299
Sources and Bibliography		**301**
Index		**307**

Abbreviations

AVC	American Viscose Corporation
BHS	British Home Stores
BNS	British Nylon Spinners
EEC	European Economic Community
F,C&W	Foister, Clay & Ward
GATT	General Agreement on Tariffs and Trade
HATRA	Hosiery and Allied Trades Research Association
HRD	Human Resources Department
ICC	Inter Company Comparisons
ICI	Imperial Chemical Industries
IRC	Industrial Reorganization Corporation
KB	Kayser Bondor
KFAT	National Union of Knitwear, Footwear and Apparel Trades
KIF	Knitting Industries Federation
M&S	Marks & Spencer
MFA	Multi-Fibre Arrangement
NMC	Nottingham Manufacturing Company
NUHKW	National Union of Hosiery and Knitwear Workers
PRC	People's Republic of China
STA	Short Term Arrangement
WTA	Wholesale Textile Association

Preface

WHEN I first entered the industry in 1966 I had no idea that it would provide a life-long interest and that I would be writing this book over four decades later. I cherish memories of factory owners, directors, managers and shop floor workers, customers and suppliers and many others that it has been my privilege to meet since that time, and many have become personal friends.

There were prosperous years that provided employment for many thousands of us particularly in the East Midlands and the Borders of Scotland. Sadly, during the long and painful decline of this old industry many moved on to new work or retired and we have lost touch but I hope that this book will revive happy memories.

While researching this subject I have become indebted to a large number of people, only a few whom I can mention here. These include many academics, researchers, archivists, librarians and industry experts who have given their time very generously and explained the background to the events examined here. Without them the whole project would have been impossible.

A special word of thanks must be given to Professor Emeritus Stanley D. Chapman of the University of Nottingham Department of History, who guided me through my early research; to Professor Chris Wrigley, Head of the Department of History, who has been a constant source of encouragement throughout; and to Professor John Wilson of the Nottingham Business School and now Director of Newcastle Business School. Their advice and expertise have been invaluable and it has been a pleasure to work with them.

I am grateful to Akzo Nobel UK Ltd, successors to Courtaulds plc, the National Union of Hosiery and Knitwear Workers, Sara Lee Courtaulds and to Ruddington Framework Knitters for allowing me access to their archives during the time I was researching my Ph.D. Their curators' advice has been invaluable and their knowledge of the industry has seemed inexhaustible. I have also had the pleasure of discussing the statistics of the industry with the late Jack Smirfitt, former Librarian of the Hosiery and Allied Trades Research Association who had a vast store of knowledge of the textile industry and was

Curator of the Ruddington Framework Knitters' Museum. Their friendship, help and encouragement was vital to the completion of my thesis and this book.

None of those referred to above bear any responsibility for any errors or for any opinions expressed; these are entirely my own.

Every reasonable effort has been made to trace copyritght holders, but if any items requiring clearance have been unwittingly included, amendments will be made at the earliest opportunity.

Finally I want to thank my wife Joy for the encouragement she has given me without which this book would never have been commenced, let alone completed.

Bramwell G. Rudd
2014

Glossary of terms

acrylic A manufactured fibre in which the fibre-forming substance is any long-chain synthetic polymer composed of at least 85% by weight of acrylonitrile units.

cellulosic *see* man-made fibres.

circular knit Weft knit fabric made on a circular needle-bed knitting machine which presents the fabric in tubular form. Circular stockings are frequently referred to as 'seamfree'.

crape Originally plain silk gauze. This was later altered by the introduction of an embossing process in which the fabric was passed between heated embossed rollers. The fabric became known as 'crêpe Anglais'.

cut and sew The manufacture of garments from fabric cut to shape from rolls of fabric or flat unshaped panels.

filament Filament yarns are produced by an extrusion process and each filament can be many miles long. Filament yarn can also be cut into short lengths before being twisted to form yarn. (*See also* staple fibres.) When used in cigarette filter tips it is called 'tow'.

fully-fashioned Fabric knitted flat into shaped panels. The garments or stockings are assembled using seaming machines.

interlock A special fabric used extensively in underwear manufacture. It is smooth on both sides and has low elasticity.

lockstitch machine A term used in the trade to describe the industrial equivalent of the domestic sewing machine.

lycra A proprietary manufactured fibre in which the fibre-forming substance is composed of a polyurethane further reacted to give a complex network characterised by high elasticity. The generic names are elastanes (Europe) and spandex (USA).

man-made fibres Cellulosic fibres are chemically regenerated from natural fibrous material. Synthetic fibres are synthesised from non-fibrous materials, i.e. simple chemicals. Both were referred to as 'man-made', although this term is now being replaced by 'manufactured'.

nylon 6 and nylon 66 A manufactured fibre in which the fibre-forming substance is a long-chain synthetic polyamide. Nylon 6 and 66 have slightly different properties and chemical constructions.

overlock An overlock machine trims and oversews fabric for edging, hemming and seaming. It is used for garment assembly in cut and sew manufacturing.

staple fibres Natural fibres such as raw cotton, wool, hemp and flax have varying fibre lengths which can be twisted to produce yarn.

Introduction

OVER the past thirty years or so, the clothing industry of the United Kingdom has suffered a period of almost terminal decline yet historians have largely ignored this phenomenon, notably in the case of the hosiery and knitwear branch of the industry.

Professor S. D. Chapman has written the only book of real substance dealing specifically with the entire UK hosiery and knitwear industry to be published in recent years. Chapman and F. A. Wells have described the hosiery and knitwear industry in general terms, but this present book is the first to examine in depth the latter years of the rise and fall of the industry, using the experience of Courtaulds in that context. Wells[1] wrote too early and both he and Chapman[2] covered a long time span. Others have written about closely related industries; again, these[3] have been more broadly based. Owen's recent book is written from the corporate angle and focuses on the worldwide reshaping of the man-made fibres industry using Courtaulds as his case study.[4]

Owing to the lack of published material, reliance is placed extensively on information gathered from private files and from interviews with former workers and managers in the industry. The combination of these sources allows the period from 1960 to the end of the twentieth century and beyond to be examined in detail and follows much of the work in the three-volume history of Courtaulds by D. C. Coleman,[5] and the text brings together two separate and very different

---

[1] Wells, *The British Hosiery Trade: Its History and Organisation* (Curwen, London 1972). This book is based on earlier work from 1935.
[2] Chapman, *Hosiery and Knitwear: Four Centuries of Small-Scale Industry in Britain*, c.*1589–2000* (OUP, Oxford 2002).
[3] Singleton, *Lancashire on the Scrapheap* (OUP, Oxford 1991). Honeyman, *Well Suited: A History of the Leeds Clothing Industry, 1850–1990* (OUP, Oxford 2000).
[4] Owen, *The rise and fall of great companies: Courtaulds and the reshaping of the man-made fibres industry* (OUP, Oxford 2010).
[5] Coleman, *Courtaulds: An Economic and Social History*, vol. 1, *The Nineteenth Century – Silk and Crape* (Clarendon Press, Oxford 1969), vol. 2, *Rayon* (Clarendon Press, Oxford

historic strands: Courtaulds, the chemical and industrial conglomerate; and the hosiery and knitwear industry.

Background

Courtaulds' known history goes back to the Huguenot refugee Courtauld family that came to England from France in the late 1600s and set up as wine merchants. The second generation became famous silversmiths, and subsequent generations entered the silk crape industry and under family leadership amassed a fortune. Around the end of the nineteenth century the crape industry began to decline and in response to this threat the firm was reorganised, new products were introduced, and the business was launched as a public company in 1904. Courtaulds' management can be categorised into broad and recognisable classic headings; partnership and family-owned business, followed by the introduction of professional management, which augmented the family directors and led to the development of one of the greatest fibre-producing companies in the world.

Courtaulds' problems

By the 1950s Courtaulds faced severe contraction in sales of viscose rayon, its major product, but it was not immediately recognised that this was not simply a fashion change, or the end of the post-war boom. In 1961 there was a hostile takeover bid for Courtaulds by the competing fibre manufacturing firm, ICI. This was repulsed, and it fell to the dynamic new managing director Frank Kearton to produce the improved results promised at the time of the takeover bid.

C. F. (Frank) Kearton was a 'larger than life' figure who came to power during a period when viscose rayon, the firm's basic product, was under threat from other fibres in which Courtaulds had little established business and the whole future of the company was in doubt. Share prices and profits were low and this had made Courtaulds vulnerable to takeover. The cellulosic products that made up 96% of the production were causing acute problems: viscose rayon was in decline, Dicel was in decline as a fashion fabric, and Tricel sold in low volumes. An acrylic product, Courtelle, at that time still only a minor part of the firm's business, was vulnerable to competition from Monsanto's Acrilan and DuPont's Orlon. Nylon was a product with tremendous potential, but the firm had no manufacturing capacity of its own other than a small pilot plant at Spondon, Derbyshire.

The firm's strategy was to try the classic and traditional methods of meeting the downturn. These were reducing selling prices, more aggressive selling, making sure that all possible sales outlets were covered, and giving priority to product

---

1969), vol. 3, *Crisis and Change, 1940–1965* (Clarendon Press, Oxford 1980).

improvement; but the problems were still not arrested. There was no simple alternative strategy. There was no prospect of the firm developing a commercially successful new 'wonder fibre', no prospect of selling unsuccessful rayon-producing plants and, having just repelled the ICI bid, largely on the basis of projected improved profits, there was no possibility of selling the whole business (at a knock-down price) to a competitor such as DuPont. This would have led to job losses and was too politically sensitive.

Diversification

Kearton sought new sources of profit and market power by embarking on a programme of acquisitive vertical diversification, development of Courtaulds' Courtelle and Courtaulds' nylon (Celon) sales, and moving into cognate industries. There began a series of acquisitions in the spinning and weaving industries aimed at safeguarding its market for fibres, and between 1963 and 1968 there was a big move into the hosiery and knitwear industry when Courtaulds acquired over twenty firms and groups of firms in the trade. The development of this manufacturing chain, vertically trading from fibre manufacture to factories producing finished garments, took place in an era when the hosiery and knitwear industry was still expanding in the UK.[6]

Detailed histories of hosiery and knitwear businesses are not common for the period after World War Two. A section of this book is devoted to the story of the acquisitions, and for most of these firms this is the only history that has been completed. It allows the reader to gain some understanding of the diverse nature of these firms and the complexity of the problems faced by Courtaulds' managers in their task of attaching them to the parent company and moulding them into product- or client-based divisions.

There is therefore a need to examine in detail the problems that faced the various single and multi-product, and single and multi-location UK hosiery and knitwear manufacturing firms, with their individual inherent cultures, when attempts were made to integrate them into Courtaulds, a large international, industrial, chemical and fibre conglomerate.

The business faces trouble

The text examines how Courtaulds, a highly funded and previously successful multinational manufacturing conglomerate, with access to the UK's greatest retailers, reacted to changing domestic and global trading conditions and why its hosiery and knitwear manufacturing sector went into almost total oblivion.

---

[6] 1974 proved to be the high point of the industry and from then on it was in relentless decline.

Tesco, Baldock, a former Kayser Bondor factory. Photograph © 2007 Traveler100.

In particular, it focuses on the following challenges and Courtaulds' response:
- increasing competition in the fibres industry
- changes in the nature of the retail trade
- the relationship with Marks & Spencer
- globalisation and the supply chain

There will also be discussion of the following theoretical issues
- leadership and corporate governance
- organisation and structure
- scale and scope in the hosiery and knitwear industry

This exposes three major issues
- that the Kearton inspired vertical supply chain approach was unsuited to the business environment in which it subsequently had to operate
- that globalisation of trade opened up the UK clothing industry to intense low-cost competition that could not be countered, the outcome being inexorable decline

- that the fate of the firm, and its hosiery and knitwear businesses, in good times and bad, was at the mercy of Marks & Spencer's fortunes in a way that was outside Courtaulds' control

Problems for Kearton's successors

By far the biggest problem faced by the hosiery and knitwear trade was low-cost imports. To some extent the trade had, in the Kearton era, been helped by the increasing demand for knitted goods during a period of increasing prosperity. Also, from 1961 to 2005, the UK industry benefited from a series of measures that limited the imports of clothing into the UK, the most important being The Multi-Fibre Arrangement (MFA) of 1974. Towards the end of the 1960s, trade became more difficult as the industry operated in a more competitive environment, and from the mid-1970s there was a relentless phasing out of restrictions on imports of garments from low-cost countries. There followed an even more hostile environment for trade. UK manufacturers had to face the reality that competitive advantage was lost. Employment in productive industries fell by 63%[7] in the period 1974–2002, but in the hosiery and knitwear industry the fall was far worse, at around 88%[8] over the same period.

There was no superior technology exclusive to the UK factories. Closeness to the customer was of less advantage as transport became faster and information technology allowed instant transfer of information between customers and suppliers.[9] Labour and other costs in the developing world were only a fraction of UK costs, and capital that might previously have been invested in the advanced economies was being diverted to low-cost countries.

The vertical trading system set in place by Kearton also proved to be a hindrance to the firm's own factories as the customers demanded wider choice of yarn. The quality of Courtaulds' yarn was somewhat suspect and prices at which the yarn was transferred from the yarn mills to the garment manufacturing units were above the competitive market price, and the whole concept of the 'vertically integrated clothing conglomerate' constrained the clothing businesses and protected the yarn mills from price and quality pressure.

Chain stores and multiples

As multiple stores expanded, their power over the suppliers became stronger. They were the only outlets that could provide the big orders needed to keep the large

---

[7] Office of National Statistics. Abstract of Statistics – All Employment.
[8] Refer to Tables 3.1, 3.2 and 3.3.
[9] The suppliers normally used English as the common commercial language.

manufacturers in worthwhile business. However, as the man and woman in the street became more demanding and fashion-conscious and expected more choice, bulk production for mass markets gave way to complex production for the same mass market. The manufacturers then had to cope with shorter production runs and more complex distribution problems.[10]

The chain stores were in fierce competition with each other and began to acquire, often via existing UK suppliers, an increasing proportion of goods from low-cost countries. The aggressive competition in the retail clothing sector, which by the 1990s included superstores such as Tesco and Asda, brought increasing pressure to supply goods made in low-cost countries at prices that Courtaulds' UK factories could not match. This off-shore sourcing was a strategy which Courtaulds' leaders had to embrace in a bid to survive.

The power of Marks & Spencer

The Marks & Spencer connection was absolutely critical to the fortunes of Courtaulds' clothing businesses. Marks & Spencer provided expansion over many years and only faltered seriously in the late 1990s. M&S demanded loyalty, cooperation and dedication to their needs in a way that was not equalled by other customers. This required the manufacturers to make and hold large stocks in anticipation of further sales, often without a formal contract and entirely at their own risk. If sales did not materialise the manufacturer could be forced to liquidate these stocks at a considerable loss. Furthermore, should sales of a product be slow M&S might require the supplier to take a damaging reduction in the price, sometimes retrospectively.[11]

Unfortunately for Courtaulds, M&S held on too long to its 'buy British' policy, which it exploited heavily in its advertising, and this hindered an orderly transfer of purchases to low-cost overseas factories and led to the inevitable under-cutting of the M&S pricing structure by its competitors.

Corporate and organisation structure

Even when Kearton was still in command it was becoming increasingly clear that Courtaulds' policies were hindering his subordinates and that there were serious failings in the concept of a business that was vertically structured from forestry and the production of wood-pulp,[12] or from other primary materials,[13] right through to the manufacture of the finished garments; in practice there were

---

[10] Particularly when supplying new emerging retailers such as Next.
[11] This was referred to as 'making a contribution'.
[12] The basic raw material for cellulosic fibres.
[13] For example, acrylonitrile for acrylic fibres and caprolactam for nylon 6.

a vast number of exceptions to the rule. Kearton's legacy was an organisation structure that was weak and did not operate as a modern multidivisional business.

Kearton's successors were faced with trying to organise a management structure for the clothing businesses. These had been added piecemeal, and from the earliest days of their acquisition until the final demise were in a state of flux, with changing managements, changing client bases, and the normal fluctuations of a fashion industry. Their unsettled nature and complicated product mix made even the construction of an organisation chart showing clear lines of command almost impossible.

The situation was complicated further by the mixture of acquisitions in the spinning and weaving, plastics, paint, packaging, forestry, chicken farming and many other industries, and the acquisition policy brought with it complexity of organisation on a scale that Courtaulds had not faced before. By the 1960s the firm was operating as a loose divisionalised multinational organisation with features of a holding company, and at the same time was attempting to integrate a newly acquired hotch-potch of garment and hosiery and knitwear firms.[14]

The installation of a 'multidivisional' head office highly centralised and controlling all functions including sales, personnel, purchasing, and technical advice never showed any likelihood of success and was never seriously attempted. Although the UK clothing acquisitions' shares became fully owned by Courtaulds, the conglomerate was run as a type of hybrid 'holding company' with most management functions being retained under the control of each management group.[15]

Decline and irresistible price pressure

Kearton's successors needed to respond to worsening trading conditions and were forced to make strategic changes. There were major reorganisations, devolution of control and reductions in capacity. These changes took place under a new style of management with a more modern consensual nature – an issue that will be discussed later at some length. It was under this new management that the global threat to the UK textiles and garment industries was formally recognised and

---

[14] Further diversification in the 1960s included the acquisition of a large stake in the Lancashire cotton industry. This subject is covered more extensively in Knight, *Private Enterprise and Public Intervention: The Courtaulds Experience* (George Allen and Unwin: London, 1974), Chapter 3.

[15] Multidivisional head office control was favoured by American business theorists. Chandler, in *Scale and Scope: the Dynamics of Industrial Capitalism* (Belknap, Harvard 1994) and Channon *The Strategy and Structure of British Enterprise* (Harvard Business School Press, 1984). This American structure was highly suitable for large corporations with a relatively simple product range.

new strategies were put in place in response to the conditions and the challenges of the times.

Ultimately the industry was overwhelmed by low-cost imports. The cost of the basic materials, that is, yarn, packaging, buttons and zips, and sewing thread in the UK, without any other costs,[16] was often even higher than the total price paid to the Far East producers for the importation of completed knitted garments into the UK. Therefore it is manifestly clear that it was impossible to meet price competition and there was no possibility of increasing volumes of production to make economies of scale because higher sales actually led to greater losses.

---

[16] To sell competitively the UK manufacturers would not fully recover the cost of the material or any of the labour and overheads and would make no contribution to profits.

ONE

Origins: Courtaulds – The Hosiery and Knitwear Industry

Courtaulds c.1685–1963

IN ORDER TO ESCAPE religious intolerance Augustin Courtauld, a Huguenot, came to England from France some time between 1685 and 1700.[1] In the latter part of the sixteenth century the Courtauld family was known to be living on the island of Oléron off the Atlantic coast near La Rochelle. Through the generations this industrious trading family had prospered, so it must be no surprise that Augustin continued in his familiar trade of wine merchant in England.

It is not known why his sons did not carry on in the same trade but were apprenticed to goldsmiths and silversmiths and then established their own business in St Martin-in-the-Fields where they became master craftsmen prospering moderately in eighteenth-century London. For three generations the family produced sumptuous silverware for the London aristocracy, but, in another change of trade, George Courtauld I set the family on a new course when he entered the silk throwing trade as an apprentice in Spitalfields, London, in 1775. By 1800 he was manager of a silk mill at Pebmarsh, Essex, and around 1815 he entered into a partnership in a Braintree silk mill, but this partnership was dissolved in 1823 after a dispute with his partner, and he died in 1834.

---

[1] The historic background given here relies upon information taken from Ward-Jackson, *A History of Courtaulds* (Curwen 1941), and Coleman, vol. 1. (1969).

Samuel Courtauld

It was George's son, Samuel Courtauld, who set the family on the path to fortune. Samuel commenced work at the age of fourteen in the Pebmarsh mill. In 1816, around the time when his father was in dispute with his partner, Samuel set up his own business as a silk throwster at Bocking. The firm commenced making mourning crape in 1830. This was a popular fabric in Victorian Britain, and Samuel Courtauld & Co. developed a special powered loom for the production of this material that gave them a considerable financial advantage over the competing hand-power producers operating at that time. The factory was technically advanced by 1840 having gas lighting and 240 steam-power operated looms. By 1850 the firm had become the biggest and most successful of the English crape manufacturers.

While the firm also manufactured a range of coloured crape gauzes on the power looms, production of mourning crape continued to rise, from 2,000 packets in 1830 to about 25,000 in 1850, when this product dominated the firm's production. The years 1850 to 1885 were the golden years of black crape production. Debts were cleared and mills were acquired at Braintree, Chelmsford and Earls Colne, all in Essex. The existing mills were extended and updated, and electric lighting was installed in the 1880s. At that time Samuel Courtauld & Co. was one of the biggest employers in the silk industry, with around 3,000 employees, and became the largest provider of manufacturing employment in the area.

There had been a severe shortage of work and much poverty in East Anglia in the early nineteenth century. Many of the old cloth manufacturing firms did not survive, but Courtaulds was highly successful. The firm built schools and cottages for the employees, started reading rooms, libraries and coffee-rooms; long service

Queen Victoria in mourning © Royal Photographic Society / NMeM / Science & Society Picture Library

workers were paid pensions, and salaried staff and skilled men had paid holidays. Wages for skilled men were high for the times, but this does not reflect the real cost of labour as the industry was largely dependent on lower-paid girls and young women, many under the age of sixteen, to operate its plant, as Table 1.2 shows.

Wages were low for the large number of women and girls who worked on machine tasks such as winding, throwing, drawing, doubling and spinning. There was little alternative work available in the area, but for many years the firm offered expanding employment and although Samuel would not tolerate trade unionism, many families were attracted to work for the firm.

Figures for 1833 show that, fortunately for Samuel Courtauld Ltd, female employees' wages in the silk industry in East Anglia were considerably lower than those in other parts of the country, notably in the Lancashire cotton industry.

Table 1.1 *Employment in silk and cotton factories, 1833*[2]

	Females as percentage of all employees	*Females under 11 as percentage of all female employees*	*Females under 16 as percentage of all female employees*
Silk			
Norfolk, Suffolk and Essex	96	14	53
Somerset	80	12	39
Derbyshire	63	8	35
Cotton			
Lancashire	50	4	33

Table 1.2 *Average weekly wages of girls and young women in silk and cotton factories, 1833*[3]

Ages	Below 11 s. d.	11–16 s. d.	16–21 s. d.	21–26 s. d.	26–31 s. d.	31–36 s. d.
Area						
Norfolk, Suffolk and Essex (silk)	1 5	2 7	4 0¾	5 0	4 11	4 4
Derbyshire (silk)	1 11	3 6½	5 11	7 0½	7 7	7 0½
Lancashire (cotton)	2 4¾	4 3	7 8½	8 5	8 7¾	8 9½

[2] Quoted in Coleman, vol. 1. p. 97.
[3] Quoted in Coleman, vol. 1. p. 98.

Samuel's drawings from the firm were enormous by the standards of that time: £46,000[4] per year on average for the last ten years of his life. He retired in 1865 and died in 1881, 'the very embodiment of the Victorian success story in industry he ended his days ... rich, lonely and unhappy in a vast country mansion'.[5]

Crisis in the crape industry

George Courtauld II controlled the firm from 1865, but, while things continued very much in the same conservative manner and the owners received substantial profits for some years, it was too good to last. Selling prices fell sharply, and profit falls turned into heavy losses. Reduced profitability was a feature of several sectors of the economy at that time but in the black mourning crape industry there were severe problems, particularly the decline in the Victorian fashion for formal mourning wear. Moreover, by 1891 the firm was using outdated technology, with over 1,000 looms of 1830s design and the original steam engines still in use. As technology had advanced in the traditional textile areas of the north of England, Essex had not kept pace. Either the owners had not recognised the need for action or, having noticed it, had failed to act in time.

Eventually remedial action was taken by the family. The firm was reconstituted as a private liability company with seven shareholders. George Courtauld remained a substantial shareholder along with his younger brother and son, but of vital importance to the future of the firm was the hard-driving new appointee Frederick Nettlefold, a member of the important Midlands grouping Chamberlain-Nettlefold. Other directors brought in at that time were D. H. Browne, a friend of Nettlefold and a London stockbroker with interests in several mining and railway companies, as well as two Warren brothers who were closely associated with Browne. These new directors brought no new experience of the textile industry, but they did recognise the need to spend money to introduce new technology. New talent was also recruited when Henry Tetley was appointed head manager and Thomas Latham, sales manager. These two men, who were not related in any way to the Courtauld family, had day-to-day control of the firm and made a vital contribution to its success over the next twenty-five years.

Within a few years the old steam engines were replaced along with many of the old looms. A chemist was employed and a programme of diversification was undertaken which widened the product range. High costs were attacked, the quality of the mourning crape was improved, and at the same time new but cognate products were introduced, such as coloured chiffon and other fabrics in

---

[4] *International Directory of Business Histories*, vol. 5. This is a modern equivalent of *c*.£2.3 million per annum.

[5] Anonymous author. *The Origin and Development of Courtaulds between 1700–1986.*

silk. For less affluent customers, cotton and lower-priced crape were added to the product range. In response to the falling demand for mourning crape, the firm developed the export market, particularly in the years 1884–86, and slowed an otherwise dangerous decline. The demand for mourning crape fell considerably after the death of Queen Victoria in 1901. However, by 1903 total sales had recovered, mainly through exports, but profits were at a lower level than in former years. For the closing years of the nineteenth century the profits were highest in 1885, at £110,633, and lowest in 1889, at £10,240.[6]

Tetley's high risk strategy

Faced with static profits at around only thirty per cent of those in the early 1880s, and tariff barriers rising in one country after another, Director Tetley recognised the need for a new source of profits to replace the crape profits. Tetley's high-risk proposal, made in April 1904, was to purchase the UK patent rights to produce artificial silk fibres. This was turned down by the board, but the owner of the patent (C. H. Stern) was persuaded to delay the sale for a short time while Courtaulds was engaged in converting the firm into a public company. The launch was highly successful, and sufficient funds were then made available to buy the UK patents for the newly discovered artificial silk (viscose filament-rayon)[7] manufacturing process for £25,000.

Table 1.3 *Paid up capital at launch in 1904*

Ordinary shares	£200,000
5½% Cumulative preference shares	£200,000
4½% First mortgage debenture stock	£200,000

Source: *The Origin and Development of Courtaulds between 1700 and 1986.*

The risk was enormous. At a time when the British were notoriously conservative about scientific education, none of the directors knew anything at all about chemistry.[8] The firm purchased the rights to an undeveloped patent and had no means of knowing if the problems of this unreliable process could be overcome or at what cost. Moreover, if successful, the new artificial silk would be in direct competition with the firm's existing products. Despite the risks, a new rayon producing factory was set up in Coventry, workers were employed, and the chemist employed in Essex was sent to be the manager. Fortunately

---

[6] Coleman, vol. 1 1969. Appendix.
[7] In the 1920s *Artificial Silk* became known as rayon.
[8] See Sanderson, *The Universities and British Industry* (Routledge 1972), p. 17.

Rayon advertisement from *Textile Mercury and Argus*, 29 June 1934, designed to show the superiority of Courtaulds Rayon.

Courtaulds already had technical skills in silk-throwing, weaving, dyeing and finishing that could be employed in the daunting task of developing the new product to commercial standards at a remarkable pace. Despite all the problems, the factory started production in 1905, and by 1908 had become profitable, with the main quality and consistency problems having been overcome by 1911. By 1909, the yarn profits had exceeded those from the old textile section of the firm, so that in 1917 when Tetley became Chairman he was the head of a highly successful business.

In 1909 the firm paid £31,000 for the American rights to produce rayon, a deal that was to have an enormous impact. A new subsidiary, The American Viscose Company (AVC)[9] was set up at Marcus Hook, Chester, Pennsylvania in 1911 and for several years massive dividends flowed back to the UK. Subsequently, as Table 1.4 shows, the firm expanded out of all recognition over the next five decades

---

[9] The American Viscose Company was later renamed the American Viscose Corporation.

or so, developing substantial interests in chemicals, packaging, paint and related industries and by 1960 Courtaulds was the largest fibre producer in the world.

Table 1.4 *Courtaulds' diversification*

Year	Development
1816	Silk
1825	Fabrics
1905	Rayon yarn
1905	Engineering
1916	Chemicals
1918	Rayon staple
1920	Acetate yarn and fibre
1920	Plastics
1930	Packaging film
1937	Garments
1937	Rayon tyre cord
1937	Protein fibre
1941	Nylon yarn and fibre (with ICI)
1946	Alginate yarn
1950	Triacetate yarn and fibre
1951	Rayon pulp
1951	Bonded fibre fabric
1951	Polyolefin yarn
1957	Acrylic fibre
1958	Paint
1958	Packaging containers
1958	Steel tyre cord
1959	Paper pulp
1960	Fluted paper

Key: (shaded): fibres/ yarns/ fabrics
(unshaded): allied and new fields

Source: Courtaulds Report and Accounts 1959–60.

Samuel Courtauld IV

Tetley died in 1921 and was succeeded by Samuel Courtauld IV, great nephew of the founder of the family silk firm. Samuel was the leader of the firm until 1946, the year before his death. As a well known industrialist he represented the firm

Augustine Courtauld silver cake basket. © Museum of Fine Arts, Houston.

very effectively to the government and it was under his leadership that Courtaulds achieved a position of respectability in the world of manufacturing enterprises. Unfortunately, it was not until the initiative was lost with the development of nylon by Courtaulds' USA competitor DuPont that Samuel realised that this was a science-led business. By then it was quite late in his career and it was left to others to rectify the lack of effective research and development within the firm.

It is ironic that the name Courtauld will be remembered not so much as an outstanding worldwide manufacturing firm but for Samuel's other interests. Samuel set up the world famous 'Courtauld Institute of Art'. He gave his house (in memory of his wife) so that the Institute could be established and gave his collection of impressionist paintings as the foundation of the gallery which was opened in 1958. The Courtauld Galleries at Somerset House, London, now hold the fabulous Courtauld Silver Collection and famous impressionist and post-impressionist masterpieces and is part sponsored by Akzo Nobel, the successor firm to Courtaulds plc.

The rayon production boom and the impact of war

The interwar years from 1919 to 1939 were boom years for rayon output. World output expanded from 29 million lbs to over 2,200 million lbs, an increase of 7,600%.[10] As rayon proved to be a highly versatile product it was possible to produce cheap hosiery, underwear, furnishings, and dress materials in rayon and rayon mixtures. However, the firm, in common with many throughout the world,

---

[10] *The Origin and Development of Courtaulds between 1700–1986*, p. 14.

began to suffer difficulties in the 1930s and despite the increasing output of rayon the profits failed to equal those of the 1920s. As the patents expired, the most famous 'name' in the UK industry became the competitor, British Celanese, a chemicals firm that also had a large presence in the warp knitting industry.[11] In the USA, there were dire problems. Sales and profits there were badly down from 1928 until 1932, taking a long time to fully recover. Profits from European subsidiaries were also badly affected.

One venture was to have an enormous impact on the fibres industry. Just prior to World War Two Courtaulds entered into an agreement with ICI to produce nylon, the new wonder fibre that had been developed by DuPont and for which ICI had obtained the UK rights. The joint ICI/Courtaulds enterprise, British Nylon Spinners (BNS) at Pontypool, began production in 1940 but production for civilian purposes was delayed until after the war. When war broke out in 1939 Courtaulds had just pioneered a new development, a high tenacity rayon tyre cord, a product with high potential in a growing market. The war had a serious effect on the firm which had to contend with shortages of labour and materials, increased taxation, and the Coventry air raids in 1941. Yet none of these problems hit the company as much as the loss of the American Viscose Corporation (AVC) which Courtaulds was forced to sell as part of the 'lend lease' deal negotiated by Winston Churchill. Britain was buying armaments on a massive scale and running into large trading deficits and as a consequence, John Hanbury-Williams, a director of both Courtaulds and the Bank of England, was forced by a deal between the British and American governments to part with 95% of AVC. Eventually compensation of £27,125,000 was paid by the British Government and at the end of the war Courtaulds was cash-rich and held over £32 milion in government securities.[12]

After the war – rayon under threat

After the war, while sales of rayon recovered, they failed to exceed pre-war levels, because nylon was taking over from rayon for stockings and crease-resistant treated-cotton was becoming popular for use in other garments. Fortunately rayon began to be used increasingly for tyre cord and staple fibre production.[13] The firm addressed the problem of the lack of investment during the war by setting up new rayon plants in Carrickfergus in 1950 and Grimsby in 1957 and also setting up capacity in Australia and re-entering the American market with a new plant in Alabama.

---

[11] Wells (1972), p. 196. After British Celanese was acquired by Courtaulds the warp knitting plants of the two firms were merged to form Furzebrook Knitting Co. Ltd. Possibly the biggest warp knitting plant in Europe.

[12] *The Origin and Development of Courtaulds between 1700–1986*, p. 19.

[13] Cellulose diacetate was a closely related product used for cigarette filter tips.

Courtaulds' rayon was used extensively in tyre manufacturing from 1937. This advert appeared in *Punch* magazine.

Problems loom close

The good years were soon over. A takeover bid for Courtaulds by ICI (joint partner in the BNS nylon plant) was repulsed in March 1962. As part of the ultimate financial settlement Courtaulds sold its shares in BNS to ICI and Courtaulds was left with only a small nylon plant at the British Celanese (by then a Courtaulds subsidiary) nylon site at Spondon, Derbyshire, that was still only at the development stage. Worsening trading conditions faced Courtaulds fibre manufacturing plants as the firm was still almost totally dependent on rayon, a declining product. With the arrival of the competitors' new fibres, which were rapidly becoming available, there was a weakening customer base for the firm's products which must have struck fear into the hearts of the Courtaulds management.

Frank Kearton

It was left to the key figure and driving force, Frank Kearton, to counter these threats.[14] In an attempt to develop a captive market for rayon and the increasing output of nylon and the new acrylic fibres, actions included the acquisition of a large stake in the hosiery and knitwear industry and other 'downstream' industries. 'Vertical expansion' proved to be highly problematical as attempts were made to graft a fashion based industry on to this high volume chemical engineering firm, a dream that ultimately failed.

The Hosiery and Knitwear Industry c.1580–1960

Hand knitting has been an established method of producing garments for thousands of years, certainly since the time of the pharaohs. However, due to its slowness it has long gone as a major commercial activity, it is now mainly a hobby and in the right hands superb garments can be produced on two knitting needles. The mechanised hosiery and knitwear industry has a history going back over four centuries.[15]

Development depended on two pieces of technology. The barbed needle, reputedly invented around 1589 by William Lee, a country parson at Calverton in Nottinghamshire, was used in the early mechanical knitting frame and the more complex latch needle, invented about 1849 by Matthew Townsend, a Leicester hosier, has been used extensively in the knitting industry as it has developed.

The early centre of hand and foot powered framework knitting was London. However, the East Midlands knitters had a plentiful supply of wool which encouraged a migration of knitters from London in the early eighteenth century. Cheaper labour and freedom from the restrictive practices of the London-based Worshipful Company of Framework Knitters also encouraged this trend.[16] Until the 1840s, the industry had been mainly cottage based. By the time mechanisation had become a viable reality in the 1850s, the industry had become firmly centred in the East Midlands, and in Hawick and the Scottish Borders. Despite many setbacks, including a depressed period in the

---

[14] Davis, *Merger Mania* (Constable 1970), Chapter 5.
[15] A detailed history of the invention of the stocking frame can be found in Felkin (1867). A reprint has been produced with a new preface, Felkin (1967), Chapter 3. For a comprehensive overview of the early history of the industry see Chapman (2002), Chapter 1.
[16] Gurnham, *History of the Trade Union Movement in the Hosiery and Knitwear Industry* (NUHKW, Leicester 1976), p. 3.

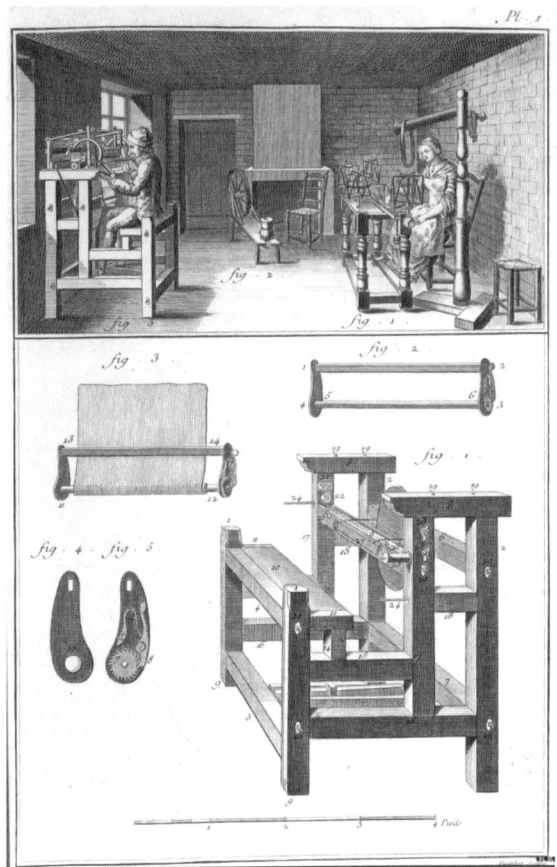

Early knitting machine © Science Museum / Science & Society Picture Library

first half of the nineteenth century when labour prices were forced down,[17] the industry thrived, generally in the form of family owned businesses.[18]

The factory system began to take off with the introduction of steam power in the 1850s, following which there was rapid technical progress from the 1870s. By the start of the twentieth century the factory system was firmly established and firms that feature in this account, such as J. B. Lewis (later renamed Meridian), I. & R. Morley, R. Walker (Wolsey), Rowley, and Corah were already leaders of the industry.

---

[17] Chapman (2002), Chapter 3 'In the Doldrums.'

[18] The machine knitting industry was based on the invention of the 'knitting frame', c.1589. The early history of the industry is covered in much detail by Wells in his invaluable aid to the study of the foundation of the industry. Wells (1972), Part 1.

Martin Green, the last traced commercial framework knitter 2013, working a William Lee knitting frame. Photo courtesy of Martin Green.

World War One

There were significant problems during the First World War due to the shortage of raw materials. However, the shortage of labour was by far the most important limiting factor with conscription, introduced in 1916, making the situation even worse. There was a big increase in the number of 'substituted' female workers who were paid identical wages to the men.[19] To counter these pressures, there was an increase in shift working and a drive for more efficiency. The industry survived the war remarkably well and was able to complete massive military contracts.

---

[19] Gurnham (1976), pp. 78–79.

The interwar years

After the First World War the industry, in common with many others, enjoyed a very short boom and then a period of short but severe recession late in 1920. Around this time the trade unions had little difficulty in removing those 'substituted women' who were on 'men's wages'. However, the growing trend for women to work in industry and forsake more genteel employment and domestic service had accelerated during the war. Subsequently they joined a labour market that could exploit the low cost of female labour, particularly in the expanding cut and sew sector of the industry. As a result, the number of people employed in the industry was over 50% greater in 1924 than in 1912.[20]

Difficult trading conditions were again encountered during the worldwide slump of the early 1930s. In that period the government encouraged the development of industry in deprived areas. Examples of firms that expanded in this way were Kayser, in South Wales[21] (aided by government grants), and Pasolds Ltd[22] at Langley (Buckinghamshire), but these developments were very small when compared to employment in the traditional centres of the trade.

Despite high and persistent unemployment in parts of the North of England, South Wales and parts of Scotland, the industry benefited from the nation's increasing spending capacity. A League of Nations report on household earnings in 1936 identified Leicester as the 'second most prosperous city in Europe'[23] and one has only to visit the prosperous suburbs at Stoneygate and Knighton to see how some of the money was spent by the factory owners on large and prestigious houses.

Technology improved and despite the worldwide economic problems of the 1930s, and the threat from low-cost imports,[24] government intervention enabled the trade to develop behind a shelter of import tariffs, the 'permanent' tariff being set at 20% in 1932. There was an exception for artificial silk (rayon) goods, on which customs duty was set at 33.33% in 1925 and silk and artificial silk hosiery duty was increased to 43.33% in 1932.[25]

---

[20] Wells (1972), p. 169.

[21] For a history of Kayser Bondor see Chapter 3.

[22] For the history of Pasolds Ltd see Pasold, *Ladybird Ladybird: a Story of Private enterprise* (MUP 1977).

[23] Chapman (2002).

[24] By 1936, Japanese cotton textiles were subject to quantitative restrictions in forty markets. Silberston (1984), p. 17.

[25] Wells (1935), p. 228.

Fashion and technology

While the import tariffs were vital to survival, the fashion scene was favourable. In an era of higher living standards, there was increasing demand for variety and at the same time 'less patching and darning and more replacement'.[26]

In the interwar years the women's hosiery industry benefited from the fashion for shorter skirts, and fine-gauge machines were introduced to produce expensive fully-fashioned silk stockings, but the cheaper rayon became increasingly popular in the rapidly expanding circular-knitted seamless hosiery trade. The men's sock sector also benefited from the general move away from boots to shoes, making fancy socks more desirable. For women, knitted outerwear, such as twin sets, became more fashionable and lighter knitted underwear was also in increasing demand, particularly in the new 'interlock' fabric.[27]

World War Two

During the Second World War, the clothing industries were placed on a war footing, and this entailed a massive reduction in the size of the UK hosiery and knitwear industry, with many employees entering the armed forces or transferring to other occupations, particularly engineering. A number of firms within the industry were concentrated[28] into nucleus groups which produced large government contracts and a limited quantity of 'utility' civilian merchandise.[29] In combination with rationing of civilian clothing this concentration took capacity out of production that would otherwise have been under-utilised (due to limited yarn supplies and the wartime shortage of labour), and as a result a considerable amount of floor space was released for other essential industries.

The period after World War Two

After the war, many of the workers who had been directed to other employment or entered the armed forces did not return to the industry. As clothes rationing ceased[30] and demand increased, the depleted industry became extremely short of

---

[26] Wells (1972), p. 171.
[27] See Meridian Ltd Chapter 3.
[28] Comprehensive details of concentration can be found in the *National Hosiery Manufacturers Federation. Provisional Register of Members 1943.*
[29] The Ministry of Defence and the Crown Agents were large customers that traditionally placed their orders in the UK both in war and peacetime. With the end of the 'Cold War', and the advent of the EEC with cross boundary purchasing this business was vastly reduced. Interview D. Pick 22 March 1999.
[30] Clothes rationing ended in 1949.

workers, as did other textile industries.³¹ At this time the shortage of workers was a limiting factor for output and with a shortage of merchandise, higher disposable incomes and the demand for comfortable informal clothing during the post-war boom, for a short time the manufacturers could sell all they could produce.

Liberalisation of trade and global trading

In the twentieth century there were major changes in international economic relations. While in the interwar years there was protection from foreign imports, following World War Two the General Agreement on Tariffs and Trade (GATT) allowed imports on a scale not encountered before. It soon became ominously clear that the industry was not competitive in a world market and to limit the effects of 'disruptive' imports the Long Term Arrangement of 1962 (LTA) slowed the imports of cotton goods from developing countries. It was around this time that Courtaulds began to buy up over twenty companies and groups in the industry.³²

The structure of the hosiery and knitwear industry

Until the mid-1960s, the UK hosiery and knitwear industry was almost totally composed of small- and medium-sized firms, many under the control of hereditary leadership. The low level of capital required and the availability of second-hand machinery made it possible for a business to be started in a small way and for new entries to proliferate.³³ However, as the major chain stores increased in size, the larger manufacturers were able to supply these mass markets and benefit from the scale and scope of their large manufacturing and distribution capacity in a way that smaller manufacturers were unable to match. It was during the 1960s that Courtaulds, under Frank Kearton, expanded downstream from fibres into textiles and garments, including the hosiery and knitwear industry, but despite the arrival of the conglomerates such as Courtaulds and Coats Viyella, small and medium sized firms were still most typical of the industry.

---

³¹ The Lancashire spinning and weaving industries were hit very hard by the immediate post-war shortage of workers. Singleton (1991), Chapter 3.

³² The industry prospered until c.1974, from then there was decline. In 1990 Courtaulds was split into two companies, of which Courtaulds Textiles plc was one. In 2000 Courtaulds Textiles plc was acquired by Sara Lee Corporation and the company Sara Lee Courtaulds was formed from the textiles interests of these two firms.

³³ See Chapman (2002).

TWO

Kearton widens the conglomerate

Background to the 1960s diversification

COURTAULDS FAILED TO BENEFIT from the lessons of the past. In the nineteenth century it had depended on a single product, black mourning crape, for most of its long running wealth creation, only to suffer a serious threat to its survival as the fashion and demand for that product declined. By the 1950s the firm once again faced a similar danger as rayon, the product on which it had become almost totally dependent, no longer had the profit potential it traditionally held. For the decade 1944 to 1954, excluding a short recession in 1952, the firm had enjoyed a steady increase in profits. However, around 1956, as profits were slipping, it was clear that important issues must be addressed. Alan Harries Wilson, at that time managing director, presented a long list to the chairman John Hanbury-Williams.

> Wilson's list was formidable: the inroads that nylon was making into sales of tyre yarn; the possible insolvency of the Canadian and Australian companies; the need to raise or maintain prices as well as increase sales of both yarns and staple fibre; the desirability of getting more money from B.N.S.; the need for a successful launching of their new acrylic fibre; and the possibility of diversification.[1]

In addition to fibre production the firm was already active in engineering, chemicals, plastics, and packaging films and had subsidiaries and branches in the UK, France, Germany, Spain, USA, Canada, Australia and South Africa. But in the absence of a replacement for the rayon profits Courtaulds suffered falling share prices and was therefore a target for a takeover bid. Board member

---

[1] Coleman (1980), vol. 3 p. 147.

Frank Kearton was charged in January 1958 with examining the possibilities of diversification into 'cognate' industries and he tackled this in a thoroughly determined manner. Group Developments Ltd, a subsidiary company, was set up under him and was soon to become the driving force behind the expansion, and in this he was closely aided by Arthur Knight who eventually became his successor. Both of these men played a central role shaping the future expansion of the firm, although in later years Knight was responsible for the thankless task of undoing much of the structure that was put in place under Kearton.

Diversification

Between 1957 and 1961 there was considerable diversification. Courtaulds bought out a number of other firms, establishing a presence in such disparate products as toothpaste tubes, industrial paints, tinplate cans, lingerie, and Lego bricks. But by far the most important acquisition in this period was its competitor British Celanese which had a large rayon producing plant at Spondon, Derbyshire. This firm, in common with Courtaulds, had suffered declining profits for a number of years. The acquisition had the effect of removing some of the price competition in the UK but the significance for Courtaulds of the introduction of new markets, and the injection of expertise this acquisition brought in weaving, knitting, dyeing and finishing was of immense value. British Celanese also had the first oil-cracking plant to be established in the UK and although the purpose of this was to provide raw materials for the production of viscose, the range of possible by-products included some that could be used in the paint industry in which Courtaulds was eventually to become a major manufacturer.

The continued importance of rayon

Despite the flurry of acquisitions and expansion into new products, as late as 1961 the firm was still dependent on fibres for the major part of its profits. Courtaulds was a latecomer to the synthetic fibres market and it was vital for the firm to secure outlets for the production of new fibres that were rapidly becoming available. Viscose based rayon, and the chemically more complex Dicel, Tricel, and acetate cigarette filter tip fibres[2] were all cellulosic products, a sector of the industry in which the firm had a dominant presence, but its Fibrolane was a specialist product used mainly in the production of carpets. Courtaulds was lagging behind the current fashion because Courtelle, one of the new acrylic fibres, was still only being produced in very small quantities. But the biggest omission was the lack of manufacturing capacity in the nylon industry. Although Courtaulds held fifty per cent of the British Nylon Spinners (BNS) shares, ICI

---

[2] Cigarette filter tip 'tow' was made at the British Celanese plant at Spondon, Derby.

British Celanese Works, Spondon Derbyshire *c*.1963 Courtesy of Courtaulds plc.

held the remainder. Courtaulds had almost no control of BNS and was totally dissatisfied with the dividends it produced.

Table 2.1 *Courtaulds' output of fibres in million lbs, 1961*

Viscose Textile yarn and staple	283.0	66.30%
Viscose Industrial yarn	62.3	14.60%
Dicel Yarn and staple	40.3	9.44%
Tricel Yarn and staple	16.8	3.94%
Acetate Cigarette filter tow	7.8	1.83%
Fibrolane (Casein staple)	2.6	0.61%
Courtelle (Acrylic staple)	14.0	3.28%
TOTAL	426.8	100%

Source: Coleman (1980)

Christopher Frank Kearton 1963 (Later Baron Kearton of Whitchurch). Courtesy of Courtaulds plc.

Momentous times – The ICI takeover bid

The trading situation was so serious that failure to act might have led to catastrophe and ICI was the key to possible change. The relationship between Courtaulds and ICI had not always been smooth, the pivotal issue being the nature of BNS which was under ICI control.[3] The jointly-owned business depended on ICI for its raw material and at the same time it was in competition with Courtaulds' rayon and ICI's Terylene. There was certainly some logic in the view of Sir Paul Chambers, chairman of ICI and John Hanbury-Williams, chairman of Courtaulds, that some form of merger would be of benefit to both firms. This was particularly the case as Courtaulds was not established in nylon production in its own right whilst ICI had not moved into acrylics at a time

---

[3] ICI and Courtaulds made a licensing agreement with DuPont in 1939 but the factory did not come on stream until 1948.

when Courtaulds' Courtelle showed every sign of becoming highly successful. Informal talks took place in midsummer 1960 between the two chairmen but the matter appeared closed when in December of that year Courtaulds decided not to pursue the matter.

In December 1961, ICI launched a takeover bid for Courtaulds which became bitterly contested, acrimonious and hostile.[4] This was almost certainly set in motion by Courtaulds' decision to reduce its interim dividend and the consequent fall in the share price. Kearton was vociferous in his opposition to the bid which broke down in the following March. This led, in 1964, to the cancellation of ICI's 38% stake[5] in Courtaulds and Courtaulds' withdrawal from BNS Ltd. There was also a £10 million (balancing up) payment by ICI to Courtaulds, phased over a four-year period.

The abortive takeover bid had far-reaching and long-term effects on the shape and future of the firm. Although Courtaulds expanded its activities across a broad front before the 1960s, until then it was in the chemical production, engineering and fibre-producing sectors that the firm was mainly involved.

Table 2.2 *Financial Data, 1961–1964 £000,000*

	1961	1962	1963	1964
Turnover	171.9	173.3	185.4	227.7
Pre-tax profit	18.74	17.7	23.6	33.3
Profit retained	4.4	2.9	4.7	6.0

Source: Courtaulds Accounts

The events of 1961–62 were momentous because the firm took on a new enthusiasm, much of which was driven by the leadership of Deputy Chairman Frank Kearton, supported by finance director Arthur Knight. Kearton had been the driving force in the campaign to defeat the hostile ICI bid[6] and as a result the younger directors who supported the independence of the firm assumed a new importance from that time. It placed Hanbury-Williams and Chairman Designate Alan Wilson, both of whom appeared to support the takeover, in an impossible position and both resigned in 1962. Dallas Bernard was appointed Chairman for a short period until Frank Kearton assumed the role in 1964.

---

[4] City editor of the Evening Standard William Davis wrote an account of the abortive bid by ICI. He notes the vital and impressive role played by Kearton. At this time Courtaulds and ICI were responsible for 90% of Britain's man-made fibre production. Davis (1970), Chapter 4.

[5] This stake in Courtaulds was built up in connection with the abortive ICI takeover.

[6] See 'The Siege of Courtaulds' in Davis (1970), pp. 44–45.

The son of a bricklayer, Christopher Frank Kearton was born in 1911. He attended Hanley High School and St John's College, Oxford, graduating with a First in natural sciences. He joined ICI, but was seconded to the UK government's Atomic Energy Project. After the war, he returned to ICI, but in 1946 was recruited to be the head of Courtaulds Chemical Engineering Research Department. Kearton was made a director of Courtaulds in 1952, deputy chairman in 1961 and chairman from 1964 until 1975. A supporter of the Labour Party, he was Chairman of the Industrial Reorganization Corporation from 1966 to 1968 and was given his peerage as Lord Kearton of Whitchurch in 1970. After leaving Courtaulds, he became Chairman of the British National Oil Corporation. Other activities included membership of the UK Atomic Energy Authority and the Electricity Supply Research Council.[7]

Capital-intensive plants and the Lancashire spinning and textile industry

Courtaulds desperately needed to ensure that the UK market for its fibres was strong. In the early 1960s it was clear that there was high potential for the new acrylic fibre Courtelle that the firm had launched on the market, but safeguarding the viscose filament sales was also of vital importance to the firm's survival. Courtaulds faced an uncertain market and the firm was dependent on the weak and fragmented Lancashire spinning and weaving industries as customers for its fibres.[8] There was a belief that there was little option other than to take control of the market to secure the future. One possibility was to modernise the 'Lancashire' industry to enable it to take the large quantities of rayon produced by the new high-volume cost-efficient plants which were needed to counter the threat on world markets from the large and efficient US plants. At this time, it was envisaged that the EEC would provide a market for this production. If the market in the EEC could be captured for Courtaulds, it would then be in a position to use the resulting benefits of scale to attack worldwide markets more effectively.

The failure of the 'Northern Plan'

In 1962, Courtaulds' directors conceived 'The Northern Plan', a strategy to reorganise the spinning and weaving section of the cotton industry, a vital link in

---

[7] For an informative review of Kearton's life and career read *Christopher Frank Kearton, Baron Kearton of Whitchurch 17 February 1911 – 2 July 1992* (The Royal Society 1995).

[8] The 'Lancashire' industry used about 40% of Courtaulds' rayon fibre output. Coleman (1980), vol. 3, p. 273.

the clothing supply chain. If these outlets failed, there would be no viable market for the UK fibre producers in general, and as far as Kearton was concerned, Courtaulds in particular.

The basis of the plan was that five firms would be bought, in the first stage, by Courtaulds, while other shareholders were to be attracted later.[9] However, as ICI was still a shareholder of Courtaulds, a joint plan was devised in which Courtaulds would take 55%, with ICI taking 45%, but the whole scheme was aborted when the valuation of one of the five firms could not be agreed. However, the issue could not be avoided for long and there was soon to be an alternative regrouping, with Courtaulds acquiring Lancashire Cotton Corporation and Fine Spinners & Doublers, J. & J. Hayes and Greenhalgh & Shaw. Courtaulds' competitors, English Sewing, took over Tootal with the aid of ICI cash, and Combined English Mills was acquired by Viyella. In another move, Courtaulds and ICI both took a shareholding in Carrington & Dewhurst. As a result of these changes of ownership these firms were saved from a possible takeover by foreign firms; particularly those from the USA which would have opened the UK market to US produced yarn.

Success under Kearton

Relative to the late 1950s the firm began to take on a new lease of life under Kearton.

Table 2.3   *Courtaulds' financial data, 1965–1974 £'000,000*

	1965	1966	1967	1968	1969	1970	1971	1972	1973	1974
Turnover	301.4	340.5	349.5	394.3	576.4	626.5	659.6	681.5	777.1	956.8
Pre-tax Profit	36.4	37.0	32.2	35.8	50.9	52.1	42.0	45.5	68.2	116.3
Profit retained	10.5	13.6	4.7	3.9	7.7	8.0	5.2	17.9	36.6	70.0

Source: Courtaulds Accounts

Following ICI's failed bid for the firm, profits began to improve and the profits for 1964/5 were double those of 1961/2 and had trebled by the end of the decade. In the 1960s the firm was able to invest heavily after selling unwanted gilt edged securities and freeing capital following the settlement with ICI. The firm also benefited from the increasing sales of Courtelle and modified rayon staple

---

[9] The firms were English Sewing Cotton, Tootal, Fine Spinners & Doublers, Lancashire Cotton Corporation and Combined English Mills. The market value of their ordinary shares was about £38 million.

Courtaulds Coventry Main Works c.1970. Courtesy of Courtaulds plc.

fibre, driven to some extent by the popularity of knitted fabric produced by the hosiery and knitwear industry and by the warp knitting industry.

Vertical trading[10]

Kearton exercised almost complete strategic control. He had a vision of a manufacturing enterprise integrated from basic raw material to the final despatch. His work-load and grasp of detail was phenomenal and throughout he never abandoned his pressure on the garment firms to use materials and services produced within the group. Because Courtaulds' yarn supply far exceeded the amount that could be taken by group firms, sales to outside users were absolutely vital: cash did not flow freely because many months could elapse from the purchase or production of the basic raw material, such as wood-pulp, until the final payment for finished goods by a retail store. Therefore, for cash flow purposes it was essential to keep supplying yarn to a whole range of customers outside as well as inside the group.

Courtaulds' vision, (or more correctly, Kearton's own vision) of a fully integrated vertically organised structure was intended to encompass all stages of

---

[10] Knight (1974), p. 47 uses the word 'verticalisation' as a way to describe the process of acquiring vertically related capacity.

processing from the forestry of the wood-pulp from which rayon is manufactured, to distribution to the retail outlets.[11] But the vertical system was never carried out, even remotely, to the level he demanded and there were any number of exceptions to his rules. M&S and other customers insisted on many occasions that non-Courtaulds yarn be used and the vertical structure was far less a reality than a concept.

Kearton expands into hosiery and knitwear

As part of the vertical trading policy, Courtaulds bought out a wide spread of hosiery and knitwear firms, ranging from some of the industry's major players down to some that appear almost insignificant but were valuable as added capacity for other manufacturing units. Some were focused on a particular product, whilst others had a diverse product range but by the 1960s many firms in this industry were diversifying and merging and were no longer exclusively hosiery and knitwear producers. It is therefore almost impossible to assess the proportion of their business exposure in these fields with any real accuracy.

A captive market for Celon

Following the rift with ICI,[12] Courtaulds was left with only a small plant producing nylon and almost no sales outlets. Kearton reacted to this by making a series of acquisitions in the fine-gauge hosiery industry. The most significant of these for the sales of nylon were Aristoc, Ballito, Contour, Kayser Bondor and Blounts.[13] All were important nylon users that could become downstream outlets for the developing Celon processing division at Spondon (Derbyshire). The market for stockings yarn was not the only reason for some of these acquisitions. Important nylon sales were also provided by the Kayser Bondor lingerie business and Blounts' associate firm of locknit producers, Derby & Midland Ltd.[14]

---

[11] Courtaulds began constructing a dissolving pulp plant, Saiccor, in South Africa in 1952. This produced the raw material for Rayon and Cellophane. Knight (1974), p. 18. The Usutu pulp mill in Swaziland produced pulp for the kraft paper industry.
[12] Coleman (1980), vol. 3. p. 252.
[13] See Chapter 3.
[14] Although Courtaulds extended far beyond the hosiery and knitwear industries into home furnishings, weaving and jersey fabric, they did not take a stake in the important rope, tyre and carpet manufacturing industries that were large users of Courtaulds fibres.

Proprietary yarn brands

Kearton was also anxious to safeguard Courtaulds' other yarn interests. Cellulosic yarn was being produced under several brand names, including Fibro, Tricel, Dicel and Vincel. In addition to Celon, Courtaulds' synthetic yarns included Courtelle and Lirelle. In many cases there was little differentiation between the competing products. All were liable to substitution by very similar products, for example DuPont's Orlon for Courtaulds' Courtelle, a problem that could occur with alarming speed in a fashion-oriented industry consisting of a large number of independent firms. Acquisitions were not the only route to the expansion of Courtaulds' yarn sales: the entry into the clothing industry closed the gap between the scientific and commercial researchers employed by the firm's fibre producers and the chain store buyers.

The trend for large chain stores to specify the raw materials used in their ranges encouraged the big yarn producers to approach them direct, bypassing the garment manufacturers. This secured large estimates of yarn usage that were scheduled into production long before final orders were placed by the garment manufacturers. This was to the advantage of both the fibre producers and the garment manufacturers that had improved confidence in the reliability of the raw materials supply chain, but it made Kearton's plan to exclusively use Courtaulds yarn impossible to implement.

John Boyes-Watson, a 'Courtaulds man' appointed chief executive of Foister, Clay & Ward (F,C&W) recognised the vital importance of M&S to the supply chain and the need for direct contact between the yarn producers and the retailers.

> The contacts and influence of Courtaulds marketing staff should not be underestimated. In the case of Tricel we did rather better with our direct contacts with M&S and the Group's competitors than via the Group. With some exceptions[15] most of the Group were reluctant customers for Group yarns.[16]

The acquisition of F,C&W, a major supplier to M&S, also enabled Courtaulds' scientific and marketing staff to gain valuable practical experience using and modifying their yarns in the working situation and gaining access to the final retail outlets. Knight wrote that '… there was scope for knowing what was going on, adjusting to it, and persuasively influencing buyers when differences were marginal or illusory.'[17]

---

[15] Courtaulds' yarn prices were fixed centrally and not normally negotiable within the group, this broke traditional buying patterns. There was also some anti-Courtaulds feeling.
[16] Information from John Boyes-Watson 16 September 2000.
[17] Knight (1974), p. 47.

Problems in the hosiery and knitwear industry

Typically, the companies in the hosiery and knitwear industry, apart from a few exceptions, were small and most of the larger firms were a hotch-potch of smaller divisions producing a multi-product range. The management of many of the acquisitions had been almost exclusively in the hands of the owners or major shareholders and their families.

Of the firms that Courtaulds found open to a buyout some were short of capital, others were caught in declining sectors of the market such as supplying the private retailers, either directly or through the declining wholesale trade and others were stuck with machinery that would not produce fashionable merchandise. It will be seen in subsequent chapters that some of these firms were still profitable but faced problems in the near future that they could not tackle unaided, but most were in various stages of decline and the vendors were unable to drive a hard bargain. Many of the sales were actually instigated by the vendors in an attempt to save at least something for the owners or shareholders of firms that were in serious trouble. The acquisitions were mainly amicable, although the Kayser Bondor hostile takeover generated a great deal of ill feeling.[18]

Kearton presses ahead

Kearton pressed ahead despite the problems. The move into the hosiery and knitwear industry began in the summer of 1963, with the acquisition of Foister, Clay & Ward (F,C&W) and Bairnswear and Meridian followed within a few months. Undoubtedly he felt that the seriousness of the yarn sales problem justified the risks. Time was not on his side. The hostile acquisition of more profitable firms would have been a long and protracted operation with no guarantee of success, and would certainly have been more expensive in the short term.[19] The main considerations were the development of a captive market for Courtaulds' yarn, the widening of the customer base in which the group operated, and the price required to settle the deal. However there was no suggestion that these firms would be supported indefinitely in a semi-autonomous state should they prove unprofitable.

Opinion in the trade insisted that Courtaulds was unaware of the problems facing the industry, but copious records show that Kearton was well briefed.

---

[18] Following a period of generally declining profits, Courtaulds was unable to agree with the directors a price for the Kayser shares. Eventually Courtaulds made an offer, direct to the shareholders, over 25% higher than Kearton's previous 'highest price'. Ill will was generated because subsequent profits did not match the forecasts made at the time. *Hosiery Trade Journal*, Jan. 1966, Feb. 1966, Aug. 1967.

[19] Some of the acquisitions were bought at below the book asset value.

The main thrust and decision-making was in his own hands, but it now seems inconceivable that the general philosophy driving the expansion would have been unknown to the rest of Courtaulds' main board although there is anecdotal evidence that major decisions were taken without adequate discussion. There is also little or no evidence to suggest that these firms were taken over with undue haste or lack of reasonable diligence. For example, as far back as the end of 1959, an approach had been made by an intermediary on behalf of the main shareholders of Nottingham Manufacturing Company to discuss the sale of that highly successful firm. It is probable that this did not proceed because Courtaulds' directors were nervous that the firm's managers (the Djanogly brothers) might decide to retire and Courtaulds had no available replacements of the calibre required.

Kearton had ambitions downstream from the fibre plants during the time he was in charge of Group Developments Ltd, and before the original rift with ICI. Talks were in place with Bairnswear and Meridian in 1961 but neither of these firms was taken over until 1963. During 1963 talks were held with Ballito and Rowley but Ballito was not taken over until 1966 and Rowley until 1968.

A management misfit

Courtaulds' executives were well aware of the problems posed by these firms, particularly the top-level management problems that needed immediate action. Kearton was a man of brilliant intellect who was surrounded by staff of very high calibre, particularly those employed in the research establishments at Courtaulds, Coventry, and at British Celanese, Spondon. This fitted uncomfortably with the general level of management available in the garment factories. The former scientists, now transferring from a chemical engineering base, were quite unfamiliar with the culture in which the hosiery and knitwear industry operated. Not only was there a cultural misfit, until 1963 Courtaulds had gained only limited garment manufacturing experience, using the trade names Celanese, Gossard and Luvisca. These firms were, by the chemical industry standards, very small. The highly capital-intensive chemicals industry produced large volumes of standardised output for a carefully researched market. Customers were often large and contracted their offtake for long periods. Cigarette filter tow[20] production, for example, was highly specialised and dominated in the UK by Courtaulds. The clothing factories operated on a vastly smaller scale and Kearton misunderstood the implications.

---

[20] Cigarette filter tips were produced from 'tow' which was acetate rayon fibre.

Strategy

In a fashion orientated industry composed of a large number of small firms, each seeking to produce a distinctive product, Kearton saw bulk production and long runs as the way to profitability. However, this was difficult to achieve in practice. Even the larger businesses, such as F,C&W and Wolsey, were groups of much smaller and diverse departments operating from widespread sites.

It seems logical, if only on the grounds of lower cost, availability for takeover, and the notion that weak firms could be saved by strong management, that Kearton should target and acquire firms that were ailing, rather than those that were profitable and secure but more expensive. However, it is unclear if this view was held at the time or is only posed with the benefit of hindsight. In the early stages, the large amount of correspondence that passed between Kearton and W. T. Archer, the executive responsible for identifying possible takeover targets and handling negotiations face-to-face, gives no indication that an overall long-term strategy had been formally set down. Firms were acquired as and when they became available and although they seemed in many cases to fit comfortably together no clear indication or detailed policy document is available to confirm the existence of a preconceived plan. It should not be overlooked that there were background political pressures on Kearton from the Prime Minister (Harold Wilson) and the President of the Board of Trade (Douglas Jay) to further rationalise the textile and clothing supply chain, even though the proposed takeover of Wolsey appeared to cut across monopoly rules. Kearton's ambitions were open-ended.

By July 1967 Kearton's aspirations were no more explicit: 'Hosiery knitting – 10% with a target of 20%. Stockings – rather more than 20% – modest stakes, except in one or two areas … womens underwear … 20% for example.'[21]

There is no doubt that Kearton had the interests of Courtaulds, rather than government policy, at the top of his agenda. It was ominously clear that the firm faced severe competition from other fibre producers and diversification was seen as a promising way to counter this threat. The diversification mirrored Kearton's own philosophy which had been evident from the time of the Northern Plan.[22] In essence, his philosophy was based on the concept that weak firms with a future should be combined under the strongest possible management. This notion was set out in the White Paper setting up the Industrial Reorganization Corporation (IRC) of which Kearton was chairman:

> Many of the production units in this country are small by comparison with the most successful companies in international trade, whose operations are

---

[21] Courtaulds AGM 1967.
[22] For a concise explanation of the Northern Plan see Knight (1974), pp. 51–2.

often based on a much larger market. In some sectors the typical British company is too small to achieve long production runs; to take advantage of economies of scale; to undertake effective research and development; to support specialist departments for design and marketing; to install the most modern equipment or to attract the best qualified management. … Size and efficiency do not always go together – there are efficient small companies and inefficient large ones. What is needed is to create a structure which will enable us to make the most efficient use, in years ahead, of our resources of skill, management and capital. [23]

However, in his work with the IRC[24] the policy differed drastically from his action of acquiring a host of small hosiery and knitwear firms, (and many in other industries) and attaching them to a major conglomerate. As Channon wrote regarding the IRC: 'Here the model used was clearly one of consolidating existing resources into a new organisation of a size comparable to international competitors; product diversity was something to be consciously avoided.'[25]

Perspectives

Operating in a time when the market for hosiery and knitwear was expanding, Kearton acquired over twenty firms in the industry, some in a very opportunistic way. Whilst it is clear that the policy did help the launch of Courtaulds' new fibres its role was rather limited in the context of the size of the whole conglomerate. As Arthur Knight, who was financial director at the time and closely involved in the expansion wrote:

At no stage was the objective of Courtaulds becoming a fully-fledged vertical group explicitly enunciated, and an account in retrospect of the development makes it all seem much more logical than it appeared whilst it was going on.[26]

The history of each of these firms is examined in some detail in the following chapter and it will be seen subsequently that the rapid, and of necessity unplanned, expansion of this complex mixture of firms contributed in a big way to the serious organisational problems which beset the business for many years.

---

[23] Cmnd. 2889 1966.
[24] See Broadway, *State Intervention in British Industry* (Kaye and Ward 1969), p. 62 and also Hague and Wilkinson, *The IRC An Experiment in Industrial Intervention* (George Allen & Unwin 1983).
[25] Channon (1984), p. 243.
[26] Knight (1974), p. 46.

THREE

The History of the Hosiery and Knitwear Acquisitions

IN ITS EARLY DAYS, the industry was composed predominantly of framework knitters and their families working in their own homes and even with the advent of the workshop and factory it remained a small scale craft industry, but by the early years of the nineteenth century, larger businesses were already becoming established. Two in particular combined the manufacturing and wholesaling functions, George Brettle & Co. Ltd and I. & R. Morley Ltd, the latter a firm described by Chapman as the 'Colossus of the Hosiery Trade and Industry'.[1] Both survived to be taken over by Courtaulds in the 1960s, but by then they were only a shadow of the great firms that they had once been. Joint stock ownership was a long-established feature of business structure and organisation at the time when Courtaulds was setting up its stake in the trade, but a structure of small scale family ownership and management still predominated in this industry.

In rise and decline

During the 1960s and early 1970s the trade was doing well and could sell most of the goods it could produce, although many firms were finding it difficult to acclimatise to the changing patterns of trading at that time, particularly the increasing power of the chain stores and the decline of the private clothing shops and outfitters. During the period when Courtaulds was actively acquiring capacity in the industry, 1963–1968, the number of plants increased whilst the number of firms declined, and the average employment per firm increased from 133 to 155.

---

[1] Textile History, 28 (1) 11–28, 1997.

Table 3.1 *Data for the whole industry*

Year	Firms	Plants	Plants per firm	Total employed, 000s
1958	1112	1343	1.2	115.2
1963	937	1238	1.3	124.5
1968	867	1253	1.4	134.7
1973	895	1067	1.2	133.6
1974	998	1173	1.2	138.9
1978	1030	1166	1.3	118.8
1983	902	1022	1.1	87.9

Source: Census of Production. Note: Small firms excluded

Due to changes in the way the statistics were collected tables 3.1, 3.2 and 3.3 do not join seamlessly together, yet they do show within themselves a decline in the total number of firms, plants or enterprises and the number of employees in the whole industry. After 1974 the industry was in decline and Courtaulds made only one large knitting acquisition in the UK, Corah Sock Division in 1988, and as will be seen later, that was made for entirely different purposes than the urgent need to build up capacity described in the previous chapter.

Table 3.2 *Data for the whole industry*

Year	Enterprises	Plants	Plants per firm	Total employed, 000s
1984	1461	1579	1.08	90.1
1985	1529	1640	1.07	85.6
1986	1587	1697	1.07	84.1
1987	1612	1699	1.05	85.0
1988	1678	1758	1.05	82.9
1989	1687	1757	1.04	77.8
1990	1547	1605	1.04	67.6
1991	1429	1471	1.03	63.9
1992	1352	1387	1.03	59.6

Source: Census of Production

From 1984 to 1992 the industry continued to decline and it was in this period that Courtaulds began to plan for the massive influx of imported goods that would eventually flood the market.

Table 3.3 *Data for the whole industry*

Year	Enterprise group	Enterprises	Total Employed, 000s
1993	923	944	48.5
1994	1011	1034	45.6
1995	906	927	46.2
1996	864	887	45.4
1997	828	852	41.4
1998		808	36
1999		737	32
2000		636	24
2001		539	19
2002		505	16
2008		284	6

Source: Census of Production and Annual Business Enquiry

It was accepted by many in the trade that the decline up to 1992 was serious, but disaster was to follow. Although Table 3.3 includes figures for the very small crocheting industry, and those from 1998 are taken from a different source, it can be seen that the decline was continuing unabated.

Because the larger firms tended to be multi-product producers it is not possible to determine with absolute accuracy the numbers employed in this industry by Courtaulds' acquisitions, but these firms were generally far above average size for the industry. At the extreme Wolsey/Lyle & Scott was thirty seven times larger than average at the time of its acquisition.

Approximations of employment are available for some firms around the time of their acquisition, the largest of these being Aristoc 1,300, Bairnswear 2,200, Ballito 1,800, F,C&W 2,900, Kayser Bondor 3,100, Meridian 2,800, Morley 1,400 and the Wolsey/Lyle & Scott Group 5,800.

Background to the Hosiery and Knitwear Acquisitions

Courtaulds bought out a complex raft of existing hosiery and knitwear businesses and many of them used well known brand names. These firms ranged from some of the smallest to some of the largest, and from some of the most obscure to some of the most well known names in the industry. For many of these firms no previous written histories have been traced.

There were single and multi-product, and single and multi-location firms and as already noted two, George Brettle & Co. and I. & R. Morley Ltd had interests downstream into wholesale distribution. All these businesses were seeking to produce garments that were popular with the customer and at the same time were in some way distinctive or at least competitive and nearly all were in competition with other members of the new group as it emerged.

On balance Courtaulds acquired a mix of firms heavily weighted towards those with serious problems. Before moving on to examine in detail the histories of the individual firms it is worth considering some general problems and trends. Most were acquired while the trade was still quite buoyant yet even in this somewhat favourable business climate the few financially viable businesses had some problem or a combination of problems that needed attention. Most were in some sort of financial difficulty, some seriously so and others worked under some perceived future threat, such as a changing market or the imminent retirement of the owner-managers. Because few were making substantial profits Courtaulds was able to buy most at around their net asset value, although some did not even achieve this modest price.

Many firms needed an injection of capital to keep them in business. In addition to a shortage of capital several factors had combined to severely restrict the development of many firms after World War Two. The UK knitting-machine building industry had been forced to divert much of its engineering capacity to the war effort. From the late 1930s, and the outbreak of war, very little new machinery had been released to the home market and most firms relied on machines which were long past their best and the ability to re-equip was hampered by the difficulty in obtaining import licences for foreign plant.[2] For many firms, profits did not allow full scale replacements of old plant with the urgency required, and for most the necessary replacement of machines in a steady and orderly manner could no longer be contemplated.

Fully-fashioned styles lose favour

For those firms making fully-fashioned stockings and fully-fashioned knitwear the problems were even more severe. Having invested in this expensive, slow and non-versatile plant in the expectation of it performing well for many years, they were faced with rapid changes in fashion. Both types of machinery were largely superseded – in the case of knitwear by cut and sew machines that could produce patterned garments, and in the stockings trade by circular machines that operated at vastly higher speeds and produced the more popular seamfree stockings and tights.

---

[2] Pasold, p. 639.

Aristoc fully-fashioned stockings, in an advert from *Punch* magazine, 14 October 1953.

Table 3.4 Courtaulds' acquisitions in the hosiery and knitwear industry, *A to C*

Company	Date acquired	FF Hose	Circular Hose	Product FF Knitwear	C&S Knitwear	Knitted Underwear	Socks	Other interests
Aristoc	1966	ARI Langley Mill, ARI Belper, ARI Kirkby-in-Ashfield	ARI Langley Mill, ARI Ramsey (Isle of Man), ARI Belper, ARI Kirkby-in-Ashfield					Beauvale Furnishing
Bairnswear	1963			BAI Worksop	BAI Notts, BAI Armagh			Knitting wool Rug wool Spinning
Ballito (Hartwood) (Tor)	1966	BAL Luton TOR Matlock	BAL Luton, BAL Skelmersdale, HAR Southport					
Brettle	1964	BRE Belper	BRE Belper			BRE Belper	BRE Belper	Warehouse Wholesale
College Hosiery	1985						COLL Barwell	

THE HISTORY OF THE HOSIERY AND KNITWEAR ACQUISITIONS

Contour (Sellers) (Lockley & Garner) (Hosiery Services) (A. H. Broughton) (G. Ginns) (F. Carnall)	1968	SELL Beeston LOC Barwell (2), BRO Wigston HOS Ashby-D-Z	SELL Beeston, LOC Barwell (2), BRO Wigston, HOS Ashby-D-Z	GIN Leicester, CAR Leicester	Macclesfield Mill (Wool tops) Booton (Machines)
Cook & Watts (West Riding Hosiery)	1967–74 in stages	WES Leeds			
Corah Socks (Reliance Hosiery)	1988			COR Leics, REL Halifax	Wholesale (Main Business)

Source: Various Sources

Aristoc Ltd

Aristoc, originally A. E. Allen & Company Ltd, was founded by Albert Ernest Allen, a former director of Rowley who resigned from that firm just after the First World War.[3] Financial support was provided for the venture by two friends, Percy Aspinall and paper merchant J. H. Williams, who later became chairman and managing director. As shorter skirts made legwear more visible, *sensible* wool and lisle stockings lost favour, and as fine-gauge silk stockings were a relatively new innovation at that time Albert Allen visited America to investigate the manufacturing process. He then commenced manufacturing in an old factory at Langley Mill, Derbyshire, a traditional hosiery manufacturing area with a reservoir of skilled labour.

The interwar years

The years 1925 and 1926 were important for the firm as they saw the establishment of the Aristoc brand and the appointment of W. L. Arber Ltd as sole distributors for Aristoc in the UK. Heavy advertising of the brand became a feature of the business from that time. This meant that Arber was faced with the prospect of replacing the existing contract business with Aristoc brand sales. The period between the late 1920s and World War Two saw continual progress, and in 1934 the firm became a public company, changing its name to Aristoc. Aristoc brand had become a leader in the growing fine-gauge stockings industry in an era when other famous brands such as Ballito and Bondor were also being promoted very strongly and according to the firm's own publicity:

> ...Aristoc remained unique for two reasons: firstly because it was the largest company in the country to specialise in fine-gauge full-fashioned silk stockings and nothing else; and secondly because it was acknowledged to be the leading brand as far as quality was concerned.[4]

The effects of World War Two

World War Two proved to be a disruptive time for Aristoc, but as a nucleus firm it was able to keep its property, plant and labour force together.[5] There was however an important change, with the shortage of silk the production of those

---

[3] Rowley Board Minutes.

[4] Allen, *Background to Aristoc: an essay on the fine gauge full fashioned hosiery industry* (Aristoc 1957), p.18.

[5] For more detail of nucleus status see National Hosiery Manufacturers Federation. Provisional Register of Members 1943.

THE HISTORY OF THE HOSIERY AND KNITWEAR ACQUISITIONS

Hosiery boarding machine © Daily Herald Archive/Science & Society Picture Library

stockings was stopped, being replaced by rayon and cotton products which were new to the company.

Due to the shortage of labour at Langley Mill after the war a factory was set up at Maltby in Yorkshire, in partnership with D. Byford & Co. of Leicester, a well known sock and knitwear firm and this arrangement remained in operation until 1952.[6] The period was notable because of the introduction of nylon into the stockings industry. The foundations of a large export trade were laid, taking advantage of the larger yarn allocation that was given to exporting firms at that time. Expansion followed and a factory was set up on the Isle of Man in 1955, which was in full production by 1956. By 1957 there were still three directors who were sons of the founders of the company but by 1966 the responsibility for the firm had fallen on the elderly chairman H. E. Williams.

Courtaulds acquired Aristoc

Aristoc was amongst the more successful firms acquired by Courtaulds. The company was well managed, and had a first class public image built on the high quality standards established in the fully-fashioned era and this was supported by a rapid delivery service. The high quality of merchandise presentation, including first class packaging, was also a notable factor and Aristoc spent more than £100,000 annually on point-of-sales display material. Aristoc had a high reputation in the trade for its high quality, good design and customer service and well-established customer base.

---

[6] Byford was later a Coats Paton acquisition. Byford Ltd Board Minutes.

The acquisition was particularly attractive for Courtaulds, not only for the sales potential of Aristoc merchandise but also because the firm was a substantial user of British Nylon Spinners' Bri-Nylon, which could be a target for substitution by Courtaulds' Celon. It was seen within Courtaulds that the acquisition of Aristoc would make the launching of Celon[7] easier than would have otherwise been possible because the firm was a large user of competitors' yarns, particularly Bri-Nylon and Enkalon which could be substituted using Courtaulds' Celon.

Although the firm had built its reputation on the production of high quality fully-fashioned stockings, as early as 1959 it had taken delivery of Italian circular stockings machines.[8] Shortly after this a competitor, Meridian Ltd, had decided to recommence circular stockings manufacturing and had ordered 28 Lonati machines, with a commitment to Bentleys the machine builders to purchase another 20 machines. However by 1961 this plant had been sold to Aristoc. Aristoc had recognised the trend away from fully-fashioned to seamfree circular hosiery and, despite its history as a leader in fully-fashioned hosiery, was producing around 75% of its production on the more popular circular machinery by the time of the takeover.

At the time Aristoc was acquired by Courtaulds in 1966 the number of people employed was approximately 1,300, plus 322 workers in Beauvale, a furniture business, which was included in the purchase but was not a cognate activity in any way for the new owners. Production was around 42,000 dozens per week knitted at Langley Mill and Ramsey, Isle of Man, a relatively small production unit. Somewhat in line with most of the industry the production of fully-fashioned styles had fallen to less than 15% of total production.

Courtaulds acquired four multi-product firms that had an important influence on the development of their fine-gauge division, Aristoc, Ballito, and Kayser Bondor in 1966 and Contour in 1968. Of these, Aristoc was significant as the market leader for quality, image, and customer service, attributes that had been nurtured consistently since the foundation of the firm. Unique among these four firms, Aristoc had benefited from continuity of experienced management, but the chairman, on whom fell much of the responsibility for running the firm, was wishing to retire. The firm was still committed to heavy advertising which had been an essential feature of the establishment and development of the *Aristoc* brand. In common with many in the industry, it was suffering declining profits, but was still successful at the time it was acquired by Courtaulds.

---

[7] For the launch of Celon refer back to Chapter 2.

[8] Their rival firm Pretty Polly also took this decision at around the same time and became a market leader.

Bairnswear factory, Perry Road Nottingham 1949.

Bairnswear Ltd

The original family business was commenced in 1900 by a Mrs Sheppard, the owner of a small plant of sewing machines.[9] Production at that time consisted of children's frocks made from woven materials, but by the time it was acquired by Courtaulds it had made spectacular progress, becoming one of the UK's leading children's knitwear manufacturers. In 1921 the business was taken over by her son Sidney, (who later became the chairman of Bairnswear), and in 1925 he reformed the firm as Bairnswear Knitting Company, with headquarters in South Sherwood Street, Nottingham. Expansion was rapid and in 1935 there was a public flotation of its share capital. Also, in the same year, the 187,000 square foot factory in Perry Road, Nottingham was opened. This building was designed especially for knitwear production and ranked among the most efficient factory sites in the industry. In 1939 the decision was taken to bypass the wholesale trade and make all Bairnswear brand sales directly to retail stores, thousands of which were still functioning at that time. This tactic got off to a good start, but the normal pattern of trading was soon interrupted by the war, and serious analysis of its success at that time is not therefore possible.

Bairnswear after World War Two

After the war, Bairnswear, in common with many other textile firms, suffered a severe shortage of making-up workers in Nottingham and responded by opening a new factory at Worksop. By 1951 the firm had manufacturing capacity at Perry Road, Nottingham, which included the head office, Hucknall Road, Nottingham,

---

[9] *The Bairnswear Story* (Undated private publication *c.*1949).

Ramoth Lane, Worksop and Armagh, Northern Ireland. In addition to men's, women's and children's knitwear the firm also manufactured children's frocks, hand knitting wool and rug wool.

By the early 1960s the fortunes of the company had changed and there were serious trading problems. It was around this time that a syndicate consisting of Eric Pasold, together with his brother and other associates, personally began to build up an influential minority interest in the firm, however, Ladybird (their company) had no direct investment in Bairnswear shares.

By 1962 Bairnswear was unable to sell the large production from its factories and the shares were at the lowest they had been for many years. The chairman '…asked all members of the board to treat this as a real crisis period.'[10]

Table 3.7 *Bairnswear Cash flow problems*

	19 May 1961 £	19 May 1962 £
Bank	27,531	(283,533)
Creditors	277,000	113,000
Debtors	339,000	338,000
Stock	1,491,214	1,695,519

Source: Bairnswear Accounts

Within one year the bank position had seriously deteriorated: the amount due from customers was about the same but the amount of money tied up in stock had increased by over £200,000, a situation that was attributed to the failure of the sales organisation to meet its targets and inevitably this led to dramatically declining profits.[11]

Table 3.8 *Declining profits*

	Net profit after Tax £
1959	160,000
1960	85,390
1961	106,955
1962	7,684

Source: Exchange Telegraph

---

[10] Bairnswear board minutes.
[11] *Exchange Telegraph* report 1963.

The policy of promoting their Bairnswear brand did not enable the firm to generate sufficient sales and despite having the advantage of a large production capacity, Bairnswear had failed to respond to changing market conditions and entered the chain store market very late. Rather unfairly, responsibility for poor sales was apportioned mainly to the recently appointed sales director Glyn Hughes,[12] but it is doubtful if the 'direct to retail' sales policy that the firm still pursued could realistically be expected to produce the necessary sales volume needed for survival.

Courtaulds acquired Bairnswear

Courtaulds' offer of about £1.25 million for a takeover in 1963 was quickly accepted by the board and recommended to the shareholders. A minority of shareholders, including the Pasold brothers and their associates, who held a personal stake[13] of 500,000 shares, did not immediately accept or make a counter bid but as a minority shareholder Eric Pasold supported Kearton's subsequent board restructuring. The Pasold consortium had built up the shareholding because it seemed to be a firm to which they could introduce their efficient methods of making children's clothing as they had done at their Chilprufe factory in Leicester.

This important knitwear manufacturing company provided a potentially valuable outlet for Courtaulds' yarn production. The main works at Perry Road, Nottingham, had the capacity to knit and make up 3,000 dozen garments per week. Worksop factory produced 700 dozens per week of classic fully-fashioned knitwear garments and Armagh produced 1,200 dozens flat knitted garments. Bairnswear also had considerable interests in spinning and the manufacture of hand-knitting wool. Although there was capacity to produce fully-fashioned knitwear at Worksop, the firm had managed to avoid being dangerously over-committed to this declining sector of the knitwear trade.

Bairnswear was noted for its high technical ability but it suffered from having inadequate top management and there were serious policy errors, particularly in the selling organisation. These were almost certainly the result of poor leadership, and the failure to make an early entry into the stores business left the firm with rising stocks and a crippling overdraft, but as a big user of yarn, with a potential to use large quantities of Courtaulds' Courtelle acrylic yarn, Bairnswear was a particularly important addition to Courtaulds' downstream activities.

---

[12] *The Evening Standard* 19 June 1963.
[13] *Sunday Times* 8 September 1963.

Ballito Hosiery Mills Ltd

Best known for its stockings and tights, Ballito was also heavily committed to fully-fashioned knitwear manufacturing. The firm was set up by its German founders the Kotzin family as Ballington Ltd, a private company, in 1922, becoming Ballington Hosiery Ltd in 1929 and taking the name Ballito in 1936.

Ballito was a well-advertised brand name and the firm prospered greatly between the wars, producing the then popular silk fully-fashioned stockings. Profits from 1929, with the exception of the difficult and loss making years 1930 and 1931, show substantial growth but the firm suffered a setback during the war when most of the workforce was switched to making Oerlikon ammunition shells.

Post World War Two

Still under the founding family, Ballito recovered quickly after the war and reached maximum profits in 1955, but from then the firm was in general decline, and by the mid-1960s the decline was serious: this was the era when fully-fashioned stockings and knitwear were rapidly losing favour and the chain stores were gaining favour with the buying public.

Table 3.9 *Ballito profit/loss record*

Year ending	Profit (loss) £
1954	300,186
1955	300,919
1956	136,291
1957	151,032
1958	160,647
1959	162,598
1960	221,234
1961	191,769
1962	50,126
1963	138,903
1964	152,806

Source: Ballito Accounts

Year ending	Profit (loss) £
1965	(106,350)*
1966	(180,000)*

Source: Courtaulds' offer document
Note: * Forecast

Shortly before the takeover by Courtaulds the finishing capacity was around 40,000 dozen pairs of stockings per week although nowhere near these figures was actually being achieved.

Ballito responds to decline

Ballito had large factories in Hatfield Road, St Albans, and Bute Street, Dallow Road, and Midland Road, Luton. There were also the associate companies, Tor at Matlock and Hartwood Hosiery at Southport. The company's response to difficult trading conditions was to undertake a policy of retrenchment, and to set up a new factory in a development area at Skelmersdale, Lancashire, to be partly supported by government grants. As part of this reorganisation they attempted to sell the St Albans factory which housed the under-utilised fully-fashioned stockings plant, and stopped manufacturing fully-fashioned stockings.

Ballito reorganisation hits trouble

Disaster loomed ahead. By September 1966, the firm was fully committed to the Skelmersdale project which was running behind schedule and it had not been possible to sell the St Albans property and the under-utilised Luton factory that were potential sources of funds. At the same time the firm was faced with the heavy reorganisation costs connected with the closure of the St Albans factory.

The firm was heavily in debt with an outstanding debenture of £215,000 on the St Albans factory. The bank overdraft stood at £667,000, an increase on the previous year of £81,000, and additionally there were outstanding loans of £257,000 for the purchase of machinery, and stocks had risen by £260,000. These figures, taken in the context of a net asset value attributable to the equity of only £1,100,000, led to the conclusion that the company could not continue trading unless sheltered by a larger organisation.

Ballito stockings packaging from the 1960s.

Courtaulds acquired Ballito

The seriousness of the situation was summed up by the chairman F. V. Ault:

> ... The securing of such a sum [£1,100,000] in cash would be entirely dependent on the complete realisation of plant, machinery and stocks, at book values. In view of the general economic situation and the depressed state of the hosiery trade, such a realisation would prove an extremely difficult operation and in the final analysis would undoubtedly fall short of book values...[14]

His assessment proved very realistic because eventually Courtaulds had to destroy or liquidate over 100,000 pairs of stockings with Beatles motifs. Thirteen fully-fashioned machines, all of which were in first class working order were broken up, each of which would have had a replacement cost of over £90,000 at that time.[15] With the exception of the chief accountant, who stayed for about

---

[14] Courtaulds' offer document.
[15] Information from Denis Snook former Post-Dye Manager, Ballito Ltd.

three months, the senior managers did not continue in employment with the new owners, and the activities in the Luton area continued to decline. Quite quickly, despite the final offer to the shareholders being only around £720,000 in cash and Courtaulds' shares, which was far below the apparent net asset value, the firm passed into Courtaulds' ownership in 1966.

Ballito suffered from a lack of senior management able to deal with the downturn in fully-fashioned stockings and knitwear production. The firm had entered a decade of decline from the mid-1950s, and failed to extricate itself sufficiently from the fully-fashioned stockings and knitwear manufacturing sector. The firm's commitment to fully-fashioned knitted outerwear was also a heavy drain on its resources involving a large amount of expensive plant and expensive property in the St Albans and Luton Area. Ballito became highly unprofitable by the 1960s, so much so that Courtaulds did not retain the directors after the acquisition, attributing to them the failure of the firm. The fully-fashioned knitwear department acquired with this firm offered almost nothing to the development of Courtaulds group knitwear sector but it was as a user of Courtaulds' hosiery yarn that the firm was bought.

George Brettle & Co. Ltd

Brettles, a combined manufacturing and wholesaling enterprise, was untypical of the hosiery and knitwear companies taken over in the Courtaulds' expansion period: had this book been based on the wholesale traders acquired by Courtaulds, Brettles might equally have been selected for inclusion.

The firm had obscure beginnings in the Belper area of Derbyshire. John Ward junior was known to be involved in the business in the early 1790s and by 1799 the firm was known as Ward & Son. By 1801 Ward senior was no longer in the business and John entered into a partnership with James Carter Sharp. Together they set up a wholesale business in Cateaton Street, London, a move that was to have a far-reaching impact on the business.

In 1803 Sharp, seeing that John Ward was personally bankrupt owing to a debt contracted prior to the partnership, withdrew from the firm and as a result the business was placed in a highly precarious position. A new partner, George Brettle, was introduced, and the firm was re-established as Ward Brettle & Ward, the third partner being John's brother, William Ward.

Following appalling financial problems in the early 1800s the firm made incredible progress, and by 1808 John claimed that the firm employed between seven and eight hundred workmen. There was structural change because John Ward left the business in 1823, his brother William died in 1833 and in 1834 the firm became George Brettle & Co., and was one of the largest and most successful businesses in the industry at that time.

More change was afoot when the wealthy George Brettle died in 1835.

George left the business on trust to three friends because his sons Alfred, 13, George Henry, 15 and Edward, 16 were still too young to control the business. The management fell to a local solicitor, Benjamin Hardwick as the other two trustees revoked their interest in favour of him. The sons became partners when Alfred, the youngest son became twenty one. The sons lived the life of country gentlemen and failed to attend to the business in the same dedicated manner as their father and the business did not expand in the same way. The final owner of the firm to bear the Brettle name was George Henry Brettle, the middle son, who died in 1872.

Absentee management

Within fifteen months George's widow Helen married a country gentleman, Lt Colonel Henry Twyford. Twyford did not enter the business at that time and it continued under the control of its managers who were responsible to Helen independently of her new husband. These were hard times for the business as the trade was in a state of depression in the 1870s along with much of British industry. Helen Brettle died in 1882 and bequeathed the business to her husband, a man with no personal knowledge of the running of a clothing manufacturing and wholesaling business.

Twyford took over, but the business continued under the existing managers who had by then been made junior partners. Business improved somewhat in the 1880s continuing in its traditional manner and Twyford enjoyed a comfortable and wealthy lifestyle with homes at Cadogan Square, London, Hove and Belper where the factory was situated. He died in 1913, the sole surviving partner of the business.

After the death of the founder the organisation seems to have lacked dynamism and its leading position had been lost to I. & R. Morley. As Hart wrote:

> It seems clear that in the late nineteenth and early twentieth centuries the firm did not evidence signs of development, innovation, growth or dynamism. It was old-established; it had a sound reputation; it was a good employer, and it became content to be old-fashioned. After George Henry Brettle's death in 1872 – if not earlier – the concern lacked firm direction. There were various problems involving the working partners; there was the basic difficulty of rule by two successive absentee owners, neither with any real experience of business... By the early years of the twentieth century it was evident that the firm was being allowed to run down. Any change had, however, to await Colonel Twyford's death in 1913.[16]

---

[16] Harte (1973), *A History of George Brettle & Co. Ltd 1801–1964* (University College, London), p. 107.

The return of owner management

Colonel Twyford left the business to his two nephews Lionel and Harry Twyford. Under them there was, after a long period of absentee ownership, a return to direct management by the owners and at this time the business was reconstituted as George Brettle & Co. Ltd. Modernisation took place. There had been increasing use of new technology in the manufacturing side of the firm at Belper for many years, and in London plans were put in place to replace the three horse vans with a motor van, a motor car replaced the North London traveller's brougham and a lady typist was employed.

During the First World War the firm made rapid progress and turnover and net assets almost doubled, although there was considerable inflation at that time. New products that required new machinery were introduced probably as a result of securing large military contracts.

Following war service, Lionel Twyford (Brigadier General) died in 1920 and Harry (later Sir Harry Twyford KBE and Lord Mayor of London) became chairman. Although Brettles, in common with almost all the industry, suffered badly in 1921 and 1922 the interwar years were generally good as hosiery and underwear sales increased and knitwear became better value due to increased mechanisation at that time. The firm went public in 1938 but by then the merchandise had become staid and was in need of revitalisation.

The Second World War was devastating for Brettles. The firm did not clinch military contracts on the scale of those obtained in the First World War. The premises it had occupied in London for 130 years were destroyed in two bombing raids in the Blitz of 1940 and the warehousing was transferred to Belper, never to return.

Post World War Two

Business did pick up to some extent from 1947 but the firm never again achieved the status in the trade that it had enjoyed in the days of the first George Brettle. Brettles remained in the wholesale business serving the independent trade at the time when the multiple traders were rapidly gaining ground and by the mid-1960s the firm was suffering severe profit reductions:

Table 3.10 *Brettles' profits*

	Pre-tax profits (£)
1961	95,000
1962	82,000
1963	62,500
1964	50,100

Source: Brettle Accounts

As a combined manufacturing and wholesaling organisation the firm continued to serve the traditional retail trade using its own brand name, 'Brettles'. There is no evidence to suggest that the firm under Sir Harry Twyford, who resigned in 1963, did anything other than remain loyal to the Wholesale Textile Association. Unlike Morley, (another leading wholesale distributor and manufacturer discussed later) which had surreptitiously built up a strong connection dealing directly with Littlewoods, there is no record of Brettles having supplied chain stores prior to the takeover by Courtaulds.

In 1964 Brettles manufactured within its own factory about 50% of its requirements of socks, stockings and knitted underwear.

The manufacturing plant consisted of 60 fully-fashioned machines, which were only capable of producing a type of stocking then in severe decline, and the underwear machines were mainly old Blackburn and Mellor Bromley plain web machines. The sock machinery consisted of a small plant of 74 Bentley Komet machines.

The total staff of 240 included five buyers and forty sales representatives, who serviced 5,000 active accounts, and also the factory, warehouse, and administration staff. In addition there were also 480 factory operatives.

Having a wide spread of customers may appear at first glance to have been a logical strategy. An added strength would seem to be the capability to reduce, in difficult times, the 'bought in' element of their requirements without reducing their internal manufacturing output. However, by the time of the takeover the manufacturing plant was old and inefficient, and relative to many other firms in the industry the capacity was fragmented and small. The firm was also heavily committed to the independent sector of the retail trade at a time when the multiples were gaining ground and the poor prospects for the wholesale trade were already quite clear.

Brettles was a long-established firm that had held on to its traditional method of trading in a changing commercial scene. It had failed to grasp new opportunities and had continued to trade as a combined wholesale and manufacturing enterprise. The trade name of Brettles was well-known in the declining drapery sector of the retail trade, but had not been marketed heavily in the department store and mail order businesses.

Brettles sold a comprehensive range of merchandise, much of it bought in from other manufacturers, but the firm was relatively unimportant in any single sector of manufacturing and had not moved with the times, retaining a rather old fashioned image. Also, it had failed to enter the chain store business and was heavily committed to the fully-fashioned stockings sector which was in almost terminal decline and it also failed to modernise its plant and equipment which had become unsuitable for modern manufacturing.

THE HISTORY OF THE HOSIERY AND KNITWEAR ACQUISITIONS

A Brettles advertisement in *Country Life*, 1956, courtesy of Slenderella, Belper.

Courtaulds acquired Brettles

Brettles was taken over early in 1964. Harte writes

> ... the value of the paper issued by Courtaulds for the purchase of George Brettle & Co. Ltd was about £465,000. The firm was valued in its own books at over £780,000. Because of the circumstances Brettles found itself in at the time, Courtaulds had been able to catch a bargain ...[17]

However, the Brettle Chairman, who controlled 54% of the ordinary shares, explained the state of the business:

---

[17] Harte, p. 150.

Over capacity in the hosiery trade continues to lead to reduced profit margins. I expect that the final figures for your Company in the current year will show that the downward trend in profits has continued. You will recollect that the directors considered it prudent to reduce the interim dividend for the current year and present indications are such that the board would not be justified in recommending the maintenance of the final dividend at 6%. I do not consider any improvement can be expected in the near future without diversification which would involve expenditure of a substantial sum on new machinery. I am therefore of the opinion that the interests of the shareholders and employees are best served by the Company becoming a member of the Courtaulds group.[18]

Although the firm was in serious financial difficulties and was only a shadow of its former self it had an important asset in its large property in the centre of Belper, Derbyshire. This had potential as a manufacturing base for stockings production, although in 1964 a large amount of space was still occupied by 60 fully-fashioned stockings machines, but the wholesaling function was still operating moderately successfully at that time.

College Hosiery Ltd

This small sock manufacturing firm was established by the College family in 1948, and operated as a private company in Osborne Road, Leicester. It later moved to Barwell, Leicestershire and became part of the holding company, Lucian Knitwear Ltd.

With a turnover of over £12 million there was a pre-tax loss of £374,000 for Lucian Knitwear (the owners) in 1984. Results were better for 1985 with an overall profit of £48,000 but the sock subsidiary College Hosiery was unprofitable, dragging down the group and the decision was taken to divest Lucian Knitwear of this small subsidiary. College Hosiery was too small to survive as an independent supplier to the chain stores and closure would have involved Lucian in redundancy payments that it could ill afford.

Courtaulds acquired College's capacity

College Hosiery was an insignificant sock manufacturing firm with only 71 direct and 10 indirect operatives[19] and was a misfit as a subsidiary of Lucian Knitwear, an otherwise successful knitwear producer. Rather than close the

---

[18] Courtaulds' offer document, 1964.

[19] Direct workers were 'directly involved' in making the merchandise. Indirect workers included service workers, material movers, despatchers etc.

business it was sold to Courtaulds as an addition to its sock manufacturing capacity.

Lucian Group was heavily dedicated to M&S production and, encouraged by M&S, Courtaulds offered £325,000 for the College plant and machinery and £300,000 for the work in progress, the intention being to move the plant into the Wolsey, Leicester site and guarantee continuity of employment for at least 70 employees. College Hosiery Ltd was acquired by Courtaulds in 1985.

Contour Hosiery Ltd

Contour Hosiery Ltd was an untidy group of small firms put together by R. A. Palfreyman, a chartered accountant and graduate of the London School of Economics who owned 50% of the equity. The group was involved in manufacturing nylon stockings, men's and children's socks and also in knitting-machine building. [20]

In 1962 the firm was incorporated as International Fibres Ltd,[21] but subsequently the name was changed to Intercontinental Fibres Ltd. Until 1963 the firm had been involved in wool-top processing but as this activity was seen as not complementing later developments, the chairman re-formed that part of the business and hived it off into a separate company which he personally owned, and Intercontinental went public in 1964.

Intercontinental Fibres acquired Sellors and becomes Contour

In 1963 Intercontinental Fibres bought a majority shareholding in F. W. Sellors Ltd, the Beeston-based hosiery manufacturers, and the whole of its associated company A. M. Buswell, a Nottingham based hosiery and knitwear wholesalers and bought the remainder of the Sellors shares in 1964. Sellors was founded in 1929 and incorporated in 1936, and Buswell was founded in 1939 and incorporated in 1947, which was about the time that the close cooperation between the two firms commenced. The name Contour Hosiery, a Sellors trademark, was adopted by Intercontinental Fibres Ltd at the time of the Sellors acquisition.

---

[20] Contour subsidiaries were: Nylon hosiery manufacturers F. W. Sellors, Lockley & Garner and A. H. Broughton; Sock manufacturers J. F. Carnall, G. Ginns and Machinery builders W. E. Booton and Hosiery Services. Details from the public offer document.

[21] The name of Contour from 1962 to 1963. Details from the public offer document.

Post World War Two

Following the Second World War, Sellors had taken advantage of the government's quota allocation system for nylon which was in short supply at that time. The system favoured exporters, and Sellors concentrated on those markets. Later, when the nylon supply position eased, business was expanded, particularly in the boom years of 1953 and 1954. But from then, in common with other fine-gauge hosiery manufacturers, Sellors suffered from more intense competition and the change in fashion from fully-fashioned to circular stockings. Contour Hosiery explained Sellors' success as being the result of responding and re-equipping to meet changing fashions.

Machine building – a misfit

Although the machine-building industry does not form a central part of this study, reference must be made to the acquisition by Contour of hosiery machine builders W. E. Booton Ltd, for £410,000 in 1964. This appears to have been a shrewd deal, because the net assets were in the region of £280,000 and there was an anticipated pre-tax profit of £70,000 for the year. More significant however, there was £200,000 in cash and short-term loans.[22] However, machine building was a risky business and Contour suffered a setback in 1966 with profits falling from £246,897 to £188,039, which the chairman attributed to losses in the machine-making subsidiary. However, profits improved by 30% in the year ending 1967.

Further expansion

Further expansion occurred in 1967 when Contour acquired A. H. Broughton, hosiery manufacturers of Wigston, Leicestershire. This included two small but useful sock manufacturing firms J. F. Carnall and G. Ginns. Contour finally made another small acquisition, Lockley & Garner, hosiery manufacturers at Barwell, Leicestershire, with its associated finishing factory Hosiery Services of Ashby-de-la-Zouch.

Through the F. W. Sellors distribution organisation, Contour was selling 98% of its stockings production to Woolworths at a rate of 10–12,000 dozens per week internally produced and 4–5000 dozens per week 'bought in'. In no way can Contour be considered a famous name in the hosiery and knitwear industry. The most important branch of this firm, from the fine-gauge hosiery viewpoint, was Sellors of Beeston, Nottingham. This firm had no really well-known trademark and was almost totally dedicated to supplying Woolworths.

---

[22] *The Times* 12 March 1964.

Courtaulds acquired Contour

It was not unique for an acquisition to include a 'non-core' activity, another example being the relatively small and unimportant Beauvale furnishing within the Aristoc organisation. The implications of Contour owning Booton (the machine-building firm) are not important to the story of Courtaulds and the hosiery and knitwear industry, but it is interesting to note that Kearton recognised that Booton was lagging far behind leading machine builders in its technology. Therefore the acquisition of Contour by Courtaulds was almost certainly mainly influenced by its potential for Celon usage and the value of the Woolworths connection in building up a stake in the stockings industry, not by the desire to gain an entry to the machine building industry. Kearton may have judged that, in the context of the overall benefit of acquiring Contour, the inclusion of Booton was either a relatively minor issue or that Booton itself might eventually prove a worthwhile acquisition. Palfreyman suggested that Courtaulds might sell Booton back to him after the takeover, but very rightly, Courtaulds refused to countenance any such prior commitment because this would have placed one shareholder at an advantage over others.

Contour passed into Courtaulds ownership in 1968 following a £2,500,000 bid.[23] The Contour group was a mixed conglomerate, with all subsidiaries working as autonomous units. The overall management of this group was in the hands of the main shareholder, R. A. Palfreyman who appears to have made no attempt to form an integrated group. Palfreyman left the firm at the time of the sale but this caused no problems because the very fragmented and autonomous nature of the individual units made it a simple matter for the new owners to split up the group and allocate its constituent parts to other management groups within Courtaulds.

Cook & Watts Ltd – West Riding Hosiery

West Riding Hosiery, a very small fine-gauge hosiery manufacturing company, was established in 1936, and in 1946 was acquired by Holt & Co. (Leeds) Ltd, a wholesale distribution company which later became a subsidiary of Cook & Watts Ltd.[24]

---

[23] *The Times* 28 February 1968.
[24] Cook & Watts was a general wholesale firm taken over by Courtaulds in 1967. The retail sector was in decline in the face of chain store domination. In 1974 Courtaulds wholesale division operated from over 40 sites: Batho Taylor & Ogden Ltd, Bell Nicholson & Lunt Ltd (15 branches), Bradbury Greatorex (3 branches) Burnt Tree Cash & Carry, Cook & Watts, Brettle & Co., Samuel Farmer Ltd, Holt & Co., S. & J. Watts, Wilkinson Riddell Ltd (11 branches), S. C. Larkins, Macanie Ltd.

Stockings unprofitable

By the early 1960s the manufacture of fully-fashioned stockings became unprofitable, and Holts decided in 1965 to scale down the business. Plans were put in hand to close the fully-fashioned section and reduce the production from 4,400 to 2,400 dozens per week.

Concurrently with the cut-back, Holts' attempts to sell this fine-gauge manufacturing business to Ballito or Taylor Woods failed, but West Riding Hosiery, as part of Holts and the ultimate holding company, Cook & Watts (Sales) Ltd, soon passed into Courtaulds' ownership.

Courtaulds acquired (Holts) West Riding Hosiery

Even the 1965 plans proved over optimistic, and at the time the firm was acquired by Courtaulds it employed about 50 people, making ladies' seamless stockings at a rate of 1,200 dozens per week on Zodiac 4 feed machines. It was losing money (£16,000) by 1966.

West Riding Hosiery was developed as a packing department for other Courtaulds stockings manufacturers. The background and reasoning behind the acquisition of a presence in the wholesale trade is discussed later.

Corah Sock Division (N. Corah & Sons)

A worse start can hardly be imagined than that suffered by Nathaniel Corah and yet he went on to establish what eventually became one of the most prestigious firms in the UK hosiery and knitwear industry. He was born in 1777 in Bagworth, Leicestershire, where his father earned a living by combining farming with framework knitting. Nathaniel set up as a framework knitter when he was twenty seven but after a few years he struck hard times and was put in a debtors' prison. On release he found work in a Birmingham gun factory but became unemployed when work dried up after Napoleon's defeat at Waterloo.

Better times for Corah

Nathaniel returned to Leicester and successfully set to work buying goods from local hosiers, meeting them at the Globe Inn and his own house, and then selling his merchandise in Birmingham. The business prospered and in 1824 he bought a factory and warehouse in Union Street, Leicester but he died at the age of only fifty-five and in 1832 the business passed to his sons. Progress continued and by 1845 they had a factory in Granby Street, in central Leicester that was powered by a steam engine. Further expansion in 1866 saw the opening of the

A fully-fashioned machine in action at Corah © Daily Herald Archive/Science & Society Picture Library

St Margaret's works where electric lighting was installed in 1883. The trademark 'St Margaret' was registered in 1875 and more factories were opened around that time. During the First World War business was badly curtailed as half the male staff entered the forces and forty lost their lives. Of the production that remained, over 70% was for government contracts.[25]

St Margaret and Marks & Spencer in the interwar years

The nature of the relationship with M&S is central to the Corah story. The firm had enjoyed a long run of success but suffered a potentially devastating setback in the 1920s. Profit margins were negligible and huge losses were incurred on stocks. The firm's nationwide warehousing chain was run down and closed, there was short time working and workers were laid off and it was only by gaining a new customer, M&S in 1926, that the firm was set on a new path to prosperity. The firm's traditional supply chain through wholesalers to the retail shops then gave way to direct delivery to the high street stores.

---

[25] Jopp, *Corah of Leicester 1815–1965* (Newman Neam), p.20.

World War Two

Progress was interrupted again when war broke out in 1939. Over 2000 employees left for the armed forces or other vital work. By the end of the war the firm was reduced to half its pre-war labour strength, it had worn out equipment, one third of its floor space had been allocated to essential war work and expansion was limited by complex planning regulations.

Corah develops the M&S connection and ethos

Corah overcame its problems to become a leading supplier of knitted goods to M&S, particularly knitwear, underwear and socks and was amongst the largest and most highly regarded multi-product hosiery and knitwear manufacturing firms.

The shortage of workers in Leicester after the war forced the firm to expand in new areas such as Brigg, Bolton-upon-Dearn, Oakham, Aberbargoed, Scunthorpe, Rochdale and Birmingham and by 1965 Corah employed 6,500, was a leader in industrial relations, training, workers pay and conditions, and in technical expertise and high quality production. An understanding of the whole ethos of this firm is essential to a general understanding of the industry, and this is particularly relevant in regard to high quality production and advanced industrial relations policies, which are dealt with in detail in a later chapter. Corah incorporated many facets of M&S' ethos into its own organisation, manufacturing to high standards of quality, and providing working conditions in advance of those that generally applied in the trade. The firm developed a symbiotic relationship with M&S and Corah dedicated large sections of its manufacturing capacity to that firm and M&S reciprocated by treating Corah as its preferred supplier.

Corah split up

The volume of the sock business increased considerably from 1984 when the firm acquired another M&S supplier, Reliance Hosiery of Halifax.[26] However, by 1987, Corah plc was in serious difficulties, with almost all operating divisions losing money largely because of high UK labour costs and a loss on the clearance of sub-standard merchandise produced at Halifax.

Corah Sock Division was dedicated to M&S, its target customer, with reputedly 80% of its production being for that customer, however M&S was suffering severe price competition and Corah was unable to meet prevailing prices and became uncompetitive. Several departments were offered to Courtaulds as a

---

[26] *Hosiery Trade Journal* December 1984.

going concern but Courtaulds declined to take over the bulk of the firm but did acquire the Sock Division which was an important M&S supplying department.

There was a damaging strike against tightened labour rates that was set in motion by pressure from Courtaulds in the run-up to the takeover date. Corah had historically offered labour terms and conditions more generous than those generally found in the industry. Corah operated a 'slack bonus scheme', whilst Wolsey and Rowley (both Courtaulds) employees operated on piece rates and achieved much higher performances. Under pressure from Courtaulds, Corah had imposed a change in working conditions which removed expensive guarantees to the employees against short time working. Despite many problems, Corah Sock Division was profitable at the time of the takeover and M&S held its management in high regard.

The firm manufactured socks at Halifax and at Leicester, where they shared a site with other Corah operating divisions. The capacity was approximately 40,000 dozens per week, of which Halifax produced 55% and Leicester 45%.

Courtaulds acquired Corah Sock Division

The acquisition of the Corah sock business followed the earlier, but very much smaller, acquisition of the M&S sock supplier College Hosiery Ltd that had been consolidated into the Wolsey business a few years earlier. The proposal was that Corah sock sites would be closed, and the equipment and operatives moved into the Wolsey Abbey Meadows, Leicester property that already housed Courtaulds' Wolsey factory. The factory at Halifax would remain open.

It was estimated that Courtaulds' sock business would be doubled from £16.3 million per annum. At the same time, the Courtaulds' share of the M&S business would be increased to nearly 40%, making Courtaulds and its competitor Simpson, Wright & Lowe (Coats Viyella) the M&S main socks suppliers.

It was with the active encouragement of M&S that Courtaulds entered into negotiations with Corah's owners. Corah Socks' asset value was £8.1 million.

The threat to Corah Sock Division caused by the failure of the parent company resulted in supply continuity problems for M&S. These were resolved to their satisfaction when the takeover was organised by Courtaulds. Had this business been acquired by Coats Viyella that firm would have become an uncomfortably dominant supplier in the M&S supply chain.

Courtaulds offered £7.1 million, which was agreed in August 1988. Corah Socks passed into Courtaulds' ownership, despite this acquisition being an apparent break with the policy set out in the Courtaulds Textile Group policy document CTG 2000 that forecast extreme difficulties for UK based manufacturers. Courtaulds was well aware of the import penetration taking place, but considered that the sock industry was still defendable against this threat.

Table 3.11 Courtaulds' acquisitions in the hosiery and knitwear industry, **D to M**

Company	Date Acquired	Product							
		FF Hose	Circular Hose	FF Knitwear	C&S Knitwear	Knitted Underwear	Socks	Other interests
Derby and Midland (Blount)	1965		BLO Belper			BLO Belper		Fabric Knitting
Foister, Clay & Ward (Yates) (Queen of Scots)	1963	FOI Mansfield (Belvedere St) (Southwell Rd)		FOI Mansfield (Belvedere St) (Southwell Road)	FOI Leicester YAT Leicester QUE Irvine FOI Middlesbrough	FOI Derby FOI Middlesbrough	FOI Gt. Cent St Leicester FOI Kegworth	Dyeing & Finishing
Hendry & Spiers	1968					H S Wishaw		
Highfield Productions	1968				HIG Hucknall			
Irvine Knitters	1968				IRV Irvine			
Kayser Bondor	1966	KAY Merthyr	KAY Merthyr, KAY Baldock					Foundation-Wear, Lingerie
Kilsyth	1969				KIL Kilsyth		KIL Kilsyth	
Meridian	1963			MER Ilkeston	MER Nottingham MER Clowne	MER Nottingham	MER Notts, MER Ilkeston	Swimwear Leisurewear
Morley	1968	MOR Sutton in Ashfield	MOR Sutton in Ashfield	MOR Heanor		MOR Heanor, MOR Sutton in Ashfield		Dyeing Printing Casual wear

Source: Various Sources

Derby and Midland Mills – Blount & Co. Ltd

Blounts, the Belper based fine-gauge hosiery firm, was formed about 1922 by Freddy Blount's mother who made a living making motifs for attachment to textile products, a trade known in those days as 'chevening'. Prior to taking his apprenticeship as a millwright her son Freddy had helped his mother distribute out-work to women in the village. On completion of his apprenticeship Freddy joined his mother's business that operated from a shed at the bottom of her garden at 7 Spencer Road where they employed a small number of workers operating sewing machines.

Following complaints about noise from her neighbours they moved the business across the road and built a new, larger shed. Following a fire he bought 'Park Mount', the large property next door, and set up there as a hosiery manufacturer, registering the firm in 1927.

Impact of war

On the eve of war in 1939 several German-made fully-fashioned machines were being installed. The German mechanics left hurriedly without their tools and these were returned to them after the war. Freddy also set up a factory in Penn Street later named Ewe Hosiery Ltd which made knitwear and underwear.[27]

During the war Freddy Blount called on his skills as a millwright and part of the Spencer Street factory was turned over to war work making parts for Rolls Royce.

Change of ownership

Shortly after the war the firm passed into the control of a Polish émigré family, headed by Jacob Prevezer and his sons Samuel and Sidney, who, as substantial shareholders, also controlled the warp knitting firm[28] Derby and Midland Warp Knitting Co. Ltd of Chandos Pole Street, Derby.[29]

The success under Blount continued under the new owners. The firm's sales were far in excess of production, and in November 1966 they were producing 18,000 dozen pairs of stockings per week and buying in a further 10,000 dozen per week from other manufacturers. This strategy was not uncommon at that time, and sub-contracting regularly took place between Brettle, Kayser Bondor and Blount when these firms needed to balance their sales and production programmes.

---

[27] Information from Mary Smedley. Belper Museum.
[28] Derby & Midland were lock-knit producers. Their type of product was used extensively in the intimate apparel business.
[29] Information from S. D. Chapman.

The output of Blounts was heavily weighted towards M&S, with whom the Prevezer family shared a close relationship within the Jewish community; the family regularly contributed to M&S charities. The remainder, produced under the Stockleigh label, was sold directly to the retail trade by a team of eleven salesmen.

Stockings prices under pressure in the 1960s

There was a decline in selling prices in the 1960s, to which Blounts' owners had responded by re-equipping with new machinery concentrating on circular stockings. When acquired by Courtaulds, they were equipped with 26 Zodiac 8 feed, 72 Zodiac 4 feed, 142 Bentley twin feed, and only 41 of the much slower producing Bentley single feed machines. Employment was in the region of 600 people.

Favourable prospects for Blounts

Sales of fully-fashioned stockings were under threat and trends showed that it would be uneconomic to make this product in the late 1960s. In response to the threatened loss of trade, Blounts set up a pilot cut and sew knitwear plant and the first knitting machine had been set up at the time the firm passed into Courtaulds' ownership.[30] At the same time, ambitious plans were in hand to more than double the production of circular knitted stockings.

Not only was this firm attractive to Courtaulds as a prospective user of Celon and a growing supplier to M&S, but also as an outlet for the surplus capacity of stockings made by Brettles and Kayser. Blounts was significant as an early entrant into the M&S stockings business for Courtaulds. Its reputation for entrepreneurial flair was based on the business accumen of the founder of the firm, who had built up Derby & Midland Mills from almost nothing into a major supplier of lingerie fabric, and Blounts into a highly successful stockings producer to M&S.

The business was dependent on the owners for its drive and direction. Blounts, the stockings arm of the firm, was under the stable management and day-to-day control of Sidney and Samuel Prevezer, the sons of the founder who by this time was quite elderly. Their success was almost certainly based on their ability to spot a business opportunity and develop it, combined with the foresight and courage to discard unprofitable ventures. In this they were helped by their close working relationship with M&S which gave them an invaluable insight into the state of the market.

The stockings factory was situated very close to Brettles at Belper, a direct

---

[30] Blounts did not continue outerwear manufacturing under Courtaulds ownership.

competitor for labour. Manufacturing capacity was regularly below Blounts' sales potential. They countered a shortage of labour in the Belper area by a strategy of 'contracting out' large quantities of work to other manufacturers. M&S agreed with this arrangement provided that strict quality control procedures were in place.

It is not easy to assess with accuracy the contribution made by Blounts to the profits of Derby & Midland or Brettles' stockings section to the overall results of Brettles, however it is certain that Blounts, under Derby & Midland, were vastly bigger stocking manufacturers. This firm was highly successful but was in need of an injection of capital to re-equip for its ambitious expansion in the expanding circular stockings and increasingly popular tights market.

Derby & Midland acquired by Courtaulds

Blount & Co. Ltd was acquired by Courtaulds, as part of the much larger takeover of Derby and Midland, in 1965. Significantly for Courtaulds, Derby and Midland Mills purchased an important 40,000 lbs of Bri-Nylon per week from Courtaulds' competitor British Nylon Spinners for its warp knitting production, and this could easily be substituted with Courtaulds' Celon.

Foister, Clay & Ward Ltd

Along with Meridian and Bairnswear, Foister, Clay & Ward was one of Courtaulds' earlier acquisitions in the hosiery and knitwear industry. The founder of the firm, Maurice C. Foister, was the son of Charles, a sock manufacturer at Thurmaston, Leicester and the grandson of Thomas, a 'bag hosier' from the same area.[31] Maurice took in partners Clay and Ward during the process of building up the business at Leicester and Mansfield.

The firm was reconstituted in 1926, and by 1942 had risen to become one of the leading manufacturers in the Leicester area, ranking close to Rowley in the number of employees, though far behind Corah, Wolsey, J. B. Lewis (Meridian) and I. & R. Morley.[32]

Records of employment and the manufacturing plant have been kept. These show the very substantial status of the firm in the early 1960s when there were almost 3,000 employees working in its hosiery and knitwear operations, the Middlesbrough factory being the largest.

---

[31] Maurice Foister was a brother of Charles Foister, founder of Cherub Ltd, of Charles Street, Leicester.

[32] National Hosiery Manufacturers Federation *Provisional Register of Members* 1943.

F,C&W – three sites in Leicester

At the time of the acquisition the Frog Island factory in Leicester housed the administrative centre and also a production unit making cut and sewn knitwear, including men's and women's cardigans, jumpers and pullovers. Production was only around 1,200 dozens per week, although the capacity of the plant was in the region of 17–18,000 dozens per week. The reason given for this disastrous shortfall was the shortage of operatives to run the 250 machines in the making-up plant. It was noted that the plant was modern and well maintained and consisted of 100 power flat V bed machines.

On the upper floors of the Frog Island factory the firm had recently installed a very modern conveyor system which was one of the most advanced of its type in the UK. This was used for the transferring[33] and final inspection of children's socks and men's half hose.

Great Central Street, Leicester, was the site of the main sock knitting plant, almost certainly one of the largest in the UK at that time. There were 650 Komet machines and 50 Wildt 'Model E' machines, which were all well maintained and capable of high quality production. Additionally there were 190 linking and toe closing machines.

A. S. Yates Ltd, of Blackbird Road, Leicester, which had been absorbed by F,C&W some years previously, was a circular-knit cut and sewn knitwear factory, focused on the medium price sector of the market. Production was predominantly jumpers, cardigans and lumbers for women. The knitting machines were mainly of the RTR type and the merchandise was largely produced from Bri-Nylon and Courtolon.[34]

F,C&W – Kegworth

Sidilay Works, Kegworth was a secondary sock factory, which was used mainly for the production of men's half-hose and boys' three-quarter hose. This plant was considerably older and smaller than the Frog Island plant, and included a mixture of Komet, and elderly but well maintained Autoswift and 'Model B' machines. Disastrously, although there were 199 machines, only 70 were in use at the time of the acquisition.

---

[33] A heated 'transfer' was applied to the sock which printed the brand name onto the sole.

[34] Courtolon was a false twist nylon 66 used in the knitting industry to produce special effects.

F,C&W – Derby

Derby Works was a large making-up plant, used for processing underwear fabric knitted at Middlesbrough. Some years previously there had been a serious fire after which the site was re-equipped with new machinery; this included two automatic Phillips laying up machines and three modern band knives, three modern blanket presses and a steam calendering machine.

F,C&W – Middlesbrough

The Middlesbrough factory was the largest in the F,C&W group. In contrast to much of the sock machinery at other branches, the equipment was expensive and modern, and included 320 knitting machines and 400 sewing machines. The underwear section was equipped with a wide range of shaped-vest and pantie machines. The outerwear section was equipped with a range of 10, 8 and 7 gauge machines, with interchangeable beds to produce 5 gauge work. There were also 35 hand-flat knitting machines. Some casual wear was also produced.

F,C&W – three factories at Mansfield

Belvedere Works, Mansfield, was a fully-fashioned stockings factory. Over the previous ten years the firm had installed 46 very expensive multi-head machines. The capacity of this plant was around 6,000 dozens per week but at the time of the takeover only around 2,000 dozens per week were being produced. By 1963 the demand for fully-fashioned stockings had fallen and the firm decided not to enter the circular sector which had come under intense price pressure. The customer requirements for circular hose were being met by purchasing several thousand dozens monthly from Italy.

Redcliffe Road, Mansfield was the site of the main fully-fashioned knitwear factory and was producing 2,500 dozens of high quality garments per week. There were 30 multi-head machines and the appropriate number of rib knitting machines to balance the production. This was probably seen as a growth area because there were other machines on order.[35]

The Southwell Road, Mansfield factory was a modern making-up unit for the Redcliffe Road knitting plant. The 250 sewing and other ancillary machines were fed by automatic conveyors, and handled about 2,500 dozens per week without difficulty.

---

[35] In 1963 fully-fashioned knitwear was still being produced in large volumes.

F,C&W – Irvine, Ayrshire

Irvine Works was also a new plant producing a mixture of bulky-knit power-flat and hand-flat garments. Capacity at this plant was in the region of 800 dozens per week, although it was only running at 50% of this level. This establishment was renamed 'Queen of Scots' shortly after the acquisition.

Courtaulds acquired Foister, Clay & Ward

The general impression was that the production facilities throughout were first class, and at some sites were exceptional. However, when the overall situation is considered, the complexity of the underlying problems emerges: this was a firm with first class manufacturing capability able to produce to the highest quality, and yet unable to generate anything like sufficient sales.

The firm had no new orders for the end of the year from M&S and the business placed by them for the following spring was only at half the volume of the previous year. The stock holding had reached very high levels, due to the slow delivery instructions being issued by M&S.

Table 3.12 *Declining profits for F,C&W*

Date	Year	Pre-tax profits (£)
30 June	1955	448,169
30 June	1956	281,110
30 June	1957	430,291
30 June	1958	241,003
31 Dec.	1960	352,165
31 Dec.	1961	265,994
31 Dec.	1962	127,565

Source: F,C&W Accounts

In 1963 the firm passed into Courtaulds' ownership. P. A. C. Vincent, the F,C&W Chairman, wrote:

> As I indicated in my review circulated with the accounts for year ending December 1962, general trading conditions in that year were the worst experienced since the war and the position to date in the current financial

year is not sufficiently clear to enable me yet to make any forecast for the current years trading, and that is still the position.[36]

The management had failed to move with the times and the changing requirements of their main customer, M&S, to whom they were very much a dedicated supplier. The directors had failed to react to the move away from fully-fashioned stockings, and the very large Mansfield plant was running far below its capacity. The fully-fashioned knitwear section at Mansfield was still in production. In the sock factories some investment had taken place, but a significant proportion of the sock knitting plant, although in excellent condition, was very old and slow in production and at the same time the knitwear factory at Irvine in Scotland had recently suffered from the collapse in sales of the Chunky Knit styles.[37]

For the 5,148,000 stock units Courtaulds paid 8s. 6d., a figure of £2,187,900 against the net asset value from the firm's accounts of £2,341,952. This may have appeared to be a bargain price but the outcome, discussed later in the text, makes that doubtful.

F,C&W ranked among the larger manufacturers in the industry. The firm had large capacity in knitwear and knitted underwear and was believed to have some of the best organised factories in the industry. Ironically, this undoubted ability to produce large volumes of high quality merchandise was lost because the ageing top management failed to keep abreast with the changing technology and fashion scene. The firm had a large capacity in fully-fashioned stockings and in sock manufacturing but neither of these sections survived long enough to feature prominently in the development of Courtaulds' garment production. Only the underwear section performed well. M&S had lost confidence and reduced orders until by 1963 the firm was in a crisis.

Hendry & Spiers Ltd

This small, privately owned slumberwear company was situated in Wishaw, Lanarkshire. It employed 30 skilled sewing machinists and was of almost no significance in any manufacturing field. The property was old, but in good condition, and valued by Hendry & Spiers at £18,000. The only acceptable plant was 12 good sewing machines, the remainder being more suitable for making-up woven than knitted fabrics.

Hendry & Spiers went into talks with Prew-Smith, the large Nottingham underwear manufacturing firm, with a view to a takeover, but this was not immediately finalised because Prew-Smith began takeover negotiations with

---

[36] Courtaulds' offer document.
[37] Information from John Boyes-Watson 3 April 2001.

Courtaulds, however there was then only a short delay before both firms were acquired by Courtaulds, and Hendry & Spiers was placed under Prew-Smith control.

The Wishaw area was a rich source of labour, and the firm had active files on 50 former employees and a further list of 60 applicants. It was estimated that there was potential space for 150 operatives and the ability to make up 3,000 dozen mixed styles of basic underwear per week.

Courtaulds acquired Hendry & Spiers

Hendry & Spiers was bought as an aid to developing the fast expanding Prew-Smith underwear units producing for M&S. Its potential was recognised by Prew-Smith Ltd. who had already decided to purchase this firm before entering Courtaulds. Although the firm was almost defunct there was a waiting list for employment and the property had potential for expansion and was therefore clearly an attraction for Courtaulds.

Hendry and Spiers was near to insolvency and was purchased for approximately £25,000. It passed into Courtaulds' ownership in March 1968.

Highfield Productions Ltd

The Highfield Knitting Company was constituted in 1930, and renamed Highfield Productions Ltd in 1932. Information for 1968 shows the firm to be producers of cut and sewn knitwear, operating from a 28,245 square foot factory on a 79,540 square foot site in Byron Street, Hucknall, Nottingham. Highfields had a mixed plant of 50 power-flats, 15 rib machines and 24 hand-flats, which had a book value of £80,000. The firm employed 3 family directors, 38 knitters, 109 making-up operatives, 17 yarn stores, packing and cleaning staff, and 27 management and clerical staff: what might be considered a high proportion of non-productive staff being explained by its reliance on a large number of small customers that were difficult to service. M&S took about 35% of the production with the remainder being supplied to 240 small clients.

Figures showing the firm's financial state are sparse, but turnover declined after 1964, and profit for 1967 was particularly poor. Forward orders for M&S business were in danger because Highfield had failed to complete orders for the previous season causing M&S to lose confidence in the firm.

Table 3.13 *Calamitous results for Highfield*

	Sales (£,000)	Pre-tax profit (£)
1962	427	11,407
1963	535	23,570
1964	592	8,047
1965	572	23,269
1966	525	28,103
1967	380	2,134

Source: Highfield Accounts

Courtaulds acquired Highfield Productions

Continuity of management was in doubt as the senior managers were planning to retire after the takeover. In May 1968 the managing director, M. R. Turton, accepted Courtaulds' offer of £175,000 for the business. This acquisition was influenced by the need for production capacity within the group.

Highfield Productions was bought by Courtaulds to supplement the capacity of Bairnswear for knitted dresses. Bairnswear, a Courtaulds branch since 1963, was able to generate extra orders very rapidly. Highfield Productions had previously lost its M&S business but after a short break limited business was resumed with them. This was in a period when M&S had a shortage of goods and they were at that time prepared to deal with firms that later would be considered too small and inadequate to meet their needs or fit into their culture. The Bairnswear management team had confidence that Highfield's quality could be raised again to M&S standards.

Irvine Knitters Ltd

This family business was situated in Bank Street, Irvine and although it was described as a knitwear company, was actually a manufacturer of general clothing. Of the shares 40% were in the ownership of the manager J. E. Taylor and 40% in a family trust.

Production, at the time of the takeover, was approximately 50% knitwear and 50% dresses, with sales to Littlewoods being 90% and wholesale trade 10%. Littlewoods gave small orders and expected a fast delivery.[38] The knitting plant consisted of 20 Stibbe circulars and 60 flat machines. Yarn usage was 30% Tricel,

---

[38] Generally Littlewoods gave reasonably large orders to the trade. Some mail order contracts were small.

40% Courtelle and 30% Orlon. However these were relatively small quantities and would have little influence on Courtaulds' decision to purchase the firm.

The most significant issue in this takeover was that the capacity of the firm could be added to Queen of Scots, a former F,C&W knitwear factory based at Irvine.

Table 3.14 *Irvine assets*

Net Assets	£70,000
Excess depreciation	£9,000
Tax allowances	£8,400
Government grants and pension surplus	£6,500
TOTAL	£93,900

Source: Irvine Accounts

Courtaulds acquired Irvine Knitters

Irvine Knitters passed into Courtaulds' ownership in 1968 after Courtaulds agreed to pay £130,000 for the business.

Kayser Bondor Ltd

The Full Fashioned Hosiery Co. Ltd was formed as a single product stockings company at Baldock in 1928, and achieved considerable success manufacturing and selling fully-fashioned stockings made from silk and rayon. The firm, which was set up with a capital of £150,000, was developed under the management of John Goodenday, a property developer. Goodenday was originally a non-executive director, who agreed to become temporary managing director during a serious trade recession in 1931 and continued in office until 1960, the year before his death. Expansion was rapid and in response to a labour shortage in Baldock, he set up with government aid a factory in Merthyr, a depressed area of South Wales. Despite the grim history of unemployment, the unattractive surroundings, and the lack of skilled workers and technical colleges to train them, the venture proved highly successful for several years. John Goodenday, who was active in Jewish and other charities,[39] maintained a keen interest in the welfare of the South Wales workers.

---

[39] Keast (Private Circulation).

THE HISTORY OF THE HOSIERY AND KNITWEAR ACQUISITIONS

Kayser Bondor advertisement from *Tatler*, 1950, courtesy of Slenderella, Belper.

Kayser Bondor – a famous brand name

Before the Second World War the firm used the brand name Bondor, a rough translation from French, meaning 'Good [as] Gold'. Following an agreement made in 1936 to distribute the merchandise produced by the American firm Kayser, the firm was renamed Kayser Bondor in 1937. Kayser Bondor (KB) continued to use both the Kayser and Bondor brand names, but it became expedient to simplify the situation and combine these names together.

79

Expansion after World War Two and the M&S connection

Kayser Bondor introduced nylon stockings into their range in 1947 and by 1953 was producing 12,500 dozens per week of the fully-fashioned type, and was among the market leaders at the time. The firm responded to the fashion change to seamfree stockings by commencing circular stockings production in 1956.

From the early 1960s the chairman was Michael A. Colefax, who had over thirty years' connection with Robert Benson & Sons, City merchant bankers. He was a friend of Israel Sieff of M&S, and through him (Colefax) KB gained a big share of the M&S business.[40] Expanding from its original base as a single product company, by the 1960s the firm had become a multi-product garment manufacturer, making dressing gowns, lingerie and foundation wear, which included substantial production for M&S.

KB profits in decline

Despite this enormous expansion, from the mid-1950s the results were dismal, and by 1964 almost every division incurred losses.

Table 3.15 *KB profits in decline*

	Net profit (loss) (£)
1954	748,559
1955	618,609
1956	189,888
1957	193,779
1958	146,472
1959	177,187
1960	334,519
1961	336,951
1962	241,418
1963	163,335
1964	(42,949)

Source: KB Accounts

---

[40] Information from S. D. Chapman.

KB diversifies

There seems to be little evidence that the fine-gauge hosiery division was central to the decline of the firm and separate accounts for each division are no longer available. KB had introduced a policy of diversification and the spread of risk, which was backed up by a good brand image, but the interwar market leader lost its way in the early 1960s. Decline continued under the management of David Goodenday, the son of the previous chairman, a man who had displayed outstanding entrepreneurial flair in the interwar period. This decline was due mainly to a series of ill-fated ventures, which were designed to widen the production base.

Several initiatives during the early 1960s showed lack of good judgement. In the rush for progress the firm was over extended and the opportunity to run pilot schemes, at minimal risk, was set aside in favour of rapid and expensive expansion. A prime example was the abandonment of the rented boutique business in favour of fully owned shops. The rental system had allowed for the easy withdrawal from unprofitable sites, but many new shops had been purchased from the previous owners when they were unprofitable and they remained unprofitable under KB.

A particularly unfortunate venture was the 1961 purchase of housecoat manufacturers Wovenair which proved to be a heavy loss-maker. Management problems caused an almost complete breakdown in manufacturing at Wovenair, and a serious deterioration of quality. A similar attempt to enter the childrenswear market also met with failure. The opportunity to import, and test the market for garments designed in America, was dropped in favour of manufacturing the American designed garments on a large scale in KB's own under-utilised factories. The design of the merchandise proved to be unsuitable for the UK market, and the volume produced was too great, forcing massive price reductions.

The prospect of entry into the Common Market encouraged KB to abandon the previous policy of selling through agents in mainland Europe. The firm then set up subsidiaries in Belgium and Germany. In both cases the local management was inadequate but the larger losses were made in Germany. This was due to the allowance of over-extended credit and the policy of deliberately selling at very low margins to attract high volume business.

KB takes action

The problems within the firm forced Michael Colefax to take drastic action, and in September 1965 John E. Bywater, a former executive in the Ford motor firm, was brought in as deputy chairman to run the company over the managing director David Goodenday.

Courtaulds acquired KB

Courtaulds' takeover in the early part of 1966 was probably encouraged by KB's high usage of nylon in the stockings division; this could be secured for Courtaulds' Celon, but would be vulnerable in the event of a takeover by some other firm with nylon processing interests. However, despite the criticism that Courtaulds drove too hard a bargain with their £2,850,000 bid, KB failed to achieve the forecast results that had been personally approved by the chairman, Michael Colefax,[41] and more serious losses were to follow. Within a very short time after the Courtaulds takeover David Goodenday resigned, and John Bywater was appointed managing director. It appears that the firm suffered from a lack of consistent and experienced management after a previous chairman John Goodenday died, and his successors embarked on a series of ill-conceived ventures, all within too short a space of time.

KB had a highly recognisable brand image in the popular market and a good reputation for quality. Without doubt it had several highly competent and well organised manufacturing units that supplied both the brand and chain store outlets, including M&S, and the KB lingerie and foundation-wear businesses were also very important acquisitions for Courtaulds, although they do not form part of this study.

Kilsyth Hosiery Co. Ltd

Josiah Cleland, a Glasgow sock maker, set up in business in 1875 and operated in Cumbernauld until 1904. Due to the shortage of workers in that area the business was then moved a few miles to Kilsyth where the Burnside Factory at Allanfauld Road was built in stages as the business increased. The firm became a limited company (Kilsyth Hosiery) in 1928.

During World War Two the firm became a 'nucleus establishment' taking into its property four smaller manufacturers, but these did not operate for very long as independent firms and were soon absorbed into the Kilsyth Hosiery Co. Ltd business. This had a pivotal impact on the firm because one of these firms produced knitted schoolwear and this part of the business gradually took over as the firm was unable to compete with the mass production sock manufacturers in the English Midlands.

There were three active partners at the time of the acquisition, who were the recently appointed managing partner, J. N. Smart CA, J. H. Cleland responsible for socks and A. E. Cleland, responsible for cut and sewn knitwear. They stated that it was their intention, should they remain independent, to cease making socks and concentrate on knitwear.

---

[41] Hosiery Trade Journal, August 1967.

Courtaulds acquired Kilsyth Hosiery

Courtaulds saw Kilsyth as compatible with and complementary to Bairnswear. Bairnswear management believed that Kilsyth, a competitor, could continue and expand in this market and free them for other production. In 1969 the firm had a 70 strong labour force manufacturing 200 dozen cut and sewn knitwear garments and 300 dozen socks per week for a customer base of 500 retail accounts. However, Bairnswear, while wishing to take the major share of the chain store schoolwear market, did not want to use their existing factories for this fragmented type of trade.

The takeover coincided with a highly successful introduction of Courtaulds' acrylic yarn *Courtelle* into the business and although this was useful to Courtaulds was unlikely to have been an important motivation for the acquisition.

Table 3.16 *Kilsyth's profit history*[42]

	Turnover (£)	Net profit (£)
1966	176,000	1,272
1967	161,000	2,331
1968	154,000	8,630
1969	176,000	21,524

Source: Kilsyth Accounts

1968 and 1969 results were very favourable due to high levels of activity in the factory following the introduction of acrylic yarn which proved popular with the customers. During the negotiations for the purchase of the firm, the assets were stated by the vendors to be:

Table 3.17 *Kilsyth assets*

Buildings	£50,000
Plant	£25,000
Stocks	£60,000
Excess debtors to creditors	£6,000
TOTAL	£141,000

Source: Kilsyth Accounts

---

[42] The improved profit was explained by Kilsyth as resulting from reducing stocks, cutting out unprofitable factored items and increasing output.

After some negotiations a deal was struck at £131,000 and this small firm, operated and owned by the Cleland family for five generations, was acquired by Courtaulds in 1969. No value appears to have been placed on the relatively high profit ratio of recent profits to assets.

Meridian Limited

Meridian was established as J. Lewis & Sons in 1815 at Tewkesbury, but the founder, James Blount Lewis, moved to Nottingham in 1830. He made substantial progress and commenced manufacturing at Ilkeston Junction in 1885, forming a limited company in 1893.

An important milestone in the progress of the company was the deal set up with the American promoters of interlock, which granted the firm the exclusive UK rights to this process between 1911 and 1929. This established Meridian as one of the foremost knitted underwear producers; '...in the 1920s the new fabric brought massive success to J. B. Lewis and Sons Ltd'. [43]

Table 3.18   *J. B. Lewis profits 1917 to 1949 (£)*

1917	58,585	1928	186,600	1939	120,448
1918	77,931	1929	209,323	1940	113,685
1919	122,548	1930	207,274	1941	101,952
1920	208,534	1931	106,057	1942	87,882
1921	5,187	1932	97,889	1943	80,115
1922	138,000	1933	83,119	1944	121,854
1923	174,628	1934	103,954	1945	103,430
1924	162,416	1935	92,524	1946	80,347
1925	175,268	1936	107,469	1947	87,110
1926	166,079	1937	121,728	1948	176,526
1927	178,921	1938	103,311	1949	215,339

Source: Meridian AGM

The prestigious factory in Haydn Road Nottingham was opened just prior to World War One and by 1930 the site included a sports ground and swimming pool.

By 1942 the importance of J. B. Lewis Ltd can be seen by reference to The National Hosiery Manufacturers Provisional Register of Members 1943, which places this firm as by far the largest member of the Nottingham Association and at that time it was a much larger firm than even Wolsey at Leicester.

---

[43]   *Meridian News* 1967.

Meridian Underwear (J. B. Lewis & Sons Ltd) advertisement in *Punch* magazine, 1949.

Labour shortages in Nottingham after World War Two

In common with many other firms, Meridian suffered from a severe shortage of labour after World War Two. The decision was made to concentrate the knitting operations, which had previously been carried out at several minor sites in Nottingham, as much as possible at Haydn Road, Nottingham and making-up was then transferred to the outlying factories where labour was more readily available.

The name of the firm was changed from J. B. Lewis to Meridian Ltd at the time of its conversion to a public company in 1951. This was to avoid confusion with other businesses of a similar name, and to benefit from the popularity of the Meridian trademark.[44]

In 1960 Meridian revived its previously dormant seamless hose plant, but sold this to Aristoc in 1961. That same year the Kirkby-in-Ashfield factory was commenced but these were difficult years for the firm, with almost static turnover and falling profits.

Table 3.19 *Pre-takeover profits (£)*

	1960	1961	1962
Current total assets	2,356,263	2,656,595	2,596,574
Current liabilities	1,284,972	1,569,019	1,508,998
Turnover	3,573,971	3,833,429	3,894,763
Profit	538,029	510,115	346,639

Source: Meridian Accounts

Courtaulds acquired Meridian

The takeover offer by Courtaulds was made in June 1963. This was accepted by the directors and recommended to the remaining shareholders and took effect very quickly. In contrast to several other Courtaulds' acquisitions, Meridian was still a profitable concern.

Declining brand sales

The firm, which promoted its Meridian brand through press advertising, was faced with a declining retail client base but had taken successful steps to attack the chain store trade, including M&S and the mail order outlets. Meridian

---

[44] *Meridian News* 1965.

developed a diverse sales policy at a time when the market was being realigned in favour of the chain stores and the firm was therefore flexible enough to move as the market dictated.

A major acquisition

Meridian was one of Courtaulds' major acquisitions during its 1960s incursion into the hosiery and knitwear industry, bringing with it manufacturing units at Nottingham, Clowne, Calverton, Ilkeston and Kirkby-in-Ashfield. Despite having interests in socks, swimwear, knitwear and leisurewear, dyeing and finishing and jersey wear manufacture, it was for underwear that the company had become best known.

The management was under the control of George Bignall, whose father was chairman, and at the time of the takeover the family owned 17.5% of the company and the management of this profitable firm was highly regarded within Courtaulds.

Meridian was a major employer with 1,800 employees at the 500,000 square foot Haydn Road site, and around 1,000 spread around the other sites. It was an important acquisition for Courtaulds, its large and efficient underwear manufacturing capacity making it a major acquisition in that field. The firm was also a large producer of knitwear and socks. It also manufactured extensive quantities of leisurewear and swimwear, although these products do not feature in this study.

Meridian employed experienced and competent management and was a noted brand supplier. The firm had a reputation for good quality output and good employee–employer relations. Its main site at Haydn Road, Nottingham, was exceptionally well equipped, with facilities including the heated swimming pool and cricket pitch.

I. & R. Morley Ltd

From modest and obscure beginnings in the framework knitting industry in Nottingham and surrounding villages the business prospered. The founders, John and Richard Morley took the courageous step of opening a warehouse in Russia Row, London and moved to the much larger warehouse in Wood Street in 1799.[45]

In its early days the firm was in the hands of several partners and was initially named Chambers, Wilson & Morley. Chambers left the partnership and the business and it prospered under the management of the two brothers, John and Richard Morley. The business was noted for its large range of merchandise, all

---

[45] For an official history of Morley see Pickering (1900).

of which was of high quality, and this was backed up by a network of contacts with other manufacturers, lawyers and bankers, most from within a circle of religious nonconformists.

Progress was spectacular in manufacturing as well as wholesaling and when the two brothers retired the firm was already a market leader in the UK. The firm grew to be the 'Colossus'[46] of the industry in the nineteenth century and Morley became the outstanding wholesale house for hosiery and knitwear.

Samuel Morley – outstanding entrepreneur

Samuel Morley (1809–1886), the son of John, entered the business in the accounts department of the London wholesale business at the age of sixteen. He became manager around 1840 and by 1860 he owned the whole business including the manufacturing plants in Leicestershire, Nottinghamshire and Derbyshire. It was under his management that I. & R. Morley was set on the path to becoming reputedly the largest firm of its type in the world. Samuel, who declined a peerage in 1865, was a Liberal MP, a principal shareholder of the London Daily News, and an outstanding entrepreneur, and was the driving force behind Morley's expansion. Although he had taken on an already outstandingly successful business, it was under him that it enjoyed a long period of expansion and the Wood Street premises were rebuilt on a larger scale and the firm made rapid progress.

Expansion under Samuel Morley

By the time of Samuel's death the firm had six large factories operating in the East Midlands and two more were being set up, there were well over 4,000 employees in manufacturing apart from the wholesaling side of the business. In addition the firm employed a large number of outworkers which by 1900 also numbered over 4,000.[47] The firm stocked a comprehensive range of general clothing as well as hosiery and knitwear items. The wholesale business drew in supplies from several high quality manufacturers as well as from the firm's own factories which also made gloves, umbrellas and ties. As might be expected, a large proportion of this merchandise was in the popular mourning black, the essential fashion in the late Victorian era, a mode that had made the Courtauld family very wealthy.

---

[46] For a more detailed view of this firm's history read Chapman, 'I. & R. Morley: Colossus of the Hosiery Trade and Industry 1799–1965' in *Textile History* vol. 28 – 1.

[47] Thomas, *I. & R. Morley a record of a hundred years* (Chiswick Press 1900), p. 22.

Morley Daybrook has been converted to residential use. Picture courtesy of the author.

Samuel Morley's successors

On Samuel's death in 1886 the business passed to his three sons. The last surviving son to lead the firm, Lord Hollenden, retired in 1920 and family members then remained in control until the firm lost its independence in 1968.

I. & R. Morley was the leading member of the Wholesale Textile Association (WTA) for many years. This organisation was set up in 1912 to protect the wholesalers from the advances already being made by the chain stores. WTA members gave preference to manufacturers that did not deal with chain stores. However it was clear that by the 1930s the forward march of the chain stores could not be resisted and that the wholesalers would not, in the long run, be able to provide all the orders that the larger manufacturers needed to survive. However, decline was gradual, even in the late 1940s and much later there were still thousands of small shops operating in the UK that needed supplying via the wholesalers.

Morley in trouble after World War Two

The heady days of success in the nineteenth century were long gone. After the Second World War this family run firm remained committed for far too long to the declining wholesale business, and the WTA. They were entrenched in the less fashionable fully-fashioned stockings, knitwear and heavy underwear (long johns) manufacturing sectors of the trade. With declining profitability they were unable to invest in more modern plant, and by the mid-1960s Morley had become an inflexible medium-scale producer in a mass production industry that required rapid reaction to fashion changes to ensure survival. The long-established market leader of the nineteenth century had failed to respond fast enough to the changing conditions of the 1960s. It remained committed to the wholesale supply chain long after that way of trading had entered into serious decline.

Disastrous losses

In 1962 the firm commenced a run of seriously reduced profits and disastrous losses:

Table 3.20 *Morley in decline*

	Group pre-tax profits (loss) (£000)	Turnover (£ million)
1960	123	5.6
1961	293	5.6
1962	(31)	5.6
1963	41	5.6
1964	80	5.4
1965	(269)	5.3
1966	(288)	5.0
1967	(307)	4.5

Source: Morley Accounts

Retrenchment undertaken from around 1964 still left the firm with too many sites. It remained a specialist wholesaler within the hosiery and knitwear trade, but did not balance its manufacturing capacity to its wholesale sales. The shortfall was partly taken care of by nearly £500,000 of clandestine sales to BHS, but this was totally insufficient to halt the catastrophic losses.[48] The lack of balance in the firm resulted in a top heavy management structure and under-recovery of overhead costs and the elderly directors were unable to correct these issues.

Morley failed to modernise its capacity, remaining for too long in the glove, fully-fashioned underwear (long johns) and fully-fashioned hosiery sectors and in all of these it operated with outdated machinery. Ultimately, the losses in 1965

---

[48] As a leading member of the WTA, Morleys was, on the surface, totally committed to wholesale trading.

and the two subsequent years sealed its fate, and it was unable to survive as an independent firm. The chairman apportioned blame to external factors:

> These difficulties were brought about by the very actions of manufacturers themselves who had collectively brought about over-capacity on new, improved, and faster hosiery machinery. Over capacity urged upon them the need for seeking greater sales volume; as a result massive competition emerged and prices were forced down to uneconomic levels. Hosiery capacity remains far higher than home demand can absorb.[49]

Morley reorganises

In 1966, in an attempt to remain viable, the drastic decision was taken to concentrate manufacturing at Heanor, with Sutton-in-Ashfield as a secondary site. The underwear factory in Durham and the Leicester warehouse were closed, and these activities were transferred to Heanor, which also housed the mainly fully-fashioned knitwear plant, and Sutton where the underwear was made up. Following a disastrous fire, the Leicester knitwear factory was closed, and not reopened. Despite the sale of the subsidiary sock manufacturing firm Fuller & Hambley Ltd, and the closure of the sock manufacturing division, the sales range of merchandise in 1966 still remained quite comprehensive.

After this reorganisation the company headquarters remained in London from where the directors still operated, but the wholesaling division was still very fragmented, with the main warehouse at Heanor, a warehouse for gloves in the East End of London, with the sales, management and departmental staff having separate accommodation in the West End of London. There were severe problems for those manufacturing departments dependent on orders from the firm's own wholesale department, because the wholesale department was not made responsible or even able to sell the output of the factories.

Courtaulds acquired Morley

Prior to the takeover the board had already decided to cease manufacturing stockings at Sutton-in-Ashfield. This did, however, leave the fully-fashioned knitwear section still producing about 1,200 dozen per week. Just prior to the takeover the firm had approximately 1,400 employees.

Morley, despite being for so long the leader of the WTA, had commenced surreptitiously supplying BHS and other large retail groups and mail order

---

[49] G. Hope-Morley in *Hosiery Trade Journal* April 1966.

Morley tights street hoarding, image produced by I&R Morley Ltd.

organisations. This was of course already a step in the right direction for Courtaulds as it showed that Morley recognised the need to concentrate on the larger outlets.

The Morley family which still controlled 51% of the shares accepted an offer from Courtaulds reputed to be in the region of £1.5 million.

After the takeover in 1968 the firm soon went into obscurity, with those manufacturing sections that were successful being allocated to other management groups. Two sections that do not feature in this book, Theta Dyeworks and John Hampden Press, were able to survive for several years in the new environment.

Table 3.21 *Courtaulds' acquisitions in the hosiery and knitwear industry, P to W*

Company	Date Acquired	FF Hose	Circular Hose	FF Knitwear	C&S Knitwear	Knitted Underwear	Socks	Other interests
Percy Taylor	1967	TAY Hinckley TAY Oadby	TAY Hinckley TAY Oadby					
Prew-Smith (J. C. Clarke)	1968				PRE Nottingham PRE Bolsover CLA Arnold	PRE Bolsover CLA Arnold		
Rowley	1968			ROW Oadby	ROW Leicester	ROW Leicester	ROW Derby	Leisurewear Dyeing & Finishing
Skolnick (Beasley)	1966	BEA Hinckley	BEA Hinckley					
Stewarton	1968				STE Glasgow		STE Glasgow	
Wolsey & Lyle & Scott	1967		WOL Ilkeston WOL Kimberley	WOL Dumfries WOL Kimberley WOL Shepshed LYL Hawick LYL Burnfoot LYL Jedburgh		WOL Shepshed WOL Bruin St Leicester WOL Gainsborough WOL Ratby LYL Dunfermline LYL Gateshead	WOL Bruin St Leicester WOL Welshpool	Double-Jersey (Knitting) Elastic (Abbey Park Mills being phased out)

Source: Various sources.

Percy Taylor Ltd

Percy Taylor Ltd, user of the brand name Penguin, was established in 1927 and produced fully-fashioned stockings. Production of circular stockings commenced in 1957. This small scale Lancaster Road, Hinckley firm also had a second site at Oadby, Leicester, used for folding and packing.

In the early 1960s the decision was taken to trade 'direct to retail', concentrating on chemist's shops. Unfortunately this coincided with a serious fire at the Hinckley factory, which reduced the manufacturing capacity to far below the sales capabilities. After the fire there was no serious attempt to regain the multiple stores trade, the sales thrust being mainly concentrated on smaller retail outlets.

Courtaulds acquired Percy Taylor

Despite the fire the firm remained profitable.[50] In 1967 it passed into the ownership of Courtaulds, probably influenced by the desire of one of the owners to retire.

Table 3.22 *Percy Taylor profits*

	Profits (£)
1960	35,938
1961	61,478
1962	88,080
1963	52,904*
1964	64,688*
1965	37,541

Note: *Includes loss of profits insurance
Source: Percy Taylor Accounts

Prew-Smith (Harry) Ltd

This family firm was established in 1930 and in 1968 the family was still in control of 48% of the shares. The firm was principally involved in the manufacture of underwear at three sites. The Nottingham Road, Nottingham, factory was acquired in 1960 and Clarkes of Arnold, a subsidiary firm in the same line of business, was acquired in 1963 but by far the most important part of the business was the knitted underwear factory at Bolsover, Derbyshire.

---

[50] From 1963 50% of the merchandise was bought in from other manufacturers.

The firm was a major supplier of underwear to Marks & Spencer, which took 60% of the output. Prew-Smith took advantage of every possible sales opportunity that M&S offered. Harry Prew-Smith, the founder of the firm, who was still running the business, had built up a close working relationship with them over many years.

In contrast to many of the businesses acquired by Courtaulds, this firm had been profitable and expanding right up to the time of the acquisition. Shortly before the acquisition, Harry Prew-Smith entered into negotiations for the purchase of Hendry & Spiers so that manufacturing could be increased to match improving sales potential.

Courtaulds acquired Prew-Smith

Prew-Smith was taken over by Courtaulds in 1968. The takeover is significant and far from typical because, despite flat sales the firm showed good profits, far in advance of most of Courtaulds' other acquisitions in the industry.[51] At the time of the takeover the firm had between 800 and 900 employees.

Kearton wrote to the directors at the time of the takeover:

> The offer obviously has an enormous element of goodwill in it, justified by the excellent results of Prew-Smith under your leadership. We would therefore expect that you would work with us to apply something of the Prew-Smith techniques to other parts of Courtaulds.

Table 3.23 *Prew-Smith profits*

	Net profit after tax (£)	Sales (£ million)
1960	120,047	
1961	117,027	
1962	117,907	
1963	145,029	
1964	193,160	
1965	281,731	£2.2m
1966	163,150	£2.2m
1967	262,112	£2.2m

Source: Prew-Smith Accounts

---

[51] The Bolsover factory later featured substantially in Courtaulds' underwear development.

Prew-Smith took advantage of the boom in knitted outerwear and set up a trial knitwear section with the encouragement of M&S, but Courtaulds discontinued this after the takeover.

Apart from a short period when Prew-Smith bought out Clarks of Arnold the firm was financed by its own profits. The relatively high return on capital employed was almost certainly due to investment income, and conversely from an absence of loan costs. The firm was noted for its attention to detail, close control of materials and the elimination of waste in all forms. This gave the Bolsover factory the reputation for being one of the most efficient in the industry.[52]

R. Rowley & Co. Ltd

Founded in the latter part of the nineteenth century, Rowley became one of the most successful hosiery and knitwear businesses in Leicester, but after the Second World War it lost its early drive, and in the 1960s suffered serious financial difficulties.

Robert Rowley commenced his business in Leicester in 1867. He was the son of a Wisbech woodworker, and the Queen Street, Leicester business was established on the site of the wood yard where his father had worked when they came to Leicester in the early 1860s. In his early years he obtained yarn from the spinners which he distributed to cottage stockingers in Great Glen and Thurmaston,[53] but by 1891 Robert Rowley's factory in Leicester was mechanised, using Cotton's patent machines, which indicates that the firm had acquired or gained access to considerable capital.

By 1901, when the firm was constituted as a private limited company, the turnover had reached £174,000. Rapid recovery followed a dramatic fire in 1911, when the factory in Queen Street, Leicester was razed to the ground, and in 1912 turnover reached £300,000. The firm's success was almost certainly due to early mechanisation and low-cost production.

The interwar years

An indication of the control the wholesale trade held over the manufacturers was felt by Rowley when R. Walker & Sons, in 1919, decided to sell their Wolsey brand products directly to the retail trade. This affected Rowley very hard because it had produced fine cashmere goods to the extent of 40,000 to 50,000 dozens per year on payment of fees to Walker for use of their (Wolsey) trademark.[54] A proposal that Rowley continue to make these goods under contract to Walkers

---

[52] Prew-Smith was an active supporter of Jewish Charities.
[53] Rowley booklet 80th anniversary.
[54] Robert Rowley AGM 1919.

Rowley gutted by fire, 1911. Picture courtesy of Leicester Mercury Media Group.

was not carried forward '…because it would prejudice us with our wholesale friends'[55] – this indicates the dependence of Rowley on the wholesale trade at that time. Interestingly this loyalty does not seem to have been reciprocated, because within a few years Rowley noted that three of its major wholesale customers were reducing orders, as they had developed their own manufacturing plants.[56]

Rowley – A multi-product firm

After the First World War, Rowley grew to be a very substantial firm and by 1943 the labour statistics in *The National Hosiery Manufacturers Federation provisional Register of Members* shows Rowley as the third largest member in terms of employment in the Leicester district. However, the multi-product nature of the firm must be considered in relation to its size. Rowley was not leader in any single product, although the sock production was considerable, Rowley was never owner of a famous brand name such as Wolsey, Pick, Pex or Byford, and continued to find its market with the wholesalers.

---

[55] Robert Rowley AGM 1920.
[56] Robert Rowley AGM 1925.

Management change

In November 1936 Robert Rowley died, aged 91, leaving an estate of £813,931. He was followed as chairman by his son, Thomas Stirk Rowley, who died within six months of his appointment, and then by his nephew, Leslie C. Robertson, the grandson of the founder, whose resignation in 1962 severed the family link with the firm.

Change in the supply chain

It is significant that the booklet produced to celebrate the eightieth anniversary of the firm's foundation made no claim to it being a leader in fashion, stating

> ... the Company caters for the requirements of the average person. Though not a fashion house, the Company keeps abreast of modern trends and fashion with a view to extension and catering for the changing market. What the man or woman in the street in almost any civilized part of the world wants in the fashion line, Rowleys will endeavour to supply. [57]

In a change of policy, by 1948 this traditional supplier to the wholesale trade was developing trade with M&S. The board minutes note that M&S was suggesting that business for 1949 should be targeted at £400,000, but the firm was only prepared to allocate goods to the value of £250,000 to them. These figures cannot be placed in a meaningful context because total turnover figures are no longer available. Severe problems occurred in 1951 because competitors were beginning to increase the quantity of goods released to the home market. Rowley was indecisive and attempted to retain as many customers as possible and decided to spread the production across the whole customer base, instead of making a tactical change and concentrating on the growth of the M&S business. It is interesting to note that, as late as 1950, an application by a sales representative in the Scottish Area to open an account with a wholesaler who was not a member of the WTA needed careful consideration as it was considered that there might be a possibility of endangering relationships with large WTA wholesalers in the area.

The sock department production plan for 1952 was still weighted towards wholesale and export trade:

---

[57] Rowley booklet 80th anniversary.

Table 3.24 *Sock sales mix 1952*

Export	306,000 dozens	43%
Marks & Spencer	80,000 dozens	11%
Wholesale home trade	328,000 dozens	46%

Source: Rowley Archives

A major setback occurred in 1951 with a recession in sales. This led to the decision, taken early in 1952, to close the Coatbridge, Lanarkshire factory that had been opened in 1948 as a response to the shortage of labour in the Leicester area. However, an agreement was made with S. Mackinnon & Co. to run the factory as a new company, with a minimum shareholding by Rowley of 51%. The Coatbridge factory continued in production but eventually closed in 1962 after incurring further heavy losses.

Rowley abandons stockings manufacturing

In common with many other firms Rowley's trade in fully-fashioned stockings deteriorated in the early 1950s. This was against a background of labour shortages, a shortage of yarn supplies, particularly nylon, and the cost of replacing the machinery, which was rapidly becoming obsolete. It was estimated that the cost of replacing the fully-fashioned machines with circular machines would be £250,000. The decision was taken not to incur this expense and to close the stockings section.

Rowley in decline

In its independent form, Rowley struggled through the early 1960s, losing a great deal of money, but had two consecutive years of profit prior to the takeover, although these were poor for the size of the business.

Table 3.25 *Rowley profits (losses)*

	Total profits (losses)
1962	(73,760)
1963	(19,993)
1964	36,127
1965	(40,080)
1966	46,225
1967	10,181

Source: Drivers' offer document

A multi-product firm, Rowley manufactured cut and sewn knitwear, fully-fashioned knitwear, knitted underwear and socks. It also had substantial leisurewear interests.

Despite previously having a long history of success, after the Second World War the firm never regained the profitability of the early post-war years and suffered the total loss of the fully-fashioned stockings and the decline of the fully-fashioned knitwear departments and the loss of the small but important trade with M&S.

Courtaulds acquired Rowley

R. Rowley & Co. Ltd was not focused on any particular market sector and was reputed, by the employees in the late 1960s, to accept any order that could be obtained, except orders from M&S, which were shunned. Shortly before the acquisition, Rowley had begun to establish a connection with the Mothercare chain of shops which became vital to its survival under its new owners. The firm had become very short of capital and probably only survived, in its independent form, because of its small and inexpensive management structure and stringent cost control.

Much of the plant was old and the once impressive main factory in Queen Street, Leicester, had become very shabby. There were also industrial relations problems due to the merger of the cut and sewn knitwear making-up department formerly at Oadby into the Leicester factory, two factories that had operated with different pay rates for direct operatives.

Talks that might have led to a takeover were held between the company and Courtaulds in 1963 but were not pursued at that time. Later there were abortive offers from Nottingham Manufacturing Co. and H. L. Driver Ltd, but in 1968 the firm finally passed into the hands of Courtaulds. A dismal profit record, stagnant dividends and poor share performance hastened the firm's loss of independence.[58]

Skolnick Ltd (P. Beasley & Co. Ltd)

The manufacturing arm of this family run and owned firm was established shortly after World War Two by P. Beasley, a former mechanic. Its manufacturing plant was situated at Brick Kiln Lane, Hinckley and in 1965 the firm was merged with Skolnick Ltd, a London wholesale selling organisation.

The firm's production was approximately 14,000 dozens seamless hose per

---

[58] Despite their dismal record Bill (T. W.) Harvey, managing director, Jack Machen, sales, and Harold Dutton, production, all worked successfully in the new environment developing the Rowley group into a major supplier of childrenswear to non-M&S outlets.

week, but fortunately it was only marginally committed to fully-fashioned stockings having an output of only 600 dozens per week of that product, which by the time of the takeover in 1966, were becoming less fashionable. The plant consisted of 116 single feed Bentley machines, 327 other single feed and four sets of fully-fashioned machines.

The firm was hit very hard by the shortage of labour in the main centres of the industry and early in 1966, just prior to the takeover, suffered a severe shortage of workers for the finishing stages of the production. The problems of old fashioned plant, old property, and poor working conditions, were totally against recruitment, and the situation had reached crisis point with 90,000 dozens of pre-dye stock and a further 30,000 dozens awaiting finishing. The existing management saw no possibility of rectifying this situation, other than stopping knitting.

Courtaulds acquired Skolnick

A potential user of Courtaulds' Celon, Skolnick had a turnover of £870,000 and a profit to April 1966 of £117,000.

Three small hosiery firms in the Hinckley area were acquired by Courtaulds: Percy Taylor, Skolnick (Beasley) and Lockley & Garner. There seems to be little to commend these small family controlled firms except that they could add some capacity to Courtaulds and use its yarn. All appear to have had problems that were beyond control for their management.

Stewarton Hosiery Co. Ltd

This very insignificant knitwear company, incorporated in 1917 was owned by the Liddell family and operated in Thornliebank, Glasgow. In 1968 the total labour force was only around 70.

Table 3.26 *Stewarton profits (losses)*

	Turnover (£)	*Taxed profits (loss) (£)*
1962	103,724	3,238
1963	111,724	4,157
1964	143,769	(86)
1965	165,769	3,963
1966	144,020	(2,732)
1967	114,216	(10,668)

Source: Stewarton Accounts

Stewarton Hosiery was positioned in the middle market between the major stores and the wholesale trade. The main outlets were United Drapery Stores, Bellmans, Burton by Post, Texplant Corporation, Empire Stores, Home Bros, Charles Creed and Scottish CWS. Aggregate losses exceeded profits over a six year period.

Courtaulds acquired Stewarton

Stewarton, which had planning permission already granted for an extension to the factory, passed into Courtaulds' ownership in 1968. The firm was a small general clothing firm and was bought to add knitwear capacity to Queen of Scots, a former F,C&W knitwear department based at Irvine, Ayrshire. It was able to gain orders that the larger Courtaulds' firms, which concentrated on M&S, found to be incompatible with their main business.

(Wolsey Ltd) Lyle & Scott

Lyle & Scott was launched in 1874 by two partners, William Lyle and Walter Scott. Using borrowed capital they made rapid progress, in the early stages concentrating on knitwear produced on hand-flat machines. Very soon 200 knitters were employed. Cottons Patent power driven fully-fashioned machines were introduced around 1883, and progress was maintained right up to the First World War.

The Interwar Years – difficult times for Lyle & Scott

Lyle & Scott was best known for its knitwear, but as early as 1928 underwear output was seen as being the more important part of the business. In the interwar period the firm's trade reached its peak in 1930 and in common with many firms in the industry suffered badly during the depression. In the 1930s there was short time working, falling share prices, the directors took pay cuts and in 1936 no dividends were paid. At this time the prestigious Scottish industry was suffering from competition from the lower-cost mass-production 'fancy'[59] knitwear from the English Midlands, and from depressed export markets. Lyle & Scott was a high quality producer in competition with Peter Scott, Innes & Henderson (Braemar) and Pringle.

---

[59] Cut and sewn knitwear.

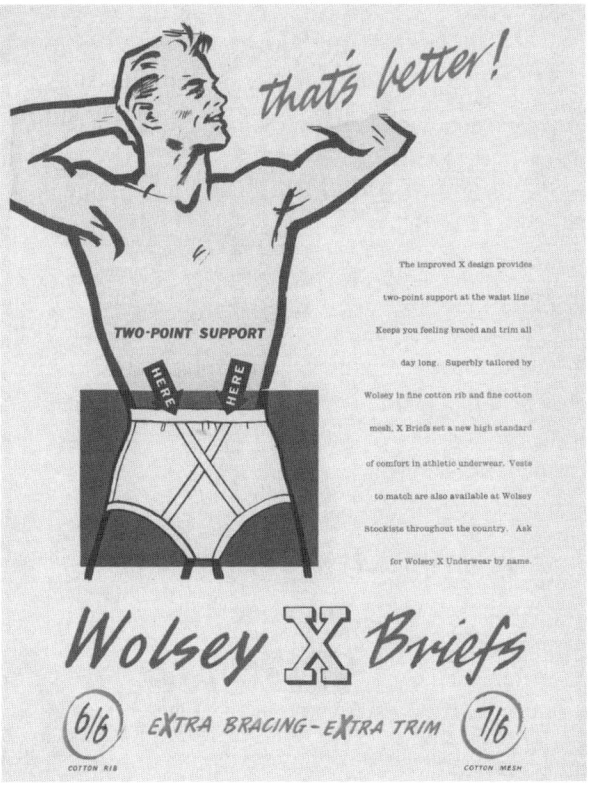

Lyle & Scott's competitor's product, Wolsey X Front, advertising their wares in 1955.

Lyle & Scott and 'Y front'

Lyle & Scott faced the possible collapse of the traditional woollen underwear that formed a vital part of its business. Success was snatched from near disaster in 1938 by a strategic move when a deal was negotiated with the American firm Cooper Inc. to produce the Cooper Bros Y Front style of men's briefs, and use that well established brand name exclusively in the UK and several European markets, paying on a royalty basis. Very different raw materials and garment assembly methods were required from those traditionally used in the high class Scottish Borders factories. However, this agreement allowed the firm to engage in mass production and break away from the trap in which they had been caught – selling expensive garments at low prices in a time of depression.

Success after World War Two

The knitwear side of the business did survive the 1930s depression and after the war the firm concentrated extensively on golf wear, developing the Lyle & Scott trademark. Sports knitwear was distributed through golf stores and the traditional Scottish knitwear remained successful and commanded high prices in top of the market stores, whilst underwear was particularly successful in department stores.

The firm prospered and to finance expansion it became a public company in 1960. The knitwear side of the business continued on traditional lines supplying cashmere, silk and cashmere mixtures, and lambswool garments to high class firms such as Harrods of London and Jenners of Edinburgh and there was little close competition for the Jockey (Cooper Inc) range of underwear other than Wolsey X Front which was much less successful.[60]

Lyle & Scott acquired by Wolsey

As a defensive measure Wolsey bought out Lyle & Scott in 1964. In the underwear business, Lyle & Scott and Wolsey were direct competitors, but Wolsey was no match for Lyle & Scott's Y Front briefs. Lyle & Scott operated as an autonomous subsidiary until 1967 when Wolsey (Lyle & Scott's holding company), was acquired by Courtaulds.[61]

Wolsey Ltd

In 1755, in the era of the framework knitters, Anne Wood & Sons commenced trading and some 70 years later this business was bought by Robert Walker who worked for the firm. Walker introduced the factory system of manufacturing and in the 1920s the firm was merged with two others, W Tyler & Co. of Leicester and the London wholesaling house, Boswell Brown Ltd.[62]

Successful policy in the interwar years

Wolsey & Co. Ltd became one of the foremost multi-product firms in the industry, and by the early years of World War Two was second only in size to

---

[60] See Gulvin, *The Scottish Hosiery and Knitwear Industry 1680–1980* (John Donald Publishers Ltd, Edinburgh, 1984).

[61] Due to the autonomous nature of this firm it is convenient to treat it separately from Wolsey.

[62] R. Walker was renamed Wolsey Ltd in 1920 and received its first Royal Warrant in 1935.

Corah in the Leicester area. A major decision was taken in 1920, to buy Boswell Brown Ltd to sell directly to the retail trade and in the subsequent three decades the firm built up a large international business, particularly under the Wolsey and Cardinal brand names. Backed by extensive advertising, a reputation for good service and top quality products and the sales expertise of Boswell Brown Ltd, this policy proved highly successful.

Challenges after World War Two

By the 1960s Wolsey was under pressure from several directions. The growth of the chain stores was a progressive threat to Wolsey as a major brand producer and a further threat came from Lyle & Scott, who competed directly as a producer of men's underwear. Lyle & Scott had an important brand advantage, because 'Y front' had come to represent the product as well as the make. Wolsey bought out Lyle & Scott in 1964 and this produced a very welcome boost for Wolsey's profits. The financial results were not sufficiently bad that Wolsey needed an urgent takeover to survive: rather it was the rapidly changing trading pattern and the ominous approaching demise of the independent retailers that most seriously threatened Wolsey's sales outlets.

In the years building up to the Courtaulds takeover the firm was still profitable:

Table 3.27 *Wolsey profits*

	Sales (£000)	Pre-tax profit (£000)
1960	7,350	607
1961	7,687	576
1962	7,856	439
1963	8,590	653
1964	11,859	873
1965	13,832	1,013
1966	14,797	873

Note: Lyle & Scott results included during and after 1964
Source: Wolsey Accounts

A. G. Scrimshaw the managing director explained: 'Those results were not bad. But we would not have survived in the existing form. ...Our strength was the brand distributed to thousands of small outfitters.'[63]

---

[63] Interview with A. G. Scrimshaw, former managing director of Wolsey, 24 April 1999.

Wolsey supplies chain stores

In response to decline in the independent retail sector, Wolsey made inroads into the chain store business from the early 1960s and was easily capable of manufacturing large contracts. Distribution to the high class men's outfitters was still an important part of the business, but this was no longer serviced by the wholesale branch of the firm. Instead it used telephone sales staff and a team of representatives. Unfortunately, the firm was incurring the heavy overheads needed for its important, but declining, traditional business, when the need to enter the chain store business (which demanded lower selling prices) was vital. Wolsey can therefore be considered a victim of its own earlier success as a supplier to the better class outfitters.

Wolsey – Corah merger talks fail

The seriousness of the decline in the private retail sector encouraged Wolsey in 1966 to seek a merger with an industry leader Corah, on the basis that Corah's strength in contract manufacturing would be complemented by Wolsey's strength in 'direct to retail' sales. The talks were essentially of a merger, but before terms were agreed a bid was made for Wolsey by Courtaulds at a price Corah could not match. The strength of Marks & Spencer can be judged, because R. L. Wessel, representing Corah, kept the M&S chairman Israel Sieff informed of developments at all stages.[64]

Courtaulds acquired Wolsey (Including Lyle & Scott)

The importance to Courtaulds of the takeover can be judged from estimates of manufacturers' sales at that time. Wolsey's contribution to the stockings sector was small, and by the time of the takeover fully-fashioned stockings manufacture had been abandoned. All other sections, particularly socks and men's knitted underwear, which more than doubled Courtaulds' share of UK production, made an important contribution to the overall manufacturing capacity of Courtaulds.

Although the Board of Trade was informed of the size and importance of Wolsey,[65] this takeover was not referred to the Monopolies Commission. It would

---

[64] Interview with A. G. Scrimshaw 24 April 1999.

[65] Wolsey factories were

Leicester	Bruin Street. Socks, Making-up U/W inc. Boxer shorts
Shepshed	FF Underwear, FF Knitwear
Kimberley	Circular Hose, FF Knitwear, Lingerie Knitting, Making-up
Dumfries	FF Knitwear 18g, 24g, 2 1/2g 5g
Gainsborough	Men's U/W Making-up unit (fabric from Lyle & Scott)

not have been difficult to defend the acquisition because although the firm was very large by the industry standards, it was not dominant in any one product.

Table 3.28 *Courtaulds and Wolsey UK market share*

	Courtaulds (%)	Wolsey (%)
Stockings	19	1.5
Men's Socks	5	7
Men's Knitwear	3	2
Women's Knitwear	7	2
Men's Underwear/shirts/nightwear	10	10*
Women's Underwear/shirts/nightwear	12	6*

*Estimated – note that imported knitted goods are not included.
Source: Figures presented to H.M. Government by Courtaulds.

Wolsey entered the Courtaulds group with a very weak contract business and was shortly to be separated from Lyle & Scott. Wolsey Socks was a very important business and survived, after many changes, to become Courtaulds' Sock Division, absorbing College Hosiery in 1985 and Corah Socks in 1988.[66]

The sock division was a leading producer making the Wolsey and Cardinal ranges in direct competition with J. P. Coats' 'Byford' socks. Within the hosiery and knitwear industry, the firm produced underwear, knitwear, and fine-gauge hosiery and the important Lyle & Scott Jockey range but other products such as woven elastics and yarn spinning do not form part of this study.

Moving towards Kearton's departure

Most of the acquisitions were made under the control of Kearton when things were generally favourable for the industry. As his time with the company drew towards its close the business had to deal with increasing competition, changing retail patterns, contraction within the trade and an increasingly difficult global

---

Ilkeston	Circular hose
Welshpool	Socks
Lyle & Scott factories were:	
Hawick Jedborough Burnfoot	Knitwear
Gateshead Dunfermline	Men's underwear

[66] Wolsey also had a large dyeing and finishing capacity and units manufacturing braid and woven elastics and processing spun yarns. The trading names were Wolsey Ltd, Lyle & Scott, Tubbs Lewis, Taylor Woods, Eminence Mens Fashions, Wolsey of Canada, Wolsey Germany and Carl Guildstrand.

business climate for clothing industries in the developed world.

The acquisitions were made piecemeal as they became available and any semblance of a cohesive structure formed by this untidy mixture of businesses was therefore more a result of fortune than preplanning.[67]

Many of the acquisitions were in fierce price competition with each other and due to the complex nature of the business were extremely difficult if not impossible to integrate. In the early stages some were still legally separate firms. It soon became apparent that during selling and price negotiations the larger customers were playing off one Courtaulds unit against the other. Early attempts at stifling price competition between group companies by informal cooperation were unsuccessful and there was a danger that this competition could drive down prices to the customer.

Although the main problems of reorganisation were left to his successors, early moves towards integrating these enterprises were simply an attempt to allocate customers to specific production units so that the firm's businesses were not in price competition with each other. It was not until the end of the Kearton era that executives were put in charge of different product types. This allowed Knight and his successors to attempt some form of cohesive management structure that could operate comfortably and effectively within an organisation that had been set up or had evolved over many decades to serve the needs of a mass production chemicals and fibres business. This was never fully achieved in this fragmented industry and it was clear that his staff would face severe problems if these acquisitions were ever to form a logical group.

Grouping the businesses together by product type began early in the acquisition era and often this was unavoidable. Some multi-product firms were split up immediately, particularly if the previous managers did not continue in employment, although it was the practice to allow incumbent managers to continue in their existing employment to test their ability.[68] As more and more firms were added it soon became obvious that management teams operated with varying degrees of success and as a simple expedient the unsuccessful production units were simply closed or attached to the more successful and their management disbanded. However, some relatively small and successful businesses remained largely autonomous for many years.[69]

It will be seen in subsequent chapters that the influence of the customer on the process of consolidation cannot be ignored. In practice, integration would be largely shaped by the market sector that the firm served, common technology

---

[67] See also 'Structure under Kearton' in Chapter 4.

[68] Some firms still had minority shareholders and these continued in the short term as autonomous accounting centres. Consolidation of the accounts was carried out at the centre.

[69] For example A. S. Yates, a former Foister, Clay & Ward subsidiary.

being only one of the issues taken into account. The power of the chain stores was a growing feature of the trade. Customer pressure affected the shaping of the Group and led to further distinct subdivisions. Where Courtaulds had a large presence in one product field, this could be sub-divided into sections that served an individual large customer or market sector. The demands of the customer, particularly M&S, were highly relevant in this context because that firm demanded that factory space, machinery and sales staff be dedicated solely to its needs. In practice it was better to dedicate capacity and sales and design staff to individual customers than to have salespeople vying with each other for the capacity that was available across a range of manufacturing sites.[70]

Within the hosiery and knitwear industry, the range of products and machine types was vast. Developing a really effective organisation structure was not simply a matter of putting technology-related production units together. Many amalgamations would only be nearing success long after Kearton's departure by which time the industry had declined to a shadow of its former size.

---

[70] The problem was further complicated because the chain stores tended to have several departments dealing with each of the major sectors e.g. men's, women's and children's, each having a dedicated buyer for separate products such as knitwear, socks and underwear. These were competing with each other for floor space and purchasing budgets.

FOUR

Kearton's Legacy

COURTAULDS' MOVE into the traditional hosiery and knitwear industry was a small but important part of the conglomerate's expansion. Outside this industry Courtaulds' record included some massive deals, notably the merger with British Celanese, the competing rayon manufacturing firm, and later the acquisition of Pinchin Johnson, the paint producers, International Paint, Lancashire Cotton Corporation Ltd and Fine Spinners & Doublers Ltd. The small scale and fragmented nature of the acquisitions in the hosiery and knitwear industry must therefore be considered in relation to the large scale nature of the parent company that was seeking down-stream outlets for its fibre production.

Complex and fragmented

It can hardly be surprising that the management of this complex mixture of acquisitions in the hosiery and knitwear industry presented problems both for the firms that had been acquired and for the management of the parent company.

In common with most of the industry, the acquisitions were facing changes in fashion and trading systems with which, in their independent state, most could not cope. Particularly devastating was the downturn in the fully-fashioned knitwear and stockings industries, which made redundant large amounts of expensive plant.

Multi-product firms featured prominently in the acquisitions.[1] Several of these owned well-known brand names and were at the same time notable as suppliers to M&S and other large customers. Corah Socks is included in this category, but was a much later acquisition and does not fit the general notion that the acquisitions were all part of the same move towards the vertical trading empire that Kearton tried to create in the 1960s. Smaller firms and single product producers were often geographically isolated and very specialised and all operated in a highly competitive, fast moving and fragmented industry, and in

---

[1] Aristoc, Ballito, Kayser Bondor, Contour, Bairnswear, Meridian, Foister, Clay & Ward, Wolsey, Corah Socks, and Rowley.

most cases were competing with each other. The nineteen sixties, during which most of the takeover activity took place, was a time when the High Street and multiple traders were continuing to gain strength. This had a weakening or even devastating effect on the manufacturers that had specialised in the development of their own branded merchandise or specialised in producing for the wholesale trade that serviced the thousands of privately owned retailers still functioning at that time.

Complication was added as there were also several instances of non-core activities being swept up as part of more important acquisitions, examples being Beauvale furnishing, Booton machine builders and the printers John Hampden Press, and these needed assimilating in some way, but the far more challenging issue was the incidence of failing and unprofitable subsidiaries and departments that dragged down what could otherwise have been successful firms.

Mixed success

While some of the acquisitions were successful businesses many were short of the capital needed to carry them successfully into the future; a problem that could be rapidly overcome by Courtaulds with its large access to capital. Chapman comments:

> Kearton's purchases were mainly 'lame ducks', or at any rate firms that had lost their way since the founding entrepreneur of the concern had died.[2] However he goes on to note: To say that a large firm bought up some 'lame duck' firms is not necessarily an indictment of it … the absorption of less by more successful firms was a common practice in the industry, particularly since 1945, and there were plenty of cases where the outcome appears to have benefited all parties involved.[3]

Considering Courtaulds' history and structure Porter's note is particularly telling:

> Reconfiguring the value chain is difficult and costly. In large firms, sheer scale also makes altering the strategy difficult. The process of modifying strategy frequently involves a sacrifice in financial performance and unsettling, sometimes wrenching, organizational adjustments. Firms without the legacy of a past strategy and past investments may well face lower costs of adopting a new strategy, not to mention fewer organizational difficulties.[4]

---

[2] Chapman (2002), p. 223.
[3] Chapman (2002), p. 224.
[4] Porter, *The Competitive Advantage of Nations* (Free Press: New York, 1990), p. 52.

Structure under Kearton

Under Kearton the formal structure of Courtaulds did not fully follow the classic theoretical pattern of the American multidivisional structure advocated so strongly by Chandler and Channon. It had long been a type of hybrid holding company and so it remained. The vertical trading strategy and diversification made new demands on the management of the clothing businesses but an appropriate structure, designed to meet these changed circumstances was not introduced at that stage, although some of the more appropriate characteristics of that system were introduced later under Christopher Hogg.

Kearton inherited a company that was fundamentally a fibre producing firm, but his rapid diversification strategy of the 1960s was not matched by structural reorganisation:

> Structurally, therefore, Courtaulds was somewhat of a mix between a holding company and a multidivisional concern. This apparent structural defect was justified by the company on the grounds that the textile trade still required the existence of a large number of small corporate units each with its own independent brands and character.[5]

Courtaulds' main board changes

Throughout the period when Kearton was in control there was very little outward change to the constitution of the main board. There were about fifteen or eighteen members of whom only two or three were non-executives and the position of Chairman and Chief Executive were combined.[6] The operation of the main board changed under Kearton and meetings were fewer – monthly instead of fortnightly as previously.

Important streamlining took place in 1962, around the time of the expansion into hosiery and knitwear, when Kearton eliminated the board committee structure. These committees had covered a whole range of functions; finance, appointments and personnel, research, customer credit, textile industry policy, subscriptions and donations and depreciation. They were replaced by only two executive committees – one dealing with 'policy' that consisted of the Chairman and two senior directors. The Policy committee dealt with long-term planning and confidential matters such as board appointments The second committee, dealing with 'operations', was also under the Chairman and had around seven

---

[5] Channon (1984), p. 179.

[6] At no time in its long history did Courtaulds have a female director. It was not until after Courtaulds Textiles plc was formed that this happened.

or eight executive directors as members and the function of the Operations Executive was to either formally agree, refer back, or block any proposed plans or management changes and to identify and take action in areas where problems were occurring.

Financial reporting channels

A new system of reporting was also set up with sixty profit centres reporting to the main board. These ranged in size from the smallest which employed capital of about £1 million to some that employed more than £30 million at that time. The firm introduced a system of reporting and budgetary control that was fast acting and, for that era, quite sophisticated, but there remained a large measure of autonomy in the many small businesses that were added to the group under Kearton.

Company structure

It seems surprising in retrospect that very early in the process of this expansion the problems of organisation structure were not addressed. It was to Kearton that this lack of structural reorganisation can be attributed. His personal intervention in all aspects of the garment industry is well known and his overpowering interference and personal decision making reached down to relatively low levels in the organisation. Arthur Knight, who succeeded Kearton, wrote:

> In the formal arrangements, the operating managements each responsible for a profit centre play the key role. The appropriate grouping of the newly acquired activities was actively debated. For example, there were many who advocated a new division to embrace the garment activities, seeing this as the best way to identify management responsibility and to provide machinery for planning and control, especially in commercial matters. But these views were consistently opposed by the Chairman, despite his public acceptance in the 1966 Bradford speech of the need for a divisional structure. His emphasis was much more on finding managers who could demonstrate success and then enlarging their responsibilities; and this view prevailed, so that those who look for a divisional pattern bringing activities into some coherent structure will not find it.[7]

It is certain that there was no preconceived corporate plan designed to integrate these diverse and relatively small businesses and that Kearton was either reluctant or unable to pass control to an executive director.

---

[7] Knight (1974), p. 75.

Writing in 1974 Knight highlights and justifies Kearton's role in the management of the firm and the manner of his direct influence on the formation and management of the Group:

> It is impossible to consider the development of Courtaulds within the [expansion] period except in the light of the extraordinary achievement of one man [Kearton]. This is no place to examine the characteristics and influences which were responsible for the combination in one man of the qualities which were crucial. ... it is sufficient to recognise that those qualities existed, and that the absence of formal organisation arrangements permitted their exercise with fewer of the restraints than would be conceivable to outsiders with preconceived ideas about business management.[8]

The new acquisitions certainly required day to day control and frequent and instant decision making that (for practical reasons) could not, owing to time constraints, be put to Courtaulds' main board for discussion. It is also certain that had control been nominally passed to another individual, Kearton would also have continued to monitor the situation and place that individual in the unhappy situation of being in charge, without having any real policy making input. It is possible that Kearton, when buying into the fragmented industry, had set something in train that was so complicated in its piecemeal construction (or evolution) that it was almost impossible for him to relinquish control and it was not until his final year that a senior executive was appointed to control the hosiery and knitwear sector of the firm.

Management reporting – non-financial

In the 1960s non-financial reporting procedures were weakly formalised and to a certain extent depended on the informal arrangement put in place by individual directors. Of these, the most interesting in the garment industries was installed by Kearton. He required a regular report from managers at all levels and he contacted the person in an organisation (not necessarily the most senior person) who was most likely to have information that he required. He also had several personal staff who visited units seeking information and reporting back to him. Kearton was also acting to remove the old slow moving 'gentlemen's club' atmosphere:

> A major effort was needed to remove traces of the old style and to engender

---

[8] Knight (1974), p. 77.

a new one more suitable to the needs. This could only stem from the top. How was it done? ... getting people to accept that information will be sought from whoever might have it without respect for hierarchy, breaking down entrenched ideas about what effective delegation means. Other techniques have been a willingness to exhort and explain face-to-face, the use of all of the skills of cajoling, bullying, rewarding and chastising (sometimes at the same time), eschewing meetings, keeping office doors open and encouraging rapid and frequent informal consultation.[9]

Despite Courtaulds' lack of attention to formal structural reorganisation, in his critique of management leadership Channon displays his admiration for Kearton:

For improvement in the level of performance, it was necessary to have strong corporate leaders who possessed both the will and the strategic ability to direct the enterprise toward the achievement of higher goals. That dramatic transformation was possible was evident from the success of the few who had achieved it. Britain truly needed more men such as Weinstock at G.E.C./E.E., Lazell at Beechams, Kearton at Courtaulds and Slater at Slater Walker.[10]

However, had Channon written only a short time later, after Kearton had resigned and moved on to new ventures and when the business had to operate in a less favourable economic climate, the failures of strategy and structure would probably have been mentioned alongside the successes.

Kearton in personal control

Kearton took a close interest in the day-to-day management of the firm and was in the habit of making decisions that directly affected the running of the fabric and garment manufacturing units. He required a regular report from all executives on the volume of group yarns and fibres consumed by their respective divisions and did not easily tolerate excuses for the use of competitors' goods or services. The firm was driven forward from the raw materials stage, and only later became more consumer-orientated. Transfer pricing of yarn was fixed centrally, and he was very rigorous in pressing for adherence to his concept of vertical trading, despite the many cases when this was not possible for technical or commercial reasons. Its logic was based on the principle that the 'upstream'

---

[9] Knight (1974), p. 82.
[10] Channon (1984), p. 227.

capital-intensive parts of the firm would gain great benefit from working at high capacity and lose profits rapidly as this drifted away.

He was convinced that the industry was not using up to date knitting equipment and large orders were placed with a range of machine builders through one of his personal assistants, Oliver Smith. The managers, designers and technical staff in the factories were not consulted and expensive machines were forced on the manufacturing sites. In many cases these machines replaced perfectly serviceable plant, loading unnecessary depreciation charges onto the business that were totally unnecessary. There were many instances where these machines were unsuited to the needs of the factory and its customers and were subsequently sold off at a considerable loss, much to the chagrin of the managers who were unable to do anything about it – some were simply destroyed.

In the early 1970s, as he approached retirement, senior executives with main board responsibilities were put in control of the very fragmented hosiery, knitwear and socks and underwear sectors of the firm. Gradually, management groups evolved with clearly defined lines of command and with a customer portfolio that left little chance of selling-price competition[11] between the various manufacturing units, but serious attempts to form a logical structure for these businesses were left to his successors.

With the benefit of hindsight, it is possible to see that the retirement of Kearton was to coincide with the high point in the history of the hosiery and knitwear industry, and that the conglomerate's large capacity in the UK industry would eventually collapse in the face of external problems such as changes in the market and the supply chain, competition from low-cost imports, and changes in fashion. It would be interesting to conjecture what Kearton would have done had he stayed with the firm after 1975 as foreign imports undercut his artificially high transfer prices which favoured the highly capital-intensive upstream fibre producing activities, '… over expansion hastened his departure and Arthur Knight and Chris Hogg picked up the pieces!'[12]

Integration and decline of the fine-gauge hosiery businesses

For just over a decade from 1963 there was rapid expansion and there were around thirty different fine-gauge hosiery manufacturing sites operating in the UK at various times. By the mid-1970s the UK fine-gauge hosiery industry had reached its zenith and from then decline set in, leaving the Courtaulds Group

---

[11] The output and designs were so varied that price co-ordination was not practical in view of the number of small manufacturing units serving the same customers and responding rapidly to their demands for price quotations.

[12] Buck, *More Ups than Downs* (Memoir Club, 2001), p. 92.

with only two manufacturing sites in action by the end of the century, one at Belper and one at Sutton-in-Ashfield.

The importance of nylon in the supply chain

Courtaulds' history and development and the abortive takeover attempt by ICI, with the subsequent loss of Courtaulds' share-holding in British Nylon Spinners Ltd, is well documented elsewhere.[13] During the 1960s there was a rapid move to build up production capacity in the stockings industry and as already explained in Chapter Two this policy was allied to the need for sales of nylon 6, which was manufactured by Courtaulds and marketed under the trade name Celon.[14] At the same time, there was the possibility that ICI, or some other large firm or consortium, might take over downstream users and secure the market for the Bri-Nylon produced by BNS. In fact, this did not happen and Kearton was able to assemble a range of captive outlets for his nylon yarn.

The factories were subservient

According to John Grew, a senior executive whose responsibilities at various times included the technical management of the large Usutu Pulp Mill in Swaziland and later the Celon Division, the needs of the garment manufacturers were made subservient to the needs of the Celon division:

> I was managing director of the Celon Division. My job was making the nylon and the big customers were all the [fine-gauge] hosiery companies – [plus] Furzebrook Knitting[15] and – the weaving people as well. Of course they had no choice; if they wanted nylon then they got Celon.[16]

Celon – a problem yarn, creates culture problems

Grew recognised that there were problems using Celon, which was difficult to knit, particularly in the early period when it produced a higher number of breaks per cone than nylon 66, its competitors' product. The captive users also had no control over its price which was artificially high, fixed, and equal to all group

---

[13] Coleman vol. 3 (1980), pp. 201–237.
[14] Courtaulds' Celon (nylon 6) differed from BNS Bri-Nylon 66 in its molecular construction.
[15] Furzebrook Knitting Company was based on the former British Celanese warp knitting firm and was probably the biggest in Europe.
[16] Interview John Grew 29 March 2000.

users, irrespective of the size of the deal. For the fine-gauge hosiery subsidiaries, nylon yarn prices were decided by a group senior executive and the final selling prices for stockings and the allocation of sales outlets to specific production units were decided at senior levels.[17]

These things were complete anathema to the people running the hosiery units. Some of these businesses, such as Aristoc and Kayser Bondor, were big names in the industry and this policy caused much frustration. Previously, they had seen themselves as manufacturers of garments for which they bought raw materials from a variety of sources, and at competitive prices, but Kearton saw their function as simply being users of Celon.[18]

The decline of the fully-fashioned stockings trade

Courtaulds' move into hosiery coincided with a period of increasing public spending on clothing. Nylon was, by this time, established as the ideal material for stockings and therefore the stocking industry was the ideal outlet for Celon.[19] Courtaulds' subsidiaries, in common with the rest of the industry, were hit hard by the decline of the fully-fashioned trade. Firms needed to invest rapidly in expensive new circular knitting plant at a time when existing equipment was not producing sufficient profits for that purpose. Fortunately, the banks were more amenable to requests for funds to be used by Courtaulds' subsidiaries, backed by the parent company's massive assets, than they were to the smaller and often less stable firms.[20]

The acquisitions

It is almost certain that the takeover of F,C&W in 1963 was a little too early to be influenced by the need for Celon sales and its potential usage of Courtelle seems to be a more credible explanation[21] and closure of their fairly small hosiery department at Mansfield was of little importance to Kearton's plans for a vertical group.

At the time of its acquisition, Aristoc still enjoyed a reasonable level of

---

[17] This indicates that a genuine division was evolving.

[18] Contrasts can be made with the other strands of the garment business, in which the yarn supply was much less important. For example, knitwear executives might manage to keep a higher level of independence provided they were profitable. Executives in other sectors of the group appeared to be under far less pressure to use Courtaulds yarn than those in the fine-gauge sector.

[19] Later extensive use was made of DuPont's Lycra.

[20] Later the allocation of capital and bank borrowing became a head office function.

[21] Coleman, vol. 3 (1980), p. 251.

success but Kayser Bondor was suffering serious profit deterioration, although how much this (if any) was due to the stockings division cannot now be established. What is certain however is that Kayser Bondor was being dragged down by its own unsuccessful subsidiaries, a problem that the management was unable to rectify. Four firms were in far more serious trouble. Ballito was bordering on insolvency, Morley had already decided to withdraw from the stockings industry, P. Beasley suffered from organisational and labour problems, and Brettles was also in serious decline. Contour Hosiery's subsidiary firms Sellors and Lockley & Garner were faring better as was Blounts (the former Derby and Midland subsidiary) and were able to sell in excess of their production capacity by contracting-out work to other producers. Contour had remained profitable, but Blounts' reputation for profitability cannot be confirmed because consolidated accounts for its previous owners, Derby and Midland Mills, do not show the profitability of the individual products. However, their large M&S market suggests they must have been competitive and efficient. F,C&W, as we have already seen, had earlier been an important M&S supplier. This ailing firm had a fully-fashioned capacity of three times their actual sales, but relied totally on imports from Italy for their circular hosiery sales. Percy Taylor, following a disastrous fire, bought in 50% of its requirements from other manufacturers. Wolsey was an exception, because it did not compete in the same market, having invested in slightly heavier gauges of machinery.

Rationalisation

The rationalisation of Courtaulds' hosiery interests was inevitable and vital to survival, although some closures were simply a tidying up process. Early closures were due to a range of factors not necessarily attributable to bad management or bad judgment by Courtaulds' executives. Some hosiery units shared factory floor space with other products that could be expanded, or were too small to contribute to the evolution of the new group with its emphasis on large chain store customers, and some sites were too isolated to be cost effective. Several were largely equipped to produce fully-fashioned stockings and were bypassed when new equipment was installed at larger and more modern sites with more potential. Also, the demise of the outdated fully-fashioned stocking frames released considerable amounts of floor space because the circular machines, which replaced the old frames, were very much faster and more compact. Therefore, the closure of Ballito in Bedfordshire, Morley, Foister, Clay & Ward and Aristoc's Isle of Man hosiery branch, seems in retrospect to have been inevitable; particularly as in the latter three cases alternative work was available to the workforce.

Had some of the acquisitions been allowed to continue unaltered, it would have been a serious financial drain on Courtaulds funds. Ballito in Bedfordshire

Wolsey stockings, in an advertisement from 1946.

was an early casualty, the decision to cease production of fully-fashioned stockings having already been taken before the firm was acquired by Courtaulds. With the failure of its knitwear operation, Ballito was unable to sustain the large property, and the cost of its central administration at its Luton site. Ballito sites at Matlock, Skelmersdale and Southport were more successful but with the total removal of the Ballito top-level management they were soon absorbed into the new 'Brettles Group' which was in the process of being set up.

A new use for the Brettle's Belper site

Ironically, the commercially threatened Brettles' Chapel Street site at Belper featured significantly in the development of Courtaulds Hosiery. As already noted, at the time of the takeover, the historic Brettles Ltd was a multi-product manufacturer that produced hosiery, knitted underwear and socks and also functioned as a clothing wholesaler. Shortly after being taken over by Courtaulds, the underwear department was closed, some machinery scrapped and the remainder transferred to Meridian. The decision was taken in November 1966 to close the sock department and also transfer that machinery to Meridian. Within a short time the Brettles wholesale division was placed under the control of the wholesale group, Cook & Watts, which joined Courtaulds in 1967. These contractions left Brettles stockings manufacturing side in a very weak position. It is not clear when the decision was taken to develop Courtaulds' hosiery manufacturing capacity as a single entity using the title Brettles Group.[22] The early intentions are unclear. Early records show little evidence that the formation of the Brettles Group was part of any real strategic plan. As early as March 1964 Kearton had decided to close the Belper site, however, despite this decision, for some reason the satellite factory at nearby Bobbers Mill (Nottingham) was retained and by the end of 1966 important integration was commencing under the management based at Blounts site at Spencer Road, Belper but why the title 'Brettles Group' was chosen is now unclear.

When the Luton firm Ballito was acquired its top management was not retained and within a couple of years the former Ballito manufacturing units at Skelmersdale and Matlock, (which also housed the selling organisation Playgirl), and Hartwood Hosiery at Southport were managed from Belper. Further consolidation of the management brought in Blounts at Belper, a new development at Carnmoney, in Northern Ireland, Sellors at Beeston, Nottingham (part of the former Contour Group), and Percy Taylor and Beasley at Hinckley.

Aristoc and Kayser Bondor which were both acquired in 1966 were still functioning largely autonomously.[23] Aristoc was a market leader producing a high quality product at their large factory at Langley Mill, but its small stockings manufacturing plant at Ramsey, Isle of Man, was closed very quickly. The business was still working in a favourable market climate and for the time being Aristoc was left alone. KB was not successful, but was allowed to run by Courtaulds as an autonomous company, partly because the KB directors had forecast very favourable profits for the firm at the time of the takeover, and partly because there were still independent shareholders in this firm. However, when poor results were published the remaining shareholders sold out to Courtaulds.

Fine-gauge hosiery – a basic commodity product

A feature of the fine-gauge hosiery industry is the heavy reliance on marketing skills and brand name development to sell merchandise that is identical or only weakly differentiated between one manufacturer and another. Sub-contracting

---

[22] The name of the firm was not necessarily important except that it was convenient to give an easily recognizable title to an accounting cost centre. Some firms were acquired with tax losses and were retained as individual firms until the tax losses were used up.

[23] Kayser Bondor still had minority shareholders.

between firms is traditional, even between fierce competitors, and is relatively easy because much of the plant is similar and the technical skills are interchangeable. Therefore, the imbalances between production and sales can be to a large extent corrected by competent administration.

It was soon clear that the acquisitions were competing with each other for the same business and so, from an early stage, the individual factories were made largely responsible for serving specific customers; Woolworths and Littlewoods at Skelmersdale, Boots and Woolworths at Beeston, Littlewoods at Chapel Street, Belper and M&S at Spencer Road, Belper. Two very small businesses, Tor Hosiery and West Riding Hosiery were mainly producing for small shops and supplementing the production of the other factories.[24]

Total integration for fine-gauge hosiery

As the group expanded and major brands were brought into Courtaulds Hosiery Limited,[25] there was need for integration to avoid the possibility that competition between group members might drive down prices to the customers. The central administration of the Hosiery Division was moved the short distance to Langley Mill in 1973. The Ballito and KB sales forces had already been amalgamated and the Aristoc brand had followed. The sales organisation also embraced the contract business that supplied the chain stores 'own label' production and the administrative task of balancing sales and production requirements was undertaken from Langley Mill, but the principle that individual factories were dedicated to specific customers was still maintained whenever circumstances allowed.

Courtaulds narrows the hosiery brand offer

Through acquisition, Courtaulds gained a host of brand names, some of which seem quaint with the passing of time and were abandoned by Courtaulds.[26] The new sales management focused on the Aristoc brand for the high-class outlets, drapery and department stores and used KB for the middle and Ballito for the lower end of the market and kept the Brettle trade name for the wholesale trade.

---

[24] Information from Sidney Clark, Brettles sales administrator 14 April 2000.
[25] A renamed successor to the Brettles group.
[26] Examples being Aristoc Dimsheen and Undergrads, Kayser Bondor Bend Easy and Ballito Town 'n' Country.

Expansion in the 1960s – but Courtaulds fine-gauge hosiery loses its way

In the 1960s, the group had been in an expansionist mode and government grants to aid employment were used to set up important manufacturing units at Dowlais in South Wales, and the integrated sites at Newtown, Carnmoney and Carrickfergus in Northern Ireland.[27] Expansion was rapid and was pressed ahead with supreme optimism, particularly so because Courtaulds had well established and strong connections with the chain stores. Business was good and in 1969 most Courtaulds factories were hard pressed to fulfil their orders for the newly popular tights but the upsurge was not long-lived and a slowdown would soon appear which would hit the industry particularly hard. By September 1972 the future was gloomy and profits were under threat with Courtaulds' factories using slow machines and paying high prices for yarn.[28]

The main reasons for poor profits were said to be worldwide over-production of tights (which led to price cutting) and low-cost import penetration, mainly from Italy. Courtaulds, having contributed to the overcapacity in the industry, was forced to respond with a massive reduction in output. The closures in the second half of the 1970s included some very important factories. The Skelmersdale factory was closed and also those set up only a few years previously with government aid at Dowlais in South Wales and Newtown, Carnmoney, and Carrickfergus in Northern Ireland.

Courtaulds fails to benefit from the improving market

The retail market picked up considerably in the period between 1980 and 1989, but Courtaulds did not benefit. It was a difficult time for the group and it was losing ground to its competitors. Despite the massive closures, the large Courtaulds factories still in operation in the early 1980s were the former Blounts, Brettles, Aristoc and KB factories at Belper, Langley Mill and Baldock. Despite the generally strong UK retail trade, Courtaulds Hosiery was performing badly and the (former KB) factory at Baldock was closed in 1983.

Hosiery business re-development project

A business redevelopment project was presented to Courtaulds' main board in 1985. Problems identified were inadequate capital investment, failure to correct an ageing customer profile in the conventional brand sector, and seeking after high

---

[27] These factories were close to or shared sites with yarn processing plants.
[28] Celon prices were kept high to Group Companies and the Booton machines were slower than those of their competitors.

volume high service-cost business in the food sector (particularly Tesco and Asda) with resulting low profit margins. Ironically this was a market that Courtaulds' competitor Pretty Polly, the market leader seems to have successfully dominated. There was also serious over-proliferation of styles in all brand ranges, inefficient manufacturing methods and the occupation of too much expensive floor space.[29]

Excess capacity in hosiery

By 1985 production had become concentrated on three sites: Chapel Street and Spencer Road in Belper and North Street, Langley Mill, and a much smaller unit at East Street Leeds. Even with these closures, there was still excess capacity and the decision was taken to close the large Chapel Street site. This decision was based on the reasoning that productivity was the lowest there and that the site was the most saleable as a development site, possibly raising £500,000. Gradually, the factory at Chapel Street was phased out with some plant and machinery being moved to Spencer Road but the Leeds factory, which was very small and subsequently quite unimportant, did survive for a short period.

Table 4.1 *Estimated UK fine-gauge capacity*

	Doz./week, 1985
Pretty Polly	220,000
Courtaulds Hosiery	136,000
Atkins	35,000
Bear Brand	35,000
Barber & Nicholls/Nicholls & Wileman	45,000
K Leigh	40,000
NMC	60,000
Adria	70,000
Couture	30,000
Tudsbury	25,000
Jennings	20,000
Melas	12,000
Berkshire	25,000
Elbeo	15,000
Others	50,000

Source: C. Powell.

---

[29] Information source: C. Powell.

Pretty Polly and Courtaulds dominated the market, but NMC and Adria were also significant forces. Ten years earlier Courtaulds' production had been 278,000 dozen tights plus 54,000 dozen stockings per week,[30] a reduction of 60% in a period when, after the problems of 1977, UK production had regained its 1975 level. It was in this period that Pretty Polly, Courtaulds' competitor, made big inroads into the supermarket outlets.

Low-cost imports

Low-cost imports were a serious problem and Courtaulds was placed in a difficult position. Customers such as Boots, M&S and Sainsbury's were demanding cheaper prices than Courtaulds could achieve from their UK factories. In response, Courtaulds procured merchandise for these clients from Italian factories. Although the Italian firms would have been happy to supply direct to the chain stores, it was a condition of these deals that Courtaulds took full responsibility for every aspect of the transaction. By 1985, Courtaulds was importing 25,000 dozens per week from Italy but did not produce fine-gauge products on mainland Europe until many years later, a tactic used by the knitted underwear sector about the same time.

Italian high quality tights

Keith White, a former chief executive, summed up his experiences:

> From the time I joined the company [1982] it went down from about 2,500 employees to under a thousand when I left [in1994]. In the 80s volume was reduced from, at one time, around 200,000 to around 100,000 dozen per week. West Mill, Belper was built in 1993 with a view to a capacity of 140,000 to 160,000.

Explaining the business relationship John Grew observed:

> These Italian manufacturers were extremely good and extremely efficient and you shouldn't look on them as inferior. Although their costs were low their quality standards were very high. In certain areas they could make the product cheaper and better than we could. These were not joint enterprise companies and were totally independent of Courtaulds.[31]

---

[30] Information supplied by C. Powell, a former Courtaulds executive.
[31] Interview John Grew 29 March 2000.

Contraction

Even more severe contraction set in from the late 1980s. Not only did production cease at Chapel Street, Belper, but the knitting, finishing and packing plant, or at least sufficient for the reduced needs, was transferred from the former Aristoc factory at Langley Mill into Spencer Street, Belper, and the small factory at Leeds was finally closed. This left an untidy situation with knitting production at Spencer Street and small storage areas remaining at Langley Mill and Chapel Street, Belper.

Deeper cuts

UK hosiery production reached a peak between 1987 and 1989, but from then there was a period of decline.[32] Courtaulds' regeneration programme had come too late. The market was contracting because increasing numbers of women were wearing trousers and socks. Both UK producers and importers were hit by falling demand and there was also a serious reduction in exports. Courtaulds entered the 1990s with a production capacity of 160,000 dozens per week and a labour force of 1,366, which was seen as too large for the business available at profitable margins, and there were considerable redundancies in the first quarter of 1990.[33]

Production and consolidation was tidied up by the move in 1993 to a new site, West Mill, Belper that employed 700 workers and produced between 100,000 and 125,000 dozens per week.[34] From then there was steep decline.

Integration and decline of the knitwear businesses

The 1960s were good years for UK knitwear manufacturing, Courtaulds acquired a major stake in the industry making eleven acquisitions that had knitwear capacity, of these the three most important to the formation of the group were Foister, Clay & Ward, Bairnswear and Meridian. The eleven acquisitions were:

Foister, Clay & Ward Ltd
Bairnswear Ltd
Meridian Ltd
Ballito Hosiery Mills Ltd
Highfield Productions Ltd
Irvine Knitters Ltd
Kilsyth Hosiery Co. Ltd
Morley [I. & R.] Ltd

---

[32] See Table 7.3.
[33] *Knitting International* April 1991.
[34] Aristoc publicity 1993.

Rowley [R.] Co. Ltd
Stewarton Hosiery Co. Ltd
Wolsey Ltd inc. Lyle & Scott Ltd

These served the wholesale, retail and chain store sectors of the trade and also used well-known brand names, including Bairnswear, Meridian, Ballito, Morley, Wolsey, Golden Eagle and Lyle & Scott. At various times after 1963, the group operated from nearly forty sites, but by the end of the century these were either closed or being closed.

Courtaulds' three major knitwear acquisitions

Foister, Clay & Ward, the ailing M&S supplier, was brought into the group in 1963. This firm had a highly skilled labour force and a high level of technical competence throughout its branches, but was operating with old technology. It had knitwear units at Redcliffe Road and Southfield Road, Mansfield, and Frog Island, Leicester. There were also two subsidiary branches, Irvine Knitters, which was renamed Queen of Scots in 1964 and A. S. Yates at Blackbird Road, Leicester.

Bairnswear was another large acquisition in 1963. Its knitwear factories were situated at Worksop, Armagh and Perry Road, Nottingham. Further factories were set up under the Bairnswear name in a rapid and optimistic expansion drive from the late 1960s. These were small factories at Askern, Ibstock and Wigston, followed in 1973 by the Barnsley and Derrymore factories and a small factory at Barwell, Leicestershire.

The third large knitwear business acquired in 1963 was Meridian, which operated at its main site in Haydn Road, Nottingham, and at Ilkeston.

Medium sized knitwear enterprises

Bedfordshire based Ballito, a household name in the stockings trade, was also heavily committed to fully-fashioned knitwear, and it was taken over in 1966, not for its knitwear business but for its fine-gauge hosiery capacity.

Wolsey with its knitwear capacity at Kimberley and Shepshed, Leicestershire and Dumfries, with its two satellite factories, Lesmahago and Annan, was brought into the Courtaulds Group in 1967. Wolsey's subsidiary, Lyle & Scott, operated at Hawick, with satellite factories at Burnfoot, Jedburgh and Carnoustie. These units were all producers for the upper end of the knitwear market.

Satellite acquisitions

A number of small factories were bought in the late 1960s solely to supplement existing capacity. Bairnswear had well established sales outlets for school knitwear and Kilsyth Hosiery was bought with the intention of manufacturing this complicated merchandise which was clogging up the main Bairnswear factories. Highfields Productions was acquired in 1968 to supplement the Bairnswear production for M&S and Irvine Knitters in Ayrshire and Stewarton Hosiery[35] were acquired as additional capacity for the Queen of Scots factory.

Morley – a mixed wholesaling and manufacturing company

Morley, acquired in 1968, was a long-established firm based at Heanor, Derbyshire, with a wholesale outlet. The appalling profit record placed a cloud over this multi-product firm which had not produced cut and sewn knitwear but had solely concentrated its knitwear production on the declining fully-fashioned style.

Rowley, a mixed product – multi-site general manufacturer

Rowley, another multi-product acquisition, had both fully-fashioned and cut and sewn knitwear departments. The firm supplied the declining wholesale trade, but was striving successfully to develop chain store connections. Prior to the takeover, the firm had been a well-established school knitwear manufacturer competing with Bairnswear.

Knitwear reorganisation commences quickly – F,C&W is split up

Despite the 1960s generally being a prosperous time, the outstanding technical ability available within F,C&W, and its important M&S connection did not ensure its commercial success. With a large and failing sock division and rapidly declining fully-fashioned stockings division, there was little point in maintaining a F,C&W head office structure. It tied up a high level of capital and produced relatively low profits and had performed badly in comparison with Meridian.[36] Kearton reacted to this problem by placing under Meridian control the three Mansfield factories (Belvedere Works, Redcliffe Road and Southfield Road)

---

[35] The title 'Hosiery' refers to its trade name not to the product this firm produced.

[36] A high level of capital investment is a recognized feature of M&S knitwear suppliers such as F,C&W, and competitors Corah and Kempton.

Morley advertising fully-fashioned knitwear.

and the factory at Frog Island, Leicester, but two subsidiaries, A. & S. Yates in Blackbird Road, Leicester, and Queen of Scots at Irvine, that were also acquired as part of the F,C&W takeover, were placed under Bairnswear management.

The Redcliffe Road and Belvedere factories at Mansfield were closed for manufacturing in 1964, due to the fall-off in orders for fully-fashioned styles. Redcliffe Road factory became a warehouse and Belvedere Works was put up for sale. In 1965, there was a catastrophic fire at Southwell Road, Mansfield, during which all its plant and equipment was totally destroyed, but both the Redcliffe Road and Belvedere Works factories were reopened and fully re-equipped within six to twelve months with brand new knitting machines, except for five which had been in store at Redcliffe Road. Despite Morleys' general decline, as high volume producers these factories were later to become a vital part of Courtaulds' knitwear interests. However, the Southwell Road factory was not rebuilt.

Wolsey fully-fashioned knitting closed

The Wolsey fully-fashioned plant was also suffering the effects of the downturn in the popularity of fully-fashioned knitwear. In 1969, knitwear production ceased at the Shepshed factory and any remaining orders were transferred to Kimberley and the factory was then utilised for underwear making-up only.

Further coordination

A half-hearted attempt was made around June 1971, while Courtaulds was still under the control of Kearton, to coordinate all Courtaulds' knitwear manufacturing interests. It was seen that the group's fully-fashioned capacity was approximately double that for cut and sewn, whereas current demand favoured the cut and sewn product which commanded a much higher price. The fully-fashioned knitwear manufacturers were Bairnswear, Queen of Scots, Ballito, Morley, Wolsey, Lyle & Scott and Rowley.

Client portfolios introduced

It was clear that something had to be done to control the selling-price competition between the group companies. Group coordinators were appointed to oversee each major UK customer. At that time no group knitwear producing company was actually precluded from trying to obtain any business they could, but instructions were given that the coordinators (who were appointed from the supplier with the highest level of business), were to be informed in detail of the plans for the account. The merchandise for M&S, the number one target customer, which was mostly produced at the Meridian and Bairnswear controlled factories, was placed under the control of the senior group executive, J. R. S. Morris (later Sir Richard Morris).[37]

Selling prices

These attempts at coordination of supply in the early 1970s did not fully resolve the problems between the various manufacturing and selling units which were, to some extent, still competitors. Attempts were made to standardise the basis

---

[37] The main allocation of customers was Bairnswear – C&A, Meridian – UDS – GUS, Rowley –Woolworths – Mothercare, Wolsey – Littlewoods – Lewis's.

on which manufacturing costs were calculated and selling prices were quoted. This meant that there was a need to continue to charge for depreciation on written-down machinery, otherwise the more modern factories would be at a disadvantage. It appears ironic that a unit with old and written-down machinery should be selling goods cheaper than a more modern, efficient and heavily invested plant. It was also found that units benefiting from government grants were passing these savings on to the customers, thereby undercutting other group firms and the general price structure.

Fully-fashioned knitwear in rapid decline

By 1972, fully-fashioned knitwear was rapidly going out of fashion and the group was in the embarrassing position of having ordered new plant and equipment which was no longer needed.

In response to the increasing demand for cut and sewn knitwear, Meridian expanded their Carlton factory in 1971 and Bairnswear opened the Derrymore factory in 1973, and around the same time set up a satellite making-up unit at Barnsley to supplement the Worksop production. Over-capacity in the fully-fashioned sector led to the closure of the knitting section of the Ballito factory at Luton in December 1971. A small making-up section at Ballito was retained as a satellite factory of Rowley's Oadby factory in 1972, but did not last long in this unfashionable product and the Rowley management closed it in 1973; the much larger (Rowley) Oadby factory, which by then was under Bairnswear control, was closed in 1975.

The brand business

The reduction in the demand for 'suppliers'-brand' merchandise, supplied largely to independent and department stores, took its toll in the middle to late 1970s with the decline of those outlets. The loss of much of the Wolsey brand business caused the closure of the Kimberley factory and the transfer of any remaining business to Ilkeston. The Morley knitwear factory at Heanor was closed about the same time and Meridian at Haydn Road, Nottingham suffered from a severe loss of business. Courtaulds was still faced with massive over-capacity. In 1979, Bairnswear management was disbanded and its factories merged into the Meridian organisation and the factories at Barnsley and Derrymore were closed followed by Askern, Ibstock, and Barwell in the early 1980s.

Retrenchment

The Bairnswear, Perry Road, plant was particularly hard hit and by 1982 was only being utilised to the extent of between 50% and 60% of its capacity, therefore it was announced that the factory, which had been in operation since 1935, and at one time had been one of the market leaders for children's knitwear, would close, along with the former F,C&W factory at Frog Island, Leicester, including the small factory at Wigston, Leicester. However, the Wigston factory was reprieved and survived for a few years making specialist children's knitwear for Mothercare under Rowley's management. This rationalisation involved the transfer of a substantial part of the Bairnswear Perry Road plant into the Meridian, Haydn Road site.

During 1983, an appraisal of the strategic opportunities for the group was undertaken by major consultants which exposed the need to improve the cost structure. Despite the earlier merger of Meridian and Bairnswear that saved management charges, the group had fallen behind in cost control and investment and a minimum of £8 million was needed to bring the plant up to date.

Meanwhile, the main competitor, Nottingham Manufacturing Company, had built up a massive lead and invested heavily both in new machinery and design services and had outstripped Courtaulds as the leading supplier to M&S, the target customer. Courtaulds' sales mix was fragmented and not totally reliant on M&S at that time.

Technology – Shaped garment panels

The former Bairnswear factory at Worksop remained in operation, although it had come under the new management grouping. The production included some of the traditional fully-fashioned and cut and sewn merchandise, as well as the new 'shaped garment' knitwear. Shaped-garment machinery became available as a result of revolutionary technology, (Courtaulds' presser foot), in the first half of the 1980s, a development which allowed shaping to be done on modified cut and sew machines. Two machine builders, Stoll and Shima, carried forward the development of this concept. The new machines combined the advantages of the fully-fashioned and the cut and sew machines and allowed shaped and patterned work to be produced with a minimum of waste. In effect, the new machines ceased to be either cut and sew or fully-fashioned in the traditional sense, but combined the advantages of both.[38]

Further retrenchment

Over-capacity remained an ongoing problem and forced the closure of the Ilkeston Junction factory that had been part of the Meridian knitwear organisation for

---

[38] Fully-fashioned machines produced un-patterned work with minimal waste. The new machines produced patterned work without the waste fabric associated with the cut and sewn method.

Shima Seiki machines were technically advanced by the 1990s. Picture courtesy of www.knittingindustry.com.

many years. The decision rested between closing one of the Mansfield factories and moving production to Ilkeston, or closing the Ilkeston factory and moving to Mansfield. Mansfield was chosen, the deciding factor being the availability of labour. The main competitors for labour were Charnos at Ilkeston and Coats Viyella at Mansfield, but Mansfield had the benefit of a much larger catchment area, and ultimately the Ilkeston building became a graveyard for redundant machinery.

After the demise of the Bairnswear organisation, the A. S. Yates factory at Blackbird Road, Leicester, was placed nominally under the Meridian Management, but was allowed to operate semi-independently: '[It] … was highly successful and the most profitable unit [relative to its size] within Meridian for many years.'[39] Around 1986 the fashion for circular knitted 10 gauge knitwear collapsed. Attempts were made to keep the Yates unit in operation, but the Meridian sales force was unable to generate sufficient alternative work for styles produced on circular knitting machinery and despite the previous good results the business was sold to Mensley Ltd, an independent operator.

---

[39] Interview, Mike Staley 15 February 2000.

Wolsey factories weakened

Wolsey management entered the 1970s in a weak position, having lost its famous sock division to Rowley and having its subsidiary, Lyle & Scott, separated off and functioning as a separate cost centre. Wolsey remained a knitwear producer (but bought in other products such as socks from Group companies to market under the Wolsey brand name). An important part of the business was Courtelle knitwear produced under stores labels for Littlewoods, Lewis's and House of Fraser. This was work that was unattractive to other parts of the Group such as Meridian, which had by this time commenced producing for M&S, who provided much larger orders. In the late 1970s there were three Wolsey knitwear factories in operation, Shepshed, producing for the lower priced chain stores, Kimberley making Courtelle fully-fashioned garments and Dumfries producing lambswool and shetland jumpers and supplementing the production with sub-contract work for Lyle & Scott. In 1980, Wolsey made a loss, was unable to generate sufficient business, and job losses resulted. In 1982 and 1983, the production capacity became concentrated at two factories only, Dumfries and Abbey Meadow Mills, Leicester. Throughout this process there was a drive up-market from the lower price chain stores and eventually a concentration on the Wolsey brand sales enabled Courtaulds to sell the brand name in a management buyout.

The non-M&S business

The creation of Courtaulds Knitwear Division from Bairnswear, F,C&W and Meridian left Rowley (Leicester), Queen of Scots (Hawick), and Lyle & Scott (Dumfries), with their satellite units which did not fit neatly into this mainly M&S orientated organisation. Following the takeover by Courtaulds, Rowley, in common with most of the medium-to-large acquisitions, was allowed a short period of semi-autonomy as a separate legal company, although Courtaulds nominees were appointed to the board. During this period Rowley, which had a history of poor results, continued its already promising drive to specialise in childrenswear for major chain stores. Following the attempts in 1971 and 1972 to bring the individual firms closer together, a more formal change in structure took place in 1973.[40] This placed all Rowley factories, for reporting purposes, in the Bairnswear group along with Queen of Scots, Irvine Knitters and Highfield Productions and brought together the pre-takeover competitors in children's knitwear, Bairnswear, Rowley and Irvine Knitting. Rowley had by this time closed its Oadby fully-fashioned unit and based its cut and sewn knitwear division at Queen Street, Leicester.

The most significant development for Rowley was the rapid development of the

---

[40] *Garment News* July 1973.

Mothercare account which was made possible by a big injection of Courtaulds' capital. In this context knitwear cannot be viewed in isolation, because from then onwards the whole Rowley business including socks, underwear and leisurewear became dedicated to Mothercare as its principal customer. As a result of the contraction and consolidation of Meridian and Bairnswear into one entity, the small unit at Wigston was taken over by Rowley for the manufacture of the infant's one-piece garments knitted on the Komet FCM machines. Despite the limited design potential and the need to have a seam on the top, rather than the underside of the sleeve, the product was highly successful for many years.

Rowley struggles on

With the break-up of Bairnswear, the non-M&S suppliers, Rowley and Queen of Scots (which had by then totally subsumed Irvine Knitters), became more self-sufficient and after the demerger of clothing from Courtaulds Ltd in 1990, Rowley became the central organisation for Courtaulds Textiles plc children's non-M&S garments. Rowley Knitwear department had met with hard times around 1985, which coincided with the final abandonment of the wholesale trade, closure was considered and claims were made for a Temporary Employment Subsidy (TES), but it struggled on and survived until the closure of the main site in 1999.

Lyle & Scott and Jockey brands

Lyle & Scott was originally acquired by Courtaulds as a subsidiary of Wolsey and operated in a semi-autonomous way because of its specialist form of trading which did not fit comfortably with the main-stream volume producers in the English Midlands. Much of the production was for golf shops but other customers included Harrods, Debenhams, Lewis, Alexander, Burberry and Dunnes, which were serviced by agents spread throughout the UK, with export business being handled by agents abroad. Lyle & Scott also produced branded merchandise using the Golden Eagle trademark. In the 1960s, the firm was producing high-quality woollen fully-fashioned jumpers which commanded top prices with even more expensive garments being produced in cashmere. Cotton's patent machines were used as well as some hand flat machines. Gradually, the cashmere business drifted away to become a very small part of the output. High quality wool garments filled the gap, but the lower-priced acrylic yarns, used extensively in the East Midlands, were never used successfully. In the 1970s, Japanese garments began to appear in the UK market and these were admitted by the very critical Hawick workers to be of excellent quality, but were retailing at about half the Lyle & Scott price.

Lyle & Scott at its main Hawick site did not suffer immediately from the downturn in the UK knitwear trade: over a period of time fringe sites were closed which saved the main site for several years. With the closure of the Wolsey Dumfries factory in 1991, that production was transferred to Hawick. Later the satellite factories at Jedburgh and Kelso were closed and work withdrawn to the Hawick factory and the seasonal shortfall was supplemented by M&S work for Meridian.

Courtaulds sells Lyle & Scott

In the late 1990s, Lyle & Scott was offered for sale by Courtaulds and continued under new ownership, keeping the Lyle & Scott name and trademark. The independent firm continued to produce a small, exclusive range of traditional knitwear. At the extreme, a very small quantity of knitted intarsia[41] garments was marketed under the Chanel trademark. These could take up to five days to produce and with a 60,000 stitch appliqué addition could retail for around £1000 at 2000 prices.

Further decline

Wolsey was operating knitwear plants at Dumfries, Shepshed, and Kimberley in 1978, but by 1988 this had been reduced to only one, Dumfries, which it has already been noted, was closed in 1991.

At the turn of the century, for the knitted outerwear trade, Courtaulds was only operating from three sites, with design, sales and administration at Worksop, and manufacturing at Belvedere Street, Mansfield, and Highfields Mills, Hucknall, Nottingham.[42]

Low-cost imports

Courtaulds was slow to respond to the threat from its overseas competitors:

> Profits were going down all the time and so businesses were not generating enough cash to invest in the better machinery and when they did they had it in the wrong place [the UK]. What began to happen was that the new machines were being put in the Philippines and the Pacific Basin and of course the designs that they were able to offer had a much greater appeal than those that were developed in the UK.[43]

---

[41] Weft-knitted fabric containing designs in two or more colours. Each area of colour is knitted from a separate yarn which is contained entirely within that area.
[42] These were closed shortly afterwards.
[43] Interview, Mike Staley 15 February 2000.

Courtaulds had a large amount of plant in the UK (making poor profits), and was unable to invest in expensive plant overseas. The competitors were selling fashionable goods for considerably lower prices.

Integration and decline of the knitted underwear businesses

In common with the fine-gauge hosiery, sock and knitwear sectors, Courtaulds entered the knitted underwear industry with the acquisition of the multi-product firm F,C&W in 1963. These 1963 acquisitions were followed by a series of others that made Courtaulds one of the most important underwear producers in the western world.

Important underwear acquisitions were:

Foister, Clay & Ward	Middlesbrough
	Derby
Meridian	Nottingham
	Clowne
	Carlton
	Kirkby-in-Ashfield
Prew-Smith / J Clarke	Bolsover
	Nottingham
	Arnold
Wolsey / Lyle & Scott	Wolsey – Shepshed
	Wolsey – Bruin St. Leicester
	Wolsey – Gainsborough
	Wolsey – Ratby
	Lyle & Scott – Dunfermline

There were also several smaller businesses:

Morley	Heanor
	Sutton-in-Ashfield
Rowley	Leicester

Much less significant in the underwear field were:

Brettle	Belper
Blount	Belper
Aristoc	Isle of Man
Hendry & Spiers	Wishaw

Women's underwear show card by Wolsey Limited Leicester, c.1963

The early shakeout

Even while the acquisitions of the 1960s were still taking place, there was already a considerable shakeout in progress. Within a very few years, the management teams of F,C&W and Morley were disbanded and their factories were allocated to other groups. Morley's heavy underwear production (such as long-johns) was no longer fashionable and its fabric knitting section was closed, although the Sutton-in-Ashfield making-up unit and circular knitting department survived and was placed under Meridian management. With the disbanding of F,C&W's management, the important knitting and making-up plant at Middlesbrough and the making-up plant at Derby also passed to Meridian control. Some early closures were due to declining demand for fully-fashioned underwear, a product that was too expensive to produce and no longer in much demand and the very small-scale underwear production units at Aristoc, Isle of Man, and Blounts of Belper were phased out for the same reason, the workers being redeployed to other work. The best of Brettle's knitting machinery at Belper was transferred to Meridian, the remainder was destroyed and the site used for fine-gauge stockings production.

Price competition

In the second half of the 1960s selling-price competition between the group businesses was a serious problem tending to drive down prices to the customers, but this was eliminated somewhat in the early 1970s by allocating non-M&S childrenswear to Rowley, the remaining heavy underwear to Wolsey, and adult non-M&S business to Meridian. All-age production for M&S was made the responsibility of Meridian Prew-Smith Division while Meridian, Wolsey and Rowley continued to supply the general retail trade using their own and their customer's brand names. Internal competition was therefore reduced as the manufacturing units began supplying fairly clearly-defined markets, with only a small amount of overlap.

Meridian and Meridian Prew-Smith Division

By far the most important management groups for underwear became Meridian and Meridian Prew-Smith Division. Prew-Smith was one of the most successful firms acquired by Courtaulds and was a vital constituent in the development of Courtaulds' underwear business.

In 1973, when there was a major reshuffle of the garment factories, Meridian and its Prew-Smith division were required to report directly to J. R. S. Morris, a main board director.[44] Ken Allen, a director of the former Prew-Smith firm, became a senior manager in the Meridian organisation and, with the authority of J. R. S. Morris he was made responsible for initiating much of the later reorganisation. As experienced suppliers to M&S, the Meridian Prew-Smith factory at Bolsover, augmented by the nearby Clowne factory, formed the core of Courtaulds' M&S underwear connection. Meridian had traditionally been a brand operator, although some experience had been gained in manufacturing for M&S as sub-contractors to F,C&W. Operating under the umbrella of the Meridian organisation, the Prew-Smith Division concentrated on supplying M&S and was central to Courtaulds' aspirations as a main supplier of knitted

---

[44] In addition to being a Courtaulds main board director J.R.S. Morris was responsible for all Courtaulds knitwear and garment companies. His other responsibilities included Courtaulds subsidiaries British Lego Ltd and the Northgate Group Ltd.

underwear of all types to M&S whilst the adult non-M&S chain-store production was based at the Meridian Underwear Division factories.

Courtaulds centralises underwear knitting

Underwear producers, in common with the hosiery and knitwear industry as a whole, traditionally combined knitting and making-up as a vertical entity although not always on the same site. The original acquisitions each had their own knitting plant, but in the first major reorganisation, commencing about 1973, the knitting sites were reduced to four plants, Sutton-in-Ashfield, Arnold, Prew-Smith at New Basford and Haydn Road, Nottingham, but by 1980 all had been consolidated into Haydn Road, Nottingham:

> Meridian management was in fact taking over the rest. They were the experts in knitted fabric which was mainly tubular. Also, as tubular machines were made in a series of fixed diameters the fabric they produced was only suitable for certain sizes. This meant that in the smaller firms certain machines were frequently left standing [to balance the production]. The central department had a greater chance of keeping the plant running. There was the idea that 'big was beautiful' and the knitting could be closely integrated with the Meridian dyeing and finishing outfit. Rowley were left with Mothercare and other children's garments because the margins were small. Wolsey heavy underwear did not fit in. Meridian were the M&S kings, we specialised in it.[45]

The growing importance of M&S as Courtaulds' major customer was clear and was firmly fixed in the ethos of the group. The requirement that M&S work must be produced in dedicated production areas led to increasing specialisation within their suppliers' factories. For example, Coleman Street factory at Derby had originally been a multi-product factory, but in a tidying up process this factory became an underwear producer, and by 1984 the New Basford factory, that had formerly been a mixed product factory, was concentrating totally on leisurewear.

The Underwear Product Group

A regrouping in the early 1980s formalised the trend towards specialisation. The Underwear Product Group Central and International Division consisted of the factories shown in Table 4.2.

---

[45] Interview with Alastair Strang, 18 October 2000.

Table 4.2 *Underwear product group customers*

Site	Principal customers
Bolsover	M&S
Clowne	M&S
Ashby	Asda, Tesco, Littlewoods, Dunnes, BHS but phasing in M&S
Arnold	Operating with Ashby
Middlesbrough	M&S plus other chain stores but phasing out M&S
Wishaw	Operating with Middlesbrough
Derby	Operating with Middlesbrough

Source: M. Lowe

The Underwear Product Group continued to perform well, despite the overall reduction in UK knitted underwear production. Despite the clothing industry's downturn that had continued unabated from the mid-1970s, Courtaulds was still successful enough in underwear to be able to convert factories from other areas of failing clothing production into underwear production. Ashby-de-la-Zouch, formerly a fine-gauge hosiery factory, had been assimilated some time previously. There followed, in the mid to late 1980s, a series of these moves which converted into underwear production the former Granby Garments leisurewear factories at Wrexham and Wishaw and the sportswear factory at Whitwick, Leicestershire. In 1991 a former S. Levine outerwear factory at Houghton-le-Spring was also incorporated into the underwear organisation. Throughout the whole period, divisional changes caused factories with common management to be joined with others, mainly as a response to changing trading patterns, but decline and closures also influenced the organisation structure.

Shortly before the demerger of Courtaulds Textiles from the remainder of the Group the underwear factories had a more rational structure that clearly reflected the dominance of M&S production.

Table 4.3 *Underwear 1989 – adult contract*

Meridian Middlesbrough	Middlesbrough	Adult Contract
Meridian Southern	Arnold	Adult Contract
	Ashby-de-la-Zouch	Adult Contract

Underwear 1989 M&S contract

Meridian underwear	Bolsover	M&S plus Fred Perry
	Clowne	M&S
	Whitwick	M&S
	Wishaw	M&S
	Wrexham	M&S
	Rhosllanerchrugg	M&S
	Morecambe	M&S

Source: M. Lowe

Note: In the 1990s, the factory at Arnold was closed as it was unable to meet foreign competition, and the Ashby-de-la-Zouch factory was converted to M&S production.

Children's underwear – non-M&S

Rowley, a multi-product business, had entered Courtaulds as a modest sized maker of children's knitted underwear. Whilst Rowley factories and sales organisations operated at arm's length from the rest of Courtaulds, the customers were made aware of the security and reliability inherent in dealing with a blue chip organisation. The strength of Rowley was its highly competitive pricing structure. There was a tight control of costs and a culture of low spending throughout the business. Much of the plant was fully written-down in the accounts, but still performed well. About 1973, the knitting was transferred to Haydn Road Nottingham in the general move to concentrate underwear knitting on a limited number of sites. From then (in the context of underwear manufacture), the Queen Street, Leicester site was used only for cutting and subsequent operations.

The Mothercare chain

A salient point in the development of Rowley was the advent of the Mothercare chain. With Courtaulds' capital, a modern factory was set up in 1970 at Allendale Road, Lincoln, dedicated at that stage to Mothercare production.[46] Lessons had been learnt from previous new set-ups and a very limited range of products was introduced in stages which allowed fast training of the totally inexperienced workers. Free from any restrictive practices and traditional methods of operating, the shop floor workers were, within a few months, trained to high levels of

---

[46] By 1972 around 80% of Rowley underwear production was for Mothercare.

performance using new plant and machinery in congenial working conditions. Within the Rowley organisation, direct costs and overheads were apportioned to products according to the costs of the factory at which they were made and not averaged across the whole organisation. This meant that the old high-cost department at Queen Street, Leicester, was constantly exposed to scrutiny and inevitably doomed when the Lincoln factory expanded and became the group's UK non-M&S children's underwear factory, there being insufficient work for both sites.

Offshore processing – children's underwear

By 1981,[47] the group recognised that imports were a serious threat to the whole business and that Rowley underwear was especially vulnerable. Mothercare had insufficient management capacity to investigate overseas sourcing and had up to that time maintained a policy of sourcing in the UK for its European stores. After consultation with Mothercare and with the full knowledge of the other major chain stores, the decision was taken in 1981 to develop a 'joint venture' manufacturing base in Portugal with an established manufacturer, Vas Ferreira. This was in full operation by 1985. The venture was not based entirely on the concept of low-cost labour. The view was taken that it would be better to concentrate on an area with established skill and management, rather than concentrate solely on low labour-costs. In retrospect, this seems to have been wise. Rowley had well established connections with the major chain stores in the UK and well developed sales and design facilities, but the organisation had been run with very tight control of costs, therefore all its management, technical and training staff was fully utilised at the UK factories. Apart from the appointment of a UK manager from Rowley, heavy reliance was placed on the technical ability of Portuguese staff, with a minimum level of input from the Leicester organisation. This venture was much earlier than the M&S-Meridian developments in Sri Lanka and was influenced much less by the technical demands of the customers. After the expansion into Portugal the highly efficient Lincoln factory was used for other customers from 1990, but even this strategy and cost-effectiveness was insufficient in the face of incessant price pressure on basic underwear from low-cost imports.

Globalisation of trade – M&S

The turning point in Courtaulds' UK underwear story came in the early 1990s. The fortunes of Courtaulds Underwear was almost totally tied up with the

---

[47] Although Morocco and Sri Lanka were considered and had lower labour costs, Portuguese labour costs were still 50% below those of the UK.

fortunes of M&S which had maintained its allegiance to the UK industry too long, almost certainly to the detriment of its own business. Meridian was already sourcing goods from Sri Lanka, Morocco, Turkey and Portugal for its non-M&S business. Relative to M&S, other chain stores became very price-competitive in the high street. As offshore suppliers grew in size and ability and the world began to open up for offshore knitters, dyers and finishers, the high street became even more fiercely competitive. It was inevitable that if M&S were to maintain its leading position in the high volume middle price market, it would have to open up the supply chain to offshore produced merchandise.

The establishment of Courtaulds' underwear manufacturing base in Sri Lanka commenced with two factories, Slimline and Slenderline, making small amounts of M&S children's underwear to establish the production, and this was followed shortly by women's garments. This was a three-way venture between Courtaulds Underwear, an American company and a Sri Lankan partner.[48] The factories were built to specifications laid down in agreement with M&S and were set up by British staff that were very experienced in the standards and procedures of the business in the UK. The established culture of M&S demanded high standards of safety, hygiene, skill and quality, backed up with top class systems and communications. From 1995, these criteria could be met, and M&S encouraged Courtaulds to supply increasing amounts of merchandise from Sri Lanka. However, whilst the expansion into Sri Lanka was building up, the Bolsover, Clowne and Houghton-le-Spring factories were still in operation employing over 600 workers.

Expansion of manufacturing in Sri Lanka was based on a concept of growth. It soon allowed M&S to offer good quality merchandise at competitive retail prices. Courtaulds had intended to average the prices between the offshore and UK production, using the offshore factories for large orders and the UK units to supplement this with a fast response service.[49] With the subsequent down-turn in the fortunes of M&S, an issue that is dealt with later, Courtaulds was faced with two choices, either to reduce the Sri Lanka production which would have upset the price balance and reduced profits, or close the UK factories which would lengthen delivery times. Ultimately Sri Lanka was the winner.

Technology

For underwear garment assembly there was a continual move towards improved technology. The level of technology varied between factories, with the large Meridian and Prew-Smith units being able to justify the use of the most up to date mechanised fabric-laying and computer-controlled cutting equipment. In the

---

[48] MAS Holdings and Mast industries.
[49] Fast response is covered in more detail in Chapter 6.

mid-1980s there commenced a movement away from circular towards open-width fabric which was an ideal application for the automated cutting equipment by then available.

Rowley was an intermediate sized business that used mechanised fabric laying equipment but shared computerised lay marking equipment with its leisurewear department. The actual cutting operations were still done with straight-knife and band-knife. Wolsey, in contrast, owing to the small scale of its output in its declining heavy underwear department, used hand controlled laying equipment, marking the fabric with yellow chalk and cutting the panels with an electric straight knife, a process almost unchanged over more than fifty years.

Basic sewing machine technology was relatively unchanged, but extensive use was made of attachments such as automatic thread trimming, stop-motions, automatic needle positioning and binding cutters. These did speed up the process and also effected a considerable reduction in wasted thread and binding.

Central Underwear Knitting closed

Changes in customer's preferences in the 1990s had a serious effect on the Meridian Prew-Smith and Meridian divisions, which after several reorganisations became known as Courtaulds Underwear. There was a general trend towards a more diverse range of fabrics and a wider variety of colours. This reduced the cost advantage of having the large circular-knitting plant and dyehouse at Haydn Road Nottingham that had been set up to produce vast quantities of white knitted fabric, and reduced the cost benefits that long production runs had provided. Inevitably as Courtaulds developed its factories in Sri Lanka most of the fabric began to be sourced offshore at vastly more advantageous prices.

Wolsey Brand

The Wolsey brand was placed at the top end of the underwear market. When Wolsey was acquired by Courtaulds in 1966, it was still involved in the production of men's heavy underwear consisting mainly of long johns and placket neck vests. With the closure of the Abbey Park Mills, Leicester, the knitting was transferred to the Meridian site at Haydn Road, Nottingham, and making-up to the Bruin Street, Leicester, factory which was mainly used for sock production. The manager, Roy Jones described the production unit: 'We had no automated cutting.... We had short runs. We were like bespoke tailors and it was a very expensive item.'

Heavy underwear was recognised, even in the late 1960s, as a declining product, but the production department survived, with some restyling, as an item of skiwear. Eventually, all fully-fashioned work was phased out and the heavy underwear was produced by cut and sewn methods. With the closure of the

Morley heavy underwear department, the manufacturing capacity in Courtaulds was reduced, but with declining sales even the small Bruin Street, Leicester, unit was able to meet the lower demand. Wolsey also produced lightweight underwear at Ratby that was knitted on RTR machines, which could knit aerated fabric. As the Ratby factory was short of labour for making-up, a small satellite factory was set up at Moira which carried on for a number of years, but the Ratby factory was later sold off.

Management buyout for Wolsey brand name

The Wolsey brand name was used in the UK and Scandinavia, both traditionally strong Wolsey markets. Wolsey branded underwear was relatively unsuccessful in the Middle East, but the Morley Theta name was still recognised there and continued to be used by the Wolsey sales organisation even after it was sold off in a management buyout. In the early part of the twenty-first century, this new independent 'Wolsey' company closed its heavy underwear manufacturing department and sourced the products from elsewhere.

Lyle & Scott 'Y' Front and Jockey

Lyle & Scott, a former subsidiary of Wolsey, was a brand leader in the 'direct to retail' sector using the trademarks Jockey and Y Front. 'Y Fronts' were manufactured at Gateshead and heavily advertised; the Courtaulds-owned X Front brand name was allowed to fade away and was dropped from the market. Lyle & Scott worked separately from the other divisions of Courtaulds and at the time of the Sara Lee acquisition of Courtaulds was sold as a going concern.

Wholesale

The high cost involved in wholesale trading was incompatible with the philosophy of chasing high volumes from chain stores. Most Courtaulds manufacturing units had withdrawn from the remaining wholesale trade by 1985.

Closure

Shortly after the acquisition of Courtaulds Textiles plc by Sara Lee Corporation the remaining UK factory at Bolsover was closed, overwhelmed by import penetration, and the production was transferred to Sri Lanka.

The integration and decline of the sock businesses

Courtaulds built up its important sock production through the acquisition of a number of multi-product firms, commencing in 1963 with the acquisition of F,C&W and Meridian. Brettles followed in 1964 and was joined in 1967 by the major acquisition, Wolsey. Contour and Rowley were acquired in 1968. College Hosiery and Corah Sock Division were added in 1985 and 1988 respectively. Despite this expansion, by the turn of the century, due to serious decline in the UK industry, the whole of the capacity was centred in the former Wolsey dyehouse and warehouse site at Abbey Meadows. Sites used by Courtaulds at various times were:

Table 4.4 *Courtaulds' sock manufacturing sites*

G Brettle Ltd	Belper
J F Carnall & Co. Ltd	St Nicholas Circle Leicester
N Corah (St Margaret) Ltd	St Margarets Way Leicester
Foister, Clay & Ward Ltd	Great Central Street Leicester
	Silday Works Kegworth
	Frog Island Leicester
G Ginns Ltd	Braunstone Gate Leicester
Meridian Ltd	Ilkeston Junction Ilkeston
	Haydn Road Nottingham
Reliance Hosiery Ltd	Hare St Halifax
R Rowley & Co. Ltd	Uttoxeter New Road Derby
	Queen Street Leicester
Wolsey Ltd	Bruin Street Leicester
	Abbey Meadow Mills Leicester
Courtaulds Sock Division	Wanlip Street Leicester
	Abbey Meadows Leicester

Foister, Clay & Ward

F,C&W's sock knitting was based at Great Central Street, Leicester, with a secondary knitting plant, Silday Works at Kegworth. The Frog Island, Leicester site was used for the final packing processes. With 700 knitting machines at Leicester and 199 machines at Kegworth, supported by 190 linking and toe-closing machines, the claim that it had the second largest plant in the UK industry seems feasible. The plant was old but in top class condition and the employees and staff had high technical ability. However, F,C&W was in decline and suffering from a shortage of orders from M&S, by far its largest customer. The problems were made worse by the shortage of labour in Leicester. F,C&W was losing money at an alarming rate and in April 1967 it was announced that production would cease and the remaining plant was to be transferred, partly to Kegworth and partly to the Meridian sock factory at Ilkeston,[50] but the Kegworth factory was closed shortly afterwards. The acquisition of this firm had failed to provide the strong entry into the M&S sock business that it had been reasonable to expect.

More sock factories

The most active acquisition period occurred in 1967 and 1968, with the takeover of Wolsey, Contour and Rowley.

Table 4.5 *Sock production from 1976*

	c.1976 (000 doz./wk)	c.1982 (000 doz./wk)	c.1988 (000 doz./wk)	c.1995 (000 doz./wk)	c.1999 (000 doz./wk)	c.2000 (000 doz./wk)
Brettle	Closed					
Great Central St	Closed					
Kegworth	Closed					
Bruin Street	20	20	20	Closed		
Wanlip Street	5	25	Closed			
Meridian	10	Closed				
Ginns	4	Closed				
Carnall	7	Closed				
Derby	8	W'house				
Queen St, Leics			15	15	3	Closed
Corah Leicester			20	Closed		
Reliance Halifax			Closed			
Abbey Meadows				45	45	40
Production total	54	45	55	60	48	40

Sources: Denis Perridge, Colin Lissaman, John Skinner.
Note: The actual capacity at F,C&W was probably over 30,000 dozen pairs per week in 1964 but was running on short time and producing approximately 20,000 dozen pairs per week. The production of Reliance Hosiery Ltd is included with Corah, its parent company.

---

[50] *Hosiery Trade Journal,* April 1967.

These firms were central to the later composition of the group because F,C&W had by then already been run down, leaving the high-cost Meridian sock division the only effective Courtaulds sock-producing unit. By far the most significant of the acquisitions was Wolsey, with its large sock manufacturing division based at Bruin Street, Leicester. The table above shows the stage that consolidation of Courtaulds' sock units had reached by six approximate dates but before 1976 Courtaulds had already lost at the very least 30,000 dozens per week with the closure of the F,C&W and Brettles manufacturing units. Despite the acquisition in 1988 of the Corah sock division which brought in a production of 20,000 dozens per week, by the year 2000 the production was down to its lowest figure, all of which was being produced at Abbey Meadows, Leicester and supplemented with Turkish imports.[51]

Rowley absorbs Contour

Two small Leicester firms, G. Ginns, manufacturers of children's socks at Braunstone Gate, and J. F. Carnall, manufacturers of men's socks at St Nicholas Street, were acquired as part of the Contour takeover. Both of these firms were housed in very old premises that were in an advanced stage of dilapidation and unsuitable for renovation, redevelopment or expansion. Both were run semi-independently, but at the time of the takeover R. A. Palfreyman the Contour chairman resigned. As this left these firms without a senior executive it was decided in March 1971 to attach them to the Rowley organisation, with its much larger stake in the children's sock industry. This enabled the two very much smaller firms to report to the centre through Rowley's accounts system. Rowley's experienced top management was then able to control capital investment, and generally take other decisions for which the management of these two firms had neither the qualifications nor sufficient status.[52] Rowley could also coordinate sales outlets and at the same time avoid the possibility that these three businesses might compete on price with each other.

Rowley – the advantage of a multi-product range

Ginns and Carnall were in many ways complementary to each other. Both made socks aimed at the middle of the market and were able to sell very competitively, but were not clearly focused on any particular customers.

---

[51] The fall in production was not halted and the factory was closed by its new owners, Sara Lee, within three years.

[52] By this time management teams did not actually decide the level of investment. Annual requests were made to the main board for specific projects. If funds were allocated the management team was responsible for the actual project.

Only Rowley owned a well-known brand name, Peter Pan, but by the late 1960s the outlets through the wholesale trade were beginning to diminish and the organisation had begun to compete successfully for non-M&S chain store business, particularly with the newly emerging Mothercare chain. In what seems to be a reversal of the then current fashion towards isolated specialist production, the sock section benefited from being able to use Rowley's dedicated Mothercare distribution service, working in effective liaison with the knitwear, leisurewear and underwear departments. Goods were picked from racks in the Rowley warehouse, packed into composite orders and forwarded to a Mothercare central distribution point for re-distribution to individual stores. Therefore, Rowley's sock factories could manufacture large orders and yet distribute them in an economical way to individual high street stores. Later, a further advantage was the close liaison between the design departments, which were in close proximity at the Queen Street, Leicester factory and could produce a coordinated product range for non-M&S chain stores.

Meridian – the minor brands

Meridian Socks operated on two sites: the pre-dye operations such as knitting and toe-closing were based at Ilkeston Junction, Derbyshire, and the packing and despatch were accommodated at the Meridian main site at Haydn Road, Nottingham. This long-established enterprise had benefited from the transfer of small amounts of business on the closure of F,C&W and Brettles. Meridian Socks was a minor 'brand' operation supplying under the trade names Meridian, Robin Hood and Maid Marian. Attempts to enter the bulk market by way of the Ministry of Defence and M&S were unsuccessful, the independent trade and the wholesale system was in decline and the Meridian sock division was unable to support itself and was placed under Rowley management.

Wolsey – the major player

Wolsey sock department, based at Bruin Street, Leicester, was best known for its Wolsey and Cardinal men's socks, produced for the better class independent trade in competition with Byford Ltd and Hall & Sons' Indestructible. During the middle of the 1960s, Wolsey responded to the decline of the independent trade by mounting an attack on the multiple stores and other large outlets. Considerable inroads were made into Littlewoods and BHS and in the less conventional outlets, such as Fine Fare and Tesco. Sales were also made to Dunnes Stores, but on a much smaller scale. Despite the pre-war decision to supply directly to retail shops, some contact was maintained with the wholesale trade and goods were produced in the customer's packaging for customers such as Gall & Co. in

Glasgow and Kingsley Forrester in Manchester,[53] but these orders only amounted to a few hundred dozens at a time. Wolsey formerly supplied socks to M&S and at one stage that business had amounted to about 10% of the total production. However, the allocation of dedicated work areas and machinery to M&S became impractical in view of the erratic orders received at that time and fitted uncomfortably with the Wolsey ethos of dedication to the Wolsey brand. M&S trade had disappeared by the time the firm was acquired by Courtaulds in 1967.[54]

Courtaulds Sock Division

By 1975, Courtaulds' sock interests had been consolidated into two operating businesses, Rowley Group and Wolsey. The decision was taken by Courtaulds' top management to join these together to form a Sock Division under a chief executive, T. W. (Bill) Harvey, at that time chief executive of Rowley, who then relinquished responsibility for Rowley Group. The new division brought together the Rowley controlled sock factories at Uttoxeter New Road, Derby, Braunstone Gate and St Nicholas Circle, Leicester, and Ilkeston Junction and Haydn Road, Nottingham, and the Wolsey factory at Bruin Street, Leicester, with distribution and administration at Abbey Meadows, Leicester.

The rationale for forming the sock division was quite convincing. At that time, with the exception of M&S, there was a broad customer base in the chain stores with *Wolsey* brand being one of the forerunners in the independent trade. With Courtaulds' capital and strong manufacturing expertise, and controlled by experienced management, the opportunities for cooperation and cost reduction seemed wide open. Also, by grouping the socks together, the lines of communication within the group could be considerably simplified.

As Colin Lissaman, factory manager at Wolsey, both prior to and during the period the Sock Division was in operation, explained:

> The division was formed without a single Wolsey person on the executive committee. Wolsey could be considered a sleeping giant with a wonderful brand name not being used as effectively as it could be. When David Mason [Production executive] and Bill Harvey [Chief Executive] hit the scene there was more attention paid to margins, and not just on paper but actual savings. They were from a more cutthroat background. The brand [Wolsey] had a tradition for much higher margins and returns. But Wolsey was struggling on the contract side. The contract was getting bigger and bigger and the brand was getting smaller and smaller and they [Courtaulds' higher management] also felt that Rowleys' expertise was not in its [Peter Pan] brand

---

[53] Information from David Swirles.
[54] Information from Denis Perridge.

which had become quite small but in contracts, [for example] Littlewoods and Mothercare – Rowley were certainly in these before Wolsey.[55]

Decline in children's socks

After 1974, the production of children's non-M&S socks became concentrated at two sites, Wanlip Street, Leicester for knitting, and Uttoxeter New Road, Derby for dyeing and finishing operations. This was made possible by the closure of the former Ginns factory on Braunstone Gate, Leicester and the transfer of the machines and operatives to the former Carnall factory at St Nicholas Circle, Leicester. This was soon followed by the consolidation of all children's sock knitting into the former Booton knitting machinery factory, built in the late Victorian era as a brewery, at Wanlip Street, Leicester. In 1978, after makeshift repairs to the decrepit property, a plant of machines was transferred from Meridian Ilkeston to produce children's socks for Mothercare. Then, knitting from Derby, Ilkeston and St Nicholas Circle was all transferred into Wanlip Street. As part of these moves, the sock operations at the former Meridian factories in Ilkeston and Haydn Road, Nottingham, were totally closed, along with the factory at St Nicholas Circle, Leicester. The closure of the sock packing department of the Derby factory soon followed.

Courtaulds Sock Division – a failed concept

There seems to have been little serious attempt to form a fully integrated sock division although all production was placed nominally under one executive, David Mason. Unfortunately there was a distinct lack of interest by Bill Harvey in the expensive advertising of the Wolsey Brand and as a consequence there was intense lobbying by John Hayes, the Wolsey executive, who wanted to control the men's sock business and re-vitalise Wolsey as a major brand, coordinated across all products. By this time Lord Kearton had retired and under his successor, Sir Arthur Knight, Hayes policy was implemented.

Fortunately for Hayes many functions had not been closely integrated and could be easily unpicked. The diverse range of children's and adults' socks should not have been any reason for the failure to integrate the sales organisations. It would have been quite practical to allocate sales people to each client and would have been equally practical to restrict the number of representatives calling on the customers but separate representation continued to be made for men's and children's socks. The sales staff remained fragmented, with John Hales in charge of the Wolsey brand and David Swirles in charge of men's contract sales from

---

[55] Interview with Colin Lissaman, 27 July 2000.

Bruin Street, the former Wolsey factory. Nigel Michael sold children's socks to contract customers and Royden Broughton sold men's socks from the Derby and Wanlip Street factories. In the early stages of the division Bill Holbrooke continued to sell Meridian brand socks. With the financial accounts still being separate it was a relatively simple matter for Hayes to claw back parts of this untidy mixture and reform the Wolsey brand operation as a single entity.

Philosophy and culture

It may be questioned why these businesses were never closely integrated. Differing philosophies drove these organisations and the sock businesses fitted uncomfortably together. Bruin Street factory, in line with its long tradition, manufactured to the highest possible standard that could reasonably be achieved without threatening viability: contract orders were made by the same people and on the same machines as the Wolsey branded socks, and to the same quality. This culture of quality production and pride in the product was reflected in all aspects of the way the business was run, including accounts, training, personnel relations, customer service and general management. The Bruin Street factory retained a strong identity and was still referred to as 'The Wolsey' by the employees. In contrast, and without implying any criticism of Rowley, that business worked on the principle that socks were made strictly to the specification agreed with the client, no more, no less, and cost-cutting in all aspects of the business was foremost in the management ethos. During the rationalisation process, the other factories lost their identity and were soon referred to as 'Wanlip Street' or 'Derby' by the employees.

Consolidation

There is little evidence that there were substantial savings made in administration costs as a result of the formation of the sock division, and heavy costs were incurred in a series of closures and site moves. As the Sock Division evolved, all the consolidation of sites that did occur was within the non-Wolsey manufacturing units. This was inevitable and would have occurred under Rowley management without the formation of the Sock Division: the lease was due to expire on the Ginns site and road alterations forced the closure of part of the Carnall site whilst Meridian was unable to survive after the loss of the wholesale trade.

Sock division disbanded

In a move that seems to presage a later trend towards grouping by customer type rather than by product sector, the ill-fated Courtaulds Sock Division was disbanded in the mid-1970s. The factories that had formed the former Rowley

Management Group, which included knitwear, leisurewear, underwear and all of Courtaulds' children's socks, plus some of the men's knitting plant from Ilkeston, were again placed together and Bill Harvey was reappointed Rowley chief executive. The Wolsey sock factory at Bruin Street and the warehouse at Abbey Meadow Mills were placed under the newly-appointed executive for Wolsey branded business for all products, John Hayes, who was charged with ensuring the continuance of the Wolsey brand name.

Courtaulds and Marks & Spencer

Courtaulds' sock business had been drifting in the market for some years, having failed to establish a major presence in the rapidly developing supermarket trade and with the vitally important M&S chain. However, there remained at Courtaulds' main board level the commitment and determination to sell to M&S and make it the priority client. This was the most important sock outlet missing from Courtaulds' wide-ranging sales portfolio. Wolsey sales people were able to reopen the M&S account, but unlike the previous attempt several years earlier, this was on a much larger scale and pursued with greater commitment. In the process, however, the Wolsey brand and other non-M&S businesses were put at risk. The provision of dedicated space and equipment for M&S production caused problems for the brand and other clients that were no longer regarded as core customers.

Courtaulds disposes of Wolsey brand

Small non-M&S orders became an embarrassment to the Bruin Street factory and attempts were made to produce the Wolsey brand socks at Rowley in Leicester, on redundant machinery from Reliance Hosiery. However, the small and complex orders and the high quality demands caused problems for the small management team that had been set up to control large and long running contracts. Courtaulds disposed of the Wolsey brand and a new firm, Wolsey Ltd, was set up as the result of a management buyout.[56] The new firm was able to obtain merchandise from a variety of sources in the UK and overseas and promote a whole range of coordinated clothing and further promote the Wolsey brand. At this time, the sock factory at Bruin Street dropped the Wolsey name and once again became known as Courtaulds Sock Division.

---

[56] This firm was sold to Matalan in 2002.

Children's socks centralised at Queen St Leicester

In the mid-1980s, Rowley finally severed its links with the declining wholesale trade and concentrated on chain store business. Major customers were Mothercare, Littlewoods, BHS, Woolworths, Tesco, Sainsbury's and the newly emerging Aldi.

Although the industry in general was losing ground, and underwear manufacturing at Rowley, Queen Street, Leicester, ceased in 1986, the sock industry was not yet so seriously affected. However, a considerable amount of floor space became vacant at Queen Street and the sock-knitting plant from Wanlip Street was transferred into this space. Although the Queen Street site was expensive to maintain, its facilities and suitability for sock manufacturing were vastly superior to the old and run-down Wanlip Street premises. It could also house the sales, design and administrative and accounts staff required, and failure to fill the space would have placed an intolerable cost on the other divisions of the Rowley Group.

Courtaulds Sock Division (second version)

Courtaulds bought the industry leaders, Corah Socks in 1988, the main Corah factory was closed and any machinery that was required was moved to Abbey Meadow Mills (the former Wolsey warehouse site). Manufacturing commenced immediately.

Reliance Hosiery had earlier become part of Corah, but was run separately.[57] It had serious industrial relations problems and, by M&S requirements, had low quality standards.[58] Courtaulds made a further rationalisation and closed Reliance, moving some of the plant into Abbey Meadows and some to Rowley. As the industry declined, even in Leicester, which had had many years of labour shortages, it was possible, in a climate of lost jobs, to recruit the necessary workers.

The former Wolsey Bruin Street factory was closed and the plant and machinery was moved to Abbey Meadow Mills, which by this time had large amounts of vacant floor space. Around this time, the firm introduced automatic pairing of socks by machine. This replaced a whole group of 'countermen', whose function had been to check each individual sock for quality and to put the socks into pairs, thereby reducing the visual effect caused by the length differences produced in the knitting process, which in reality were quite small. This hand

---

[57] College Hosiery had been bought out in 1985 but had been immediately closed and the plant and operatives transferred to Bruin Street, Leicester. It did not operate as a separate unit within Courtaulds.

[58] The proportion of rejects discarded in the factory was very high by industry standards.

'countering' process was outdated in an era of modern manufacturing and the savings in labour costs and the reduced floor space contributed to the survival of the enterprise for a few years.

Globalisation of trade

The UK market for socks held up much longer than the fine-gauge hosiery sector and was unaffected by swings of fashion. The major change in the global trading pattern occurred later than in other sections of the trade but in the second half of the 1990s exports began to fall away and imports gained ground. In this period Courtaulds was forced by price pressure to supplement its sock offer to M&S with imported merchandise, most notably from Turkey.[59] At the same time, the total sock sales to M&S took a down-turn.

Rowley closes

In the face of mounting import penetration, the Queen Street, Leicester factory of Rowley was closed in 1999 and the sock-knitting plant was transferred to Abbey Meadows. The Derby factory was closed almost immediately, leaving Courtaulds with only one sock-manufacturing site. A few months before closure the capacity of the Rowley plant was still in excess of 15,000 dozens per week, but, as the downturn had now become a disaster, only 3,000 dozens per week were transferred to the Abbey Meadows site, which was still functioning, although rapidly going into decline at the time of acquisition by Sara Lee Corporation in 2000.

Kearton's legacy in retrospect

Kearton took over a chemicals and fibres business that was on the edge of disaster with demand for rayon, its most important product, in rapid decline. In a bid to provide a captive outlet for the rapidly developing market for newly developed Courtaulds fibres he expanded the firm by acquiring a position in cognate industries such as spinning, weaving and hosiery and knitwear.

Many of the businesses taken over at this time were multi-product enterprises, many had serious management problems and by their very nature they included products that were unsuccessful and of necessity were closed. Some of the acquisitions were unsuccessful, were split up and their constituent parts placed under the control of other more successful managements. Many would otherwise have gone out of business had they remained independent but some could not be revived.

---

[59] The Sara Lee sock factory, originally Wolsey, Bruin Street, Leicester, closed in 2003.

Kearton had the benefit of working in a less hostile business environment than his successors and was able to build up capacity by the acquisition of a wide ranging portfolio of companies but towards the end of his tenure of leadership it was clear that hard times were ahead and the main acquisition movement came to a halt around 1968.

Kearton had taken a company that had been on the verge of losing its identity and set it on a path that enabled it to survive profitably for many years. Despite this monumental achievement Kearton was open to criticism for his lack of attention to management structure, policy and management style, issues that feature in subsequent chapters.

As has been seen, his successors were faced with a declining market for UK-produced goods, particularly after 1974, and reorganisation and decline under those that followed was gradual and largely a response to overcapacity. They were not free to make the decisions that would have been appropriate in more stable times and were unable to halt the tide of imports that overwhelmed the hosiery and knitwear industry.

The contribution of the acquisitions to the product sectors

Due to the complex structure of many of these multi-product and multi-location acquisitions, the acquisitions have been grouped together into the following themes: fine-gauge hosiery, knitwear and underwear, socks, and multi-product childrenswear (non-M&S) (the detailed case studies in Chapter 3 are in alphabetical order). Here the firms are grouped according to their position in the product range after being absorbed into the developing Courtaulds' structure. This grouping is somewhat arbitrary in nature and includes some anomalies because several of the multi-product firms influenced more than one sector of Courtaulds' garment knitting structure as it began to evolve.

Table 4.6 *Multi-product firms*

Fine-gauge	Knitwear/underwear	Socks	Non-M&S children's
Aristoc	Bairnswear	Wolsey	Rowley
Ballito	Meridian	Corah	
Kayser Bondor	Foister, Clay & Ward		
Contour			

Table 4.7 *Entrepreneurial M&S suppliers*

Fine-gauge	Knitwear/underwear	Socks	Non-M&S children's
Blount (D&M)	Prew-Smith		

Table 4.8 *Brand Concession/Scottish Knitwear*

Fine-gauge	Knitwear/underwear	Socks	Non-M&S children's
	Lyle & Scott (W)		

Table 4.9 *Wholesale/manufacturers*

Fine-gauge	Knitwear/underwear	Socks	Non-M&S children's
Brettle	Morley		

Table 4.10 *Small firms*

Fine-gauge	Knitwear/underwear	Socks	Non-M&S children's
Percy Taylor	Hendry & Spiers	College	Kilsyth
Beasley	Highfield Productions		
W. Riding (C&W)	Irvine		
	Stewarton		

FIVE

Change under Kearton's Successors: Devolution and Demerger

Devolution of control

ARTHUR WILLIAM KNIGHT WAS THE SON of a steel hardener who later became a railway porter. He left school armed with his matriculation certificate and commenced work as a clerk for the grocery company, J. Sainsbury. While with Sainsbury's he attended evening classes at the London School of Economics and gained a B.Com. degree with first class honours in 1938. He commenced work for Courtaulds in 1939 as a junior economist in the London office.

Knight served in the army from 1940 until 1946, concluding with a spell as a lieutenant-colonel at the Finance Division of the Control Commission for Austria. After the war he returned to Courtaulds and worked in the overseas investment department, rising to be a senior executive and was promoted to the main board in 1958. He then worked closely with the newly appointed managing director Frank Kearton and was soon appointed finance director. In this capacity he was involved with Kearton in repelling the takeover bid launched by ICI, and when Kearton became chairman in 1964 he was already a very influential member of the board. On Kearton's retirement in 1975 Knight (by then Sir Arthur) was appointed chairman. Knight had worked alongside Kearton in the massive programme of expansion, diversification and acquisition and set up the organisation and finance by which this was achieved, undertaking much of the negotiation involved. Knight in his former capacity as head of finance seemed remote from the manufacturing units and their executives, but as chairman he was found to be much more approachable than Kearton.

When Arthur Knight took over the leadership from Kearton in 1975, at the end of a long run of expansion, the effects of recession were being felt and Knight was faced with enormous challenges. Although Noel Jervis, later a chief executive of Courtaulds Textiles plc, was reflecting on the position of Courtaulds plc as a whole, he might well have been talking specifically about the experience of just the hosiery and knitwear businesses described in the previous chapter:

> What followed, apart from an economic disaster, was a period of aftermath, indigestion and significant retrenchments – pretty much a wholesale rejection of many previous policies and especially so in the light of the emerging competitive environment.[1]

The firm was open to the criticism that the entrepreneurial flair of the middle managers had been lost because their decision-making authority had been removed. It was being questioned whether the vertical trading policy, put in place in the 1960s, was equal to the demands of the 1970s. Courtaulds' own yarn manufacturers knew they were being protected because they had a captive market for inferior goods at prices dictated by Kearton.[2] Yarns that were not good enough for the next users down the line were forced on them. Opening up the nylon procurement to full competition by allowing the firm's own businesses to purchase nylon from outside suppliers would have forced Courtaulds' own chemical engineers and spinners to sort out the product. It would also have highlighted the quality and price problems to the top management if garment manufacturers had not bought the firm's own products. Protecting the firm's own fibre makers and spinners from market forces was not good for either end of the business.

Economies of scale

Although Courtaulds expanded downstream from its chemicals and industrial business as a defensive strategy aimed at protecting its markets for fibres, it would also have been reasonable to expect benefits in the form of economies of scale from the acquisitions.[3] In the clothing trade there was nothing to equal the

---

[1] Noel Jervis, The Cyril Hurd memorial lecture 1994.

[2] Information supplied by Dr J. B. Smith. The major problem was in Celon (Courtaulds' nylon) which was launched on the market before the product was fully developed. Other yarn was not necessarily inferior. Courtaulds Courtelle was technically sound but over-priced at £3.30 kilo. The competing Leacryl from Sunray Dyeing (Leicester) was £3.05 kilo (1980 prices).

[3] The reasoning was never clearly set out by the firm but, as the Lancashire spinning industry was in serious decline, securing the market for the firm's fibres was seen as essential for the long-term survival of Courtaulds. Specifically regarding the knitting industry the vertical policy made selling the firms products such as Courtelle and Celon easier in the

Sir Arthur Knight – Chairman of Courtaulds plc 1975–1980. Photo courtesy of Courtaulds plc.

scale of grocery items such as Flora margarine, Persil or Heinz Beans. Despite the perceived theoretical and practical advantages, in practice the process of actually integrating this complex mixture of businesses into a cohesive form and attaching them to a large scale chemicals and industrial enterprise produced serious challenges for the firm, and met with only very limited success.

Knight realised that the search for economies of scale was mostly chasing an illusion. As Chandler notes: 'In the more labor intensive industries[4] ... the large integrated firm had few competitive advantages.'[5]

From the mid-1970s the main factor limiting the UK knitting industries was the ability to produce goods at a price the customer was prepared to pay, rather than any real shortage of workers or plant and machinery. Neither was extending the product range and scope of the factories on the agenda. The opportunities for entering other branches of the clothing trade would have almost certainly

face of American competition. See Knight (1974), p. 47.
[4] Such as publishing and printing, lumber, furniture, textiles, apparel, leather etc.
[5] Chandler (1994), p. 45.

meant competing with other products that were already being produced within Courtaulds and were equally under threat, and therefore as the UK clothing industry shrank, the hosiery and knitwear industry businesses were forced to shed capacity.

The short production runs needed constant attention from all levels of management and there were limits to the range of products that could be understood and controlled by individual managers, frequent and rapid decision-making being needed to control the host of small orders that are a feature of the clothing industry. Tight control of stock and supply chain expertise was absolutely vital and making goods without an order would be almost suicide in what was rapidly becoming a more contract based industry. Consolidating factories together to make larger units was almost impossible because the size of each factory was generally limited by the available labour, rather than by any geographical constraint.[6] A less obvious but important factor was that multi-product sites needed a common labour policy and this was difficult to achieve, because as each business became more responsible for its own profits this affected a whole range of issues including the important matter of pay and working conditions.[7]

The strengthening power of the chain stores continued. Customer pressure affected the shaping of the Group and led to the establishment of distinct subdivisions, particularly when the growth of the supermarkets altered the balance of power between the retailers. Where Courtaulds had a large presence in one product field, the larger factories could be sub-divided into sections that served an individual customer or market sector. Channon argues regarding the textile industry '… it was the deliberate or accidental managerial failure to coordinate integrated activities accumulated rapidly by acquisition which made the strategy actually one of diversification.'[8]

This statement does not comfortably match the Courtaulds situation. The firm expended considerable effort attempting to coordinate the acquisitions in the hosiery and knitwear field, but its failure to do so was neither a result of deliberate policy or unknown reasons or misfortune. It was simply that coordination was attempted but found not to naturally fit the realities of the situation. Rather it could be argued that it was the notion that coordination of these small enterprises was an achievable prospect that was misconceived rather than lack of implementation being failure.

---

[6] The geography is discussed in Chapter 8.
[7] Labour issues are discussed in Chapter 6.
[8] Channon (1984), p. 178.

Courtaulds' structure

Describing earlier research Channon notes:

> All the textile companies examined had adopted a partial multidivisional structure yet still containing many features of a holding company. Those structures were especially ill-suited to coordinated integrated operations, since great autonomy was permitted to the operating units, and very few central office services had been developed.[9]

Courtaulds' central organisation could certainly be described as containing features of a holding company, which in fact it was, having many part owned and other legally separate corporate subsidiaries. In practice great autonomy was actually necessary to the operation of the clothing manufacturing units. To function in the fashion industries a large measure of autonomy was required because the customers actually demanded close attention and rapid reaction to their needs from decision makers, designers, planners and technicians. Indeed the larger customers demanded production units and management staff that were totally dedicated to their needs.

Knight's response

Knight responded to the problem of managers' loss of motivation, initiative and the ability to manage their own profit centres by relaxing the tight central control that had previously been exercised by Kearton. He is probably most remembered as the leader under whom much of the strategy put in place by Kearton was reversed, and under Knight the value of the vertical trading concept was challenged. Gradually, it became possible for individual managers to negotiate on such matters as the purchasing of non-Courtaulds yarn. The breakdown of the vertical trading policy was very evident in the hosiery and knitwear sector. To the delight of the garment factory managers increasing use was made of non-group services, and the Group's dye-houses were put in open competition with outside dyers. In addition, the large underwear fabric knitting and dyeing and finishing unit at Haydn Road, Nottingham, developed after the closure of several fragmented knitting plants, became exposed to direct competition from independent knitting firms.

No longer did Group businesses support each other in difficult times, and with increasing over-capacity in the industry the customers, particularly the High Street chain stores, squeezed down prices and inevitably as shown in previous chapters there were large scale plant closures.

---

[9] Channon (1984), p. 178.

Courtaulds garment industries continued to suffer from divided ambitions, trying to supply the wholesale trade with its myriad of specialist labels and small orders, promoting its own brands and supplying the major chain stores. These problems were recognised by Christopher Hogg who was responsible for the garment industries, and together with the challenge of low-cost imports were issues that challenged the leadership during Knight's tenure, however it was to be several years before a formal plan, set out to address these problems, was put in place.

Chairman of Courtaulds Textiles plc 1990–93 and 1993–1995

In contrast to the self-made Kearton and Knight, Christopher Hogg had the advantage of being born into more affluent circumstances and was from a very different social class than Kearton and Knight. He was educated at Marlborough College and from there he went to Trinity College, Oxford. This was followed by a period at Harvard Business School, where he gained his MBA. After military service he spent time as a Harkness Fellow at Lausanne. In 1963 he moved to Hill Samuel (investment banking), and in 1966 to the Industrial Reorganization Corporation, where he worked closely with Kearton until 1968 when he joined him at Courtaulds. An establishment figure, well known in the city, Hogg was Courtaulds' Chief Executive from 1979 until 1991, and also chairman from 1980 to 1996. He became Chairman of Reuters in 1985, held various directorships and Honorary Fellowships and a directorship of the Bank of England, and was knighted in that year.[10]

Weakening trading conditions

Trade was difficult during Knight's tenure of command but worse was to follow. In the 1980s, the UK clothing industry suffered increasing competition from the developing low wage-cost countries in the Far East. Over-capacity became more pronounced in many of Courtaulds' textile-related businesses. Hogg was forced to reappraise the structure of the firm and divest it of many businesses that were not perceived to have a successful future within the group. This meant that in order to meet the dividend requirements and interest payments strict budgets had to be enforced and the capital requirements of businesses seen as having long term potential were met from funds released by closing or reducing the size of weaker businesses.

---

[10] See *Who's Who* (Palgrave Macmillan, Basingstoke 2000).

The breakdown of vertical trading

Massive cuts were made in manmade fibre production with the withdrawal from polyester and the almost total withdrawal from nylon and reductions in acetate yarn and viscose staple production. The upstream textile sector was also affected by reductions in cotton-type spinning, filament weaving, warp and jersey-knitting and domestic textiles.[11]

The gradual move towards downstream management autonomy in the textiles and garment businesses destroyed much of the original reason for the development of the vertically structured parts of the conglomerate – mutual support.

Forced vertical trading led to the perception that it gave support to parts of the group that were ailing. Units were retained for longer than they probably would have been had they formed part of a smaller organisation. The very fact that Courtaulds was so large and had financial strength allowed a long term view to be taken, a luxury not available to less secure firms. However, this was not always a bad thing, sometimes a medium term view enabled a failing part of the group to be absorbed into a more successful area, but often the firm simply hung on to 'losers' for too long.

Multidivisional control

Hogg had joined the company in the late 1960s and therefore had the benefit of seeing the effect of Kearton's management style and Knight's changes and was able to learn lessons and form his own judgments. He was even more committed to devolution of power than Knight. There was a reaction against what had gone on under Kearton and a commitment to putting responsibility further down the line, making people responsible for their own decisions and their own profit centres.

The former sixty reporting centres had increased with the acquisition of many small clothing firms. Hogg took steps, in the mid-1980s, to consolidate this into six major divisional reporting centres (Fibres, Wood-pulp, Chemicals & Materials, Coatings, Films & Packaging and Textiles) each responsible to a main board Director.

Capital expenditure was strictly controlled with an annual budget. This was hierarchical. Annually there was a capital expenditure proposal put forward by the managers of each business. There were defined levels of expenditure that could be authorised at various levels of management, assuming this was inside their budget, but the divisional director had a major role in the allocation of

---

[11] During the restructuring the firm also sold some peripheral businesses, including the automotive section of International Paint, although there were also some acquisitions including a Spanish acrylic-fibre business.

Christopher F. Hogg – Chairman of Courtaulds plc 1980–1996. Photo courtesy of Courtaulds plc.

capital expenditure. Indeed, the main board would not necessarily be aware of the capital allocated to smaller units.

If something appeared to be going wrong and was an issue that was disastrous or could materially affect the group, it was the responsibility of the divisional reporting board's chief executive to report this to the main board. Less important issues were the responsibility of the executive in charge of each division and most would not be reported to the main board.

Main board retains vital powers but devolution proceeds

Despite the fact that decision making over many issues was moved to the operating management groups, real powers were retained by the main board directors. The decisions regarding the vital matter of the allocation of capital to each main sector of the firm, the re-allocation of manufacturing units between the management groups, and the acquisition and disposal or closure of businesses and many other policy decisions were all retained at the centre of the company. There was never devolution on the scale that was possible in a simple 'holding company', but nevertheless it became possible for managers to contribute to and influence their own profit centre, even if they might feel that they had little influence on the whole firm.

Executives therefore became more responsible for their own profits and were allowed the freedom to negotiate on almost all matters, including the charges for goods and services from within the group and, within certain guidelines, wages and conditions within their own units, on a plant-by-plant basis.

With this freedom came an almost complete reversal of the philosophy of vertical integration. Instead of the group being a means of pushing Courtaulds' raw materials through to the final customer the position was reversed with power passing to the end stages of production.[12]

Central aspects of control

Despite the movement towards devolution of power set in place under Knight, some functions in addition to those already mentioned were retained under central control; treasury, audit, insurance, pensions, worldwide patents, trademarks, government relations, and legal advice are examples. Foreign lawyers were checked by head office before being employed. Raising capital and borrowing money was not difficult for Courtaulds, but was under central control even for foreign operations. However, the very idea that central purchasing of manufacturing supplies might be introduced was totally abandoned. The older generation of Courtaulds managers were very sceptical about this. There was a concern that people in the centre might buy inferior quality supplies at inflated prices and there would be nothing that could be done about it.[13]

Some central functions such as the Human Resources Department were severely weakened. Under Kearton, HRD had recruited and developed staff for high level posts, but later, under Hogg it had a much less significant role. In Hogg's era many advisory functions were outsourced and in the process, head office staff was cut drastically: from having two buildings in Hanover Square, London, there remained only half of one building.

There was also a distinct change of culture after the departure of Kearton and a more open approach to management with more discussion at all levels. It was significant that under Hogg it would be very much the exception for a main board director to approach a lower level manager without, as a matter of courtesy, informing the divisional director.

---

[12] Arthur Knight provides an interesting example of centralized corporate control. '... initially, as a new and inexperienced producer, the nylon division was unable to meet competitive quality standards. ...but since the Group's needs were made manifest, the troublesome two years which would have made it impossible for a new independent producer to survive were overcome. The expanded stocking activities, also large users of nylon, bought at prices which were higher than those offered by outside suppliers ...' Knight (1974), p. 86.

[13] Interview, Ian Harrison 21 January 2003.

Specific circumstances in textiles

The textiles side of the business still demanded a disproportionately large amount of management effort. Ian Harrison, later company secretary of Courtaulds plc, explained:

> Hogg paid particular attention to the Textiles Division. Specifically for Textiles there was a slightly more detailed report. Textiles still had an unofficial 'board' although the intention was that each of the direct reporting businesses would be responsible for themselves. It is possible that Chris Hogg had considered the demerger of Textiles but if so it was not discussed openly. I think he had it in mind but was waiting for Textiles to become sufficiently solid to stand on its own two feet.[14]

Courtaulds Textiles formed 1985

As the following table shows, the complexity of the company created enormous problems for Hogg.

Table 5.1 *Product type and percentage of sales 1983*

Fibres/yarns	Viscose staple	Wood pulp	Acetate fibres	Acrylic Fibres	Spun yarns Others	35%
British cellophane	Cellophane	Film	Conversion	Non-wovens		9%
National plastics						2%
International paint	Marine protective	Industrial	Other markets			17%
Others	Courtaulds Engineering	Moy Park Chickens	Knitting (Australia)			5%
Fabrics	For apparel knitted	Domestic furnishings	Technical Industrial	For apparel woven		16%
Consumer products	Knitwear hosiery	Made up clothing	Distribution			16%

Source: Courtaulds Accounts

---

[14] Interview Ian Harrison 21 January 2003.

With seven product groups operating in the UK and sixteen countries overseas, Hogg was faced with an organisational nightmare, balancing the needs of such diverse activities as chicken farms, plastic floor tiles, yarns and paints to mention only a very few.[15]

In 1985 the first step was taken in what proved to be the final separation of textiles from the rest of the business. The Textiles Division was made up of the 'downstream' textile activities that had been greatly increased from the early 1960s under Kearton's policy of vertical integration and had been assembled to safeguard the fibre-making activities of the firm. The business had now become a large consumer goods supplier to the retail trade that was largely driven by fashion and the requirements of the end users rather than by the needs of the conglomerate's fibres plants.

Courtaulds recognises the global threat

In the mid-1980s, top executives Colin Dyer, Noel Jervis and David Suddens led the task of examining the future of all aspects of the company and for the clothing companies a report was circulated within the garment sector during April 1986 that gave their forecast of the shape of the industry at the commencement of the next century.

The whole of The Courtaulds Textile Group 2000 Report[16] was circulated to senior executives who were free to discuss this at lower levels of the organisation. This was a cultural issue. There was an open approach that had not been seen in the company before. It is inconceivable that in similar circumstances Kearton would have discussed the company's strategy in so much detail.[17] In practice the problems faced by the industry were explained right down to shop floor supervisor level, although there is little evidence that shop floor workers were made aware of the full implications.

Although the report was pointing towards a situation fourteen years or so in advance, events proved to be amazingly close to its forecasts. The report was painful to read. The executives involved said that there would be an erosion of

---

[15] Knitwear and Hosiery represented 45% of Consumer Products turnover.

[16] The principles of the CTG 2000 report were set out by Noel Jervis in the Hurd Memorial Lecture 1994.

[17] Kearton was from a secretive working environment. Before World War Two he was in chemical engineering research. During the time he was an important member of the 'Manhattan Project' involved with the development of the atom bomb. Kearton became a friend of Klaus Fuchs and suspicion fell on Kearton and Fuchs when it was discovered that secret papers were divulged to the Russians. Kearton was cleared. After the war he joined Courtaulds and formed the Chemicals Engineering Section within the research department. *Obituary (The Royal Society 1995)*.

the UK share of all manufactured consumer textile products. This would proceed unevenly with periods of stability followed by losses.

Price competition was absolutely central to the reasoning of the CTG 2000 report. The newly emerging centres of 'textile competence' would continue to be the preferred suppliers, but the Mediterranean centres of textile competence would develop quickly outside the Multi-Fibre Arrangement (MFA). The British and European manufacturers would be more involved in 'product cost averaging', with fast-delivery products being made in local plants and slower but much larger deliveries being sent from low-cost countries, the so called 'average' price being somewhere between the two. For those basic products where it was possible to predict requirements well in advance, these would move even further (than in 1986) to low-cost countries. By 2000 it was thought that the British textile infrastructure might have lost its breadth and depth and be less able to accommodate changes in the demand for the types of product in fashion at that time.

Whilst outward processing would continue to grow, there was a somewhat misplaced confidence that the European 'upstream' suppliers in the heavily capital-intensive industries, such as fibre production, would continue to supply raw materials for an important share of the product range of UK manufactured garments.

The shape of the world supply industry in 1995–2000 was seen to include growing levels of world trading, predominantly East to West, helped by the increasing use of information technology.

Hong Kong was already much too expensive for internal manufacturing and was aiming to be an entrepôt for other low-cost centres. Hong Kong was forecast to be a merchanting centre for this trade, using suppliers in the People's Republic of China (PRC) and other low-cost 'sink economies' to give lower labour-cost advantages. With Korea and Taiwan increasing the sophistication of their capital equipment as well as their expertise in product manufacture, all the low-cost countries were likely to remain at a significant cost-advantage whilst at the same time developing their own expertise and reliability.

Specific centres of supply were identified, particularly the PRC, which was destined to undergo remarkable change and in a few years become a world leader in trade, and also Thailand, Malaysia, the Philippines, and Indonesia in the Far East. In Europe, Turkey and Portugal threatened, but interestingly Greece and Spain were already forecast to become too expensive to qualify as low-cost suppliers.

Courtaulds, M&S and CTG 2000

Having set the scene so clearly, Courtaulds was unable to press on with a policy that would fully back up the CTG 2000 findings. The key role of M&S (Courtaulds' major customer) made it difficult if not impossible to implement an appropriate response with the necessary urgency. Had this report been embraced within the company, and with M&S being fully involved at a much earlier time, the effect of the globalisation of trade on Courtaulds Textiles plc would have proved less disastrous. Possibly, Courtaulds might have avoided much of the expense of keeping alive its share of the UK industry.

Demerger

After the formation of Courtaulds Textiles Division, the problems of running two differing types of business were still not resolved. Textiles, a mainly UK business, was a more labour intensive business than the chemicals and industrial side. There were enormous tensions in running these two totally dissimilar businesses. Courtaulds had created a reporting system to control Courtaulds Textiles as a homogeneous business, which it was not, and control systems which were right for one type of product within this broad based industry were not necessarily right for another. The main board was unable to concentrate on the smaller businesses within textiles, and yet was reluctant to complicate the system by reverting back to splitting textiles into a number of smaller groups:

> There were complex choices to make which could not be reconciled. One [proposal for example] was from Textiles to buy a French fashion company and another was from the Paint Division to buy a coatings and specialist aircraft sealants business in Los Angeles. If you could only afford one how could you decide between the two.[18]

Ultimately, Hogg decided that Courtaulds Textiles was a viable business in its own right. There was a view that globalisation was an inevitable trend and it was only a matter of time before the Multi-Fibre Arrangement ran its course.[19] Considered in retrospect, however, Courtaulds' management showed over-confidence at that time that their speed of response and good service would put them at an advantage over their smaller competitors – and that this would cause the customers to make purchases in the UK, ensuring the continuity of a good proportion of Courtaulds' UK factories.

Having taken the decision in principle to separate Courtaulds Textiles from the chemicals and industrial side of the business, there was some discussion as to whether it should be sold to a third party or to a management buyout, or simply demerged. One advantage of a demerger was that it was unnecessary to fix a price for the business as the market would find its own level, and in January 1990 the business was floated as Courtaulds Textiles plc.

---

[18] Interview, Ian Harrison 21 January 2003.
[19] The MFA was later set to end in 2004.

Results under Kearton's successors

Table 5.2 *Financial data, Courtaulds plc 1975–1978 (£000,000)*[20]

	1975	1976	1977	1978
Turnover	1,133.9	1,166.31	1,510.3	1,575.7
Pre-tax profit	118.2	46.3	80.9	53.7
Profit retained	67.2	9.5	29.6	4.6

Source: Courtaulds plc Annual Report and Accounts

Trading conditions became ever more difficult in the late 1970s, affecting not only the UK but business generally throughout the world. The turnover must be considered in the context of high inflation; profits were halved and the profits retained to improve the business were dramatically down.

Following the oil price shock of 1973 costs rose sharply. The price of oil doubled during 1979,[21] with a consequent slowing of the economy. This created the most severe depression since World War Two. Tight monetary policy caused further loss of competitiveness and conditions deteriorated rapidly for textiles in the UK and for manufacturing in general.

Table 5.3 *Financial data, Courtaulds plc 1979–1989 (£000,000)*

	1979	1980	1981	1982	1983	1984	1985	1986	1987	1988	1989
Turnover	1,662	1,819	1,710	1,789	1,906	2,038	2,152	2,173	2,262	2,421	2,610
Pre-tax profit	64.0	68.1	5.1	51.1	63.3	117.8	128.2	143.0	201.1	220.6	197.0
Profit retained	10.0	13.0	(117.0)	10.0	(6.0)	42.0	56.0	79.0	97.0	96.0	205.0

Source: Courtaulds plc Annual Report and Accounts

---

[20] Taking inflation into account, to equal 1975 values by 1978, turnover would need to be £1,791.6 million, pre-tax profit £186.76 million and profit retained £106.17 million.

[21] The price of oil had risen from $3.5 to $9.3 per barrel between 1973 and 1974. The oil producing countries ran massive current account surpluses with corresponding deficits for the oil importing countries. Because the oil producing countries spent only a small part of this surplus this had a deflationary effect on the world economy. During the oil crisis of 1979 the price of oil doubled and by 1980 oil had reached $32 per barrel. Interest rates rose and inflation reached 13% in 1980 and these factors, combined with tight monetary policy, had a depressing effect on the economy.

As already noted, profits were poor from the late 1970s. However, there was to be a general recovery in consumer spending and the strong dollar meant that the imports from low-cost countries were slightly more expensive as they were normally paid for in US dollars. Profits in proportion to turnover improved but the turnover was relatively poor. The turnover of £1,662 million in 1979 would have needed to increase to £3,378.8 million in 1989 to equal the general rise in retail prices (but only £2,610 million was achieved). Therefore it can be concluded that the firm was performing badly and in real terms was in steady decline.

Perspectives

Courtaulds was, in common with much of British industry, in serious difficulty, certainly from the mid-1970s. The poor financial results reflect the decline in the firm's manufacturing capacity that was seen in the previous chapter.

The new breed of managers such as Christopher Hogg fought a losing battle and failed to revive the firm's fortunes. The hosiery and knitwear acquisitions discussed in the previous chapter presented enormous problems. Organisational changes were made but the decline continued and the separation of the textiles interests from the chemical and industrial arm of the firm in 1990 saw the commencement of the break-up of this historic firm. Subsequent chapters deal with the background to Courtaulds' story and the industry in more detail.

SIX

Employment, Labour and Industrial Relations

Background

COURTAULDS ENTERED AN INDUSTRY that had a long history of unionism stretching back to the days of the eighteenth century, with the first union being formed to aid the knitters in their struggle for a living wage. Gurnham[1] writes of an industry composed of a large number of small-scale operators, the framework knitters, many of whom operated within the family home.

Early trade unions

Describing the early years of unionism, Gurnham notes discernible features of the trade: fragmentation and specialisation,[2] the differing wage rates between the town and country,[3] and the rise and decline of trade union membership associated with the rising and falling fortunes of the industry.[4] Even after the advent of mechanised factories, the industry remained fragmented, mainly consisting of a large number of relatively small units. These were still recognisable features of the industry in the latter part of the twentieth century. The UK hosiery industry never operated, for example, on the scale of the large motor works of the twentieth century or the Korean shoe factories and was always at the mercy of the whims of fashion.

Framework knitters were located in the major East Midlands towns, particularly Leicester and Nottingham and throughout the surrounding country

---

[1] Gurnham (1976), and Chapman (2002).
[2] Gurnham, p. 16.
[3] Gurnham, p. 12.
[4] Gurnham, p. 16.

districts. Specialisation was well established in the industry. Products included hosiery, gloves, socks, shirts and drawers and the framework knitter would tend to be a specialist in one sector only. Competition between the master hosiers who controlled the framework knitters was fierce and the wages in the villages were generally lower than in the major centres of the industry.

Attempts to establish uniform rates of pay for framework knitters usually failed within a short period. Towards the end of the eighteenth century, small unions began to appear, many of which were short-lived. The rise and fall of the unions tended to follow the demand for the industry's goods. In good times there was a possibility of improved rates of pay but in hard times the opposite was almost certain. Irregular workloads were normal and the framework knitters' wages dried up when no work was available.

There was no concept of a national union until the mid-1800s and associations were frequently formed to serve the needs of a small district or a small section of the trade, such as the 'point net' or 'fancy' sections of the trade. There was one slightly more successful union, 'The Union Society of Framework Knitters', but even this was only in operation for a short time around 1812 to 1814. Depression followed the Napoleonic Wars and it was not until the 1850s that there was a real movement towards trade unionism in the form that we recognise now.

Trade unionism in the factories

The introduction of the factory system in the 1850s did not immediately result in the demise of the framework knitters and trade unionism became stronger in both the slowly developing factories and the declining home based framework knitting industry. Rising living standards contributed to the increase in trade and this enabled the framework knitters to exist alongside the factory system, but from the 1880s framework knitting technology had become outdated and factory based unions were able to gain more control over wages and conditions. However, by 1880 the town factories were suffering from price-cutting by the rural based factories in much the same way that the urban framework knitters had also suffered in earlier times.[5]

Between the World Wars

The industry and its workers suffered between the two World Wars, but were affected less than many others partly because the fashion for shorter skirts created a higher demand for fashion stockings and a large quantity of knitted fabric was used in the then fashionable women's knitted suits. Men's knitwear also became fashionable in this period. During the period from 1920 to 1939 UK employment

---

[5] Gurnham, p. 21.

in the industry rose from around 90,000 to about 120,000,[6] however, short-time work was common and loyalty to the industry's unions was strongly tested as reductions in pay and working conditions were often imposed without reference to the unions. Also, in the outlying areas of the industry such as Lancashire the wages were lower, and this challenged the security of jobs in the Midlands. In an era of management anti-unionism, membership in the period 1920–1938 fell from around 34,000 to 22,000.[7]

The rise and fall of trade unionism from the 1960s

From the end of World War Two (when direction of labour ceased), until the early 1970s there was a rise in the numbers employed. Already during Courtaulds' advance into the industry in the 1960s there were signs of increasing import penetration but confidence was still high. A delegate to the 1968 union conference gave her opinion:

> We know that ours is a highly competitive industry, but provided the competition is fair we in this country have nothing to fear, because we are world famous ... for quality, style and finish. Indeed I would go so far as to say we are second to none.[8]

Miss McIntyre's analysis is open to question because 'quality, style and finish' were not the only selling points, she omitted one vital ingredient – price. From the mid-1930s the industry had operated in a protected trading climate, first by heavy tariffs against Germany and Japan, then by war controls and the availability of large military contracts, and in the 'golden years' following the war, by disruption in the offshore competitors' factories, particularly in Germany, Japan and Italy. Miss McIntyre's Scottish members were soon to face the reality that their goods were uncompetitive in a global market and what her Scottish members would consider a 'fair' wage could support several knitwear workers and their families in the emerging nations.

Decline looms

Following World War Two, the industry enjoyed a period of high demand and rising output based on rising living standards in the UK and the increasing demand for casual clothing. Until the mid-1970s the industry's workers were in a strong bargaining position. From then, the industry was in decline, and the

---

[6] Gurnham, p. 99.
[7] Gurnham, p. 101.
[8] Miss E. McIntyre (Scottish Region) NUHKW conference report 1968, p. 110.

role of the union became largely one of managing decline, and mitigating its effects on the workers.

The UK industry was no match for the external competition. Employment continued to decline and at the end of the twentieth century the decline was almost terminal. Upheaval and change was not confined to the shop floor workers. All levels of technical and management staff were affected by the changing conditions and trading patterns that accelerated from the 1960s.

Flexibility, new technology and strikes

The industry responded to outside competition with flexibility,[9] particularly by the use of sweatshops, (that would take on work from overloaded firms), and outworkers and part timers.[10] But having a flexible and low-paid stand-by work force could only delay the inroads made by merchandise from the emerging nations. Flexibility had been gained by the employment of a hidden army of home workers, frequently referred to as 'outworkers', often working on piecework for substantially lower wages than the factory workers and with little attention being paid to health and safety issues. Their employment was often very erratic and, without the benefit of a formal contract of employment, these workers were liable to be either overloaded when garments that needed their particular skills were being made, or completely without work with little or no advance warning at other times. In effect, firms were able to expand and contract to a limited extent without financial penalty.

Unlike the unions described by Singleton[11] and Honeyman,[12] the recognised union for the industry, the National Union of Hosiery and Knitwear Workers (NUHKW),[13] was cooperative in the introduction of new technology and the industry was seldom held back by restrictive practices. Based on interviews with two prominent trade union leaders, Chapman wrote a generalisation that had a large element of truth:

---

[9] The use of multi-skilled workers who could be moved to different jobs at short notice, the use of contract workers where jobs are not specific to the firm (such as electricians, drivers, cleaners, typists and canteen staff) and the introduction of factory, rather than industry-wide pay negotiations. J. Atkinson, 'Manpower strategies for flexible organizations' *Personnel Management*, vol. 16, August 1984, pp. 28–31.

[10] Here 'flexibility' describes the labour utilization within the industry rather than the transferable skills of the workers within the national industrial structure when faced with displacement.

[11] Singleton, *Lancashire on the Scrapheap* (OUP Oxford 1991)

[12] Honeyman, *Well Suited: A History of the Leeds Clothing Industry 1850–1990* (OUP Oxford 2000)

[13] NUHKW was later renamed The National Union of Knitwear, Footwear and Allied Trades (KFAT).

... the union did well for the skilled male knitters. ... New machinery was discussed with pace-making manufacturers as soon as the innovation was identified at one of the great international machinery exhibitions ... Until the 1980s, when the industry's infrastructure began to fall apart, entrepreneurs would find no better industrial relations environment in which to operate in Britain.[14]

Within a few years the decline in UK production was an ogre that cast its shadow over the trade and the efforts of the union officers to keep themselves informed about the availability of new technology was not of great benefit to the workers. They were not in any position to support workers who resisted the introduction of new plant, had they done so their members' firms, and the workers employment prospects, would have soon suffered in competition with non-union firms in both the UK and the global industry. In practice the threat by a multi-site employer *not* to install new equipment at a particular branch quickly brought the workers into line.

Strikes in the industry, and in Courtaulds in particular, were a rare occurrence, but one, at Courtaulds' competitor firm Mansfield Hosiery Mills factory in Loughborough, had bitter elements of racism.[15] In the early stages the strike was about wages but it later developed into a confrontation, in which the principal grievance over pay was over-shadowed by the deep sense of injustice felt by Asian workers denied promotion on racial grounds. (For further detail refer to Appendix 1.)

Rise and decline in employment

Employment rose gradually in the 1960s and reached its peak in 1974.

Table 6.1 *Total employed (000s)*

	1963	1968	1970	1971	1972	1973	1974
Total employment*	124.5	134.7	136.6	130.9	128.0	133.6	138.9
Membership of NUHKW	41.6	50.6	63.3	64.4	68.7	71.7	72.7
Penetration by NUHKW %	33.4	37.6	46.3	49.2	53.7	53.7	52.2

*For the industry
Sources: Census of Employment; Annual Report NUHKW

---

[14] Chapman, pp. 203–4.

[15] Neither Gurnham nor Chapman refers to this strike. See Wrigley, *British Trade Unions 1945–1995* (MUP, 1997), pp. 157–9. See Appendix 1.

Employment was in decline from the mid-1970s, but trade union membership, which had been rising for several years, was maintained at over 70,000 from 1973 until it dropped sharply in 1980.

Table 6.2 *Total employed (000s)*

	1975	1976	1977	1978	1979	1980	1981	1982	1983
Total employment*	130.6	124.7	124.8	118.8	112.2	103.6	93.6	91.9	87.9
Membership NUHKW	70.3	71.6	74.0	72.8	70.4	61.8	58.3	57.1	53.6
Penetration by NUHKW %	53.8	57.4	59.3	61.2	62.7	59.7	62.3	62.2	60.1
Courtaulds employment**	18.3	18.3	17.3	16.1	15.5	13.3	12.3	12.3	11.5
Courtaulds employment %	14.0	14.7	13.9	13.6	13.8	12.8	13.1	13.4	13.0

*For the industry
Source: **Acordis Ltd

From the years 1975 to 1983 a series of data (see Table 6.2) is available which isolates Courtaulds' employment in this industry from other sectors. The firm's employment fell in approximately the same proportion as total employment for the industry. Although the NUHKW lost around sixteen thousand members in this period, its level of membership relative to total employment was well maintained as its officers were seen to be working hard in their attempts to secure the best deals possible for workers whose jobs were threatened.

Table 6.3 *Total employed (000s)*

	1984	1985	1986	1987	1988	1989
Total employment	90.1	85.6	84.1	85.0	82.9	77.8
Membership of NUHKW	51.6	51.4	49.0	47.0	44.5	38.7
Penetration by NUHKW %	57.3	60.0	58.3	55.2	53.7	49.7

Sources: Census of Employment; NUHKW archives
NOTE: Categories for total employment were revised for 1984 onwards to give greater coverage of small firms.

Employment in the second half of the 1980s continued on its downward trend, but in this period the NUHKW suffered disproportionately.

Table 6.4 *Total employed (000s)*

	1990	1991	1992	1993	1994	1995	1996
Total employed	67.8	63.9	59.6	48.5	45.6	46.2	45.4

	1997	1998	1999	2000	2001	2002	2003
Total employed	45	36	32	24	19	16	na

Source: Census of Production

Note: Figures for total employment were revised for 1990 onwards to include the manufacture of crocheted items.

NUHKW merges to become KFAT

As trade fell away, firms suffering decline tended to close satellite factories first, and followed this by closing the least important branches.[16] In a defensive move, aimed at maintaining a viable sized membership base, the NUHKW merged with the shoe workers' union NUFLAT and from then the figures for hosiery workers cannot be isolated. Eventually, the weakened industry retreated to its traditional centres.[17]

Table 6.5 *Membership – NUHKW*

Year	Male	Female	Total	Year	Male	Female	Total
1960	10,859	30,216	41,075	1969	13,473	44,803	58,276
1961	10,765	29,042	39,807	1970	16,273	46,989	63,262
1962	10,249	29,586	39,835	1971	17,225	47,147	64,372
1963	9,869	31,701	41,570	1972	18,729	49,929	68,658
1964	10,596	34,240	44,836	1973	19,528	52,183	71,711
1965	9,889	37,476	47,365	1974	19,887	52,836	72,723
1966	10,312	38,035	48,347	1975	18,941	51,351	70,292
1967	10,285	39,153	49,438	1976	19,340	52,286	71,626
1968	10,183	40,426	50,609	1977	20,486	53,591	74,077

Source: NUHKW Conference Reports

---

[16] For further information on the number of enterprises refer to Tables 3.1, 3.2 and 3.3.

[17] The geography of the industry is discussed in Chapter 8. Refer also to Table 8.2.

Following the Second World War, the NUHKW membership tally had benefited from the rise in employment in the clothing trade and in the early 1960s, the NUHKW was the main union, but there were at least four hosiery unions and two non-hosiery unions vying for the industry's workers. The absorption, between 1969 and 1975, of six small unions brought in 7,000 members.[18] The high point in employment was reached in 1975. Union membership was high between 1973 and 1979, when there were over 70,000 members. Unionisation became well-established in the larger firms, with most, including Courtaulds, Coats Viyella and Corah, formally recognising the NUHKW as the appropriate union for their employees in the industry.

From a maximum membership of 74,077 in 1977, the membership declined to around 34,000 in 1990. Throughout the 1980s, the viability of the NUHKW as an independent entity was in question and on 1 January 1991 the National Union of Footwear Leather and Allied Trades (NUFLAT) was amalgamated with the NUHKW to form a new union, The National Union of Knitwear, Footwear and Apparel Trades (KFAT).

Table 6.6 *Membership – NUHKW*

Year	Male	Female	Total	Year	Male	Female	Total
1977	20,486	53,591	74,077	1984	13,500	38,145	51,645
1978	20,483	52,375	72,858	1985	13,636	37,721	51,357
1979	19,458	51,026	70,484	1986	13,472	35,501	48,973
1980	17,271	44,566	61,837	1987	13,276	33,962	47,238
1981	15,552	42,759	58,311	1988	11,846	32,680	44,526
1982	15,223	41,882	57,105	1989	10,503	28,178	38,681
1983	N/A	N/A	53,631	1990	9,262	24,921	34,183

Source: NUHKW Conference Reports

[18] Gurnham, p. 179.

Table 6.7 *Membership – KFAT*

Year	Male	Female	Total	Year	Male	Female	Total
1990	20,748	36,329	57,077	1996	16,953	23,577	40,530
1991	19,582	31,876	51,458	1997	16,279	21,796	38,075
1992	18,974	29,510	48,484	1998	14,520	18,104	32,626
1993	18,806	28,311	47,117	1999	12,255	14,753	27,008
1994	18,814	26,602	45,416	2000	10,129	10,521	20,650
1995	18,182	25,625	43,807				

Source: KFAT Conference Reports

The new union was established with a membership of 57,077, comprising 34,183 former members of the NUHKW and 22,894 from NUFLAT. A further small amalgamation took place in 1996 when the Rossendale Union of Boot, Shoe & Slipper Operatives, with a membership of 1,030, transferred to KFAT but by the turn of the century, the membership had slipped below 21,000 and further discussions regarding amalgamation were in progress within KFAT.

Despite the close alignment of many members of the National Executive to the Labour Party, the union was not highly politicised. However, the national conference did instruct the National Executive to lobby on a number of national issues that were not exclusively the concern of the workers within the industry. Issues perceived to be affecting the members included matters such as state pensions, the National Health Service, law and order, and anti-union legislation.

Occupations and gender specific work

The workforce was dominated numerically by women but despite this gender imbalance, men had a stronger influence on trade union affairs and filled more of the higher union positions than did their female colleagues. Moreover, women earned substantially less than men, and were less well rewarded for the skill and physical effort of many of their jobs.

Table 6.8 *Hourly earnings (pence)*

		1975	1980	1985	1990	1995
Hosiery and knitwear	Men	123.9	204.9	335.6	482.0	610.0
Hosiery and knitwear	Women	84.3	139.2	225.0	329.0	441.0
All manufacturing	Men	139.9	227.5	397.1	551.0	698.0
All manufacturing	Women	93.0	157.1	271.0	377.0	486.0

Source: Knitstats

Average earnings levels were lower in the industry than for manufacturing in general and the large differential between men's wages and women's wages continued to be a feature of the industry in line with manufacturing in general.

Table 6.9[19] shows that the manufacturers were proposing a wage for male knitters that was far in advance of that for the women who made up the garments. There was a clear divide between the pay for the higher and lower levels of skill, with 'turning' requiring significantly less skill than linking. However, the big difference between the pay for seamless hose linkers (female), which was one of the most tedious and skilled jobs in the industry, and the pay for knitters (male) is hard or impossible to justify.[20] Knitters always seemed to hold bargaining power, often earning more than their supervisor, mechanic or even sometimes their manager.

Table 6.9 *Seamless-hosiery wage scale 1961*

Operation	Suggested wage (£/week)	Traditional gender
Knitting 370 needle	15.50	Male
400–474 needle	17.00	Male
Linking	9.00	Female
Rough and dress mending	8.66	Female
Pre-examine rectify mend	8.37	Female
Mock seaming	7.50	Female
Shearing and toe seaming	7.25	Female
Box Bag Transfer Fold	7.00	Female
Turning	6.00	Female

Source: KIF Minutes

---

[19] Minutes of a meeting of the LHMF, Seamless Hose Section Committee, 5 July 1961.

[20] In correspondence Jack Matlock, former district secretary of KFAT wrote 'In dexterity and skill the knitter did not need anywhere near the dexterity and skill of an overlocker or linker' 29 May 2001.

The Leicester & District Hosiery Manufacturers' Association carried out several surveys of earnings in the late 1970s that revealed large differences in the amount of money paid for apparently identical operations. Not only did the standard wage vary enormously between firms but also the actual wage earned shows wide variations and this even occurred within identical job categories.[21]

Several factors were responsible for this situation. At various times firms may have needed to attract workers away from their competitors and increased the wage value for this purpose, but where a firm's standard wage value was exceeded by a large amount this was almost certainly due to the 'loose' setting of the piecerates or standard times for the individual task. Possibly the opposite was true when earnings were below the wage value and the piecerates or standard times were 'tight' but this would be less likely because the workers would contest such a situation. The long-standing situation – that workers could demand higher wages in areas where their skills were in high demand such as central Leicester, and less in outlying districts, must also be taken into account. For example, the standard wage value for bar tacking[22] varied from £51.39 (Firm 26) to £65.55 (Firm 43) and actual earnings from £49.68 (Firm 43) to £76.40 (Firm 23). The competition for labour, the vagaries of the piecework system with its large element of negotiation and the range of performances achieved by the employees was little changed from the situation that Gurnham noted as a feature of the industry since its early days.[23]

Despite 'equal opportunities' legislation and a more enlightened attitude towards gender inequalities, there was little evident change in the gender divide or the position of the female hosiery workers relative to industrial workers at large. Table 6.8 shows that any change in the position of women, relative to men, was marginal.

Supervisory positions were largely gender-specific. Knitting shop floor supervision was generally the preserve of men who were normally paid more highly than the female making-up supervisors. For hand cutting and machine cutting of knitwear it was normal to employ female supervisors, but underwear 'continuous-length' fabric cutting was most frequently controlled by men and maintaining the large numbers of knitting and sewing machines was also almost exclusively the province of men.[24]

During the Second World War, several jobs that had previously been male dominated, such as knitting, were also performed by women, but after the war

---

[21] The individual firms were not identified by the compilers of the statistics.
[22] Bar tacking was a simple machining operation.
[23] Gurnham, Chapter 1.
[24] In 1974 it was estimated that every year about 400 trainee knitting machine mechanics were recruited. *Knitting International* January 1974 p. 119. Almost all firms except the smaller ones would employ their own sewing and knitting mechanics.

they gradually reverted to male domination, a trend that was accelerated with the introduction of three-shift working. Band-knife cutting was regarded as men's work but sewing machine operations and hand cutting of knitwear was almost exclusively women's work. Pairing and examining socks and fine-gauge hosiery (countering) was a well paid job traditionally done by men, many of whom went to work smartly dressed. This gender divide remained entrenched in the Wolsey sock factory until the late 1980s, when countering was discontinued and the task was mechanised. At other firms, particularly in the fine-gauge hosiery sector, this gender difference tended to disappear more quickly. It may be argued that women are generally more dexterous than men, and that men are generally more suited to heavy jobs, but on both these counts it would be arguable that as a very light job, countering socks and stockings could qualify as a woman's job. Equally, from that narrow perspective, band knife cutting or electric knife cutting would be suitable for either gender, as indeed it later became. [25]

---

[25] Honeyman (2000). The writer exposes the gender divide that separated male operatives on hourly rates from females on payment by results. This particular inequality was not entrenched in the Hosiery and Knitwear industry as both sexes were generally on some form of measured work standard.

Table 6.10 Standard Wage Values and Average Earnings (£ Standard working week) 1980

Firm	Wage value Bar tack	Ave wage Bar tack	Wage value Button hole	Ave wage Button hole	Wage value Button sew	Ave wage Button sew	Wage value Exam fold	Ave wage Exam fold	Wage value Cup-seam	Ave wage Cup-seam	Wage value Cut	Ave wage Cut	Wage value Draw-thread	Ave wage Draw-thread	Wage value Fault Insp'ct	Ave wage Fault Insp'ct
10	57.60	60.00	57.60	60.00	57.60	60.00	n/a	n/a	53.53	60.00	57.60	60.00	53.53	68.05	53.53	60.00
13	n/a	n/a	n/a	n/a	n/a	n/a	n/a	n/a	n/a	n/a	70.12	83.20	n/a	n/a	n/a	n/a
14	61.73	54.80	61.73	53.19	n/a	n/a	61.73	65.02	n/a	n/a	64.87	56.18	61.73	64.70	61.73	68.32
15	n/a	n/a	51.31	55.24	51.57	67.75	63.26	64.56	n/a	n/a	52.50	63.78	47.18	55.49	n/a	n/a
16	56.25	58.39	59.94	65.47	56.25	59.58	n/a	n/a	69.37	72.04	64.71	59.60	53.81	61.43	55.84	66.40
17	n/a	n/a	66.87	60.69	n/a	n/a	65.18	52.54	n/a	n/a	96.94	79.05	65.18	63.13	n/a	n/a
18	63.25	63.25	63.25	65.15	63.25	63.88	63.25	60.09	n/a	n/a	69.00	77.28	63.25	64.54	n/a	n/a
21	59.34	64.88	59.34	58.80	n/a	n/a	62.65	62.87	71.48	57.08	62.65	46.09	58.23	45.60	n/a	n/a
22	n/a	n/a	n/a	n/a	n/a	n/a	52.80	50.80	n/a	n/a	67.00	68.40	n/a	n/a	n/a	n/a
23	67.48	76.40	67.48	58.40	67.48	58.40	52.18	57.73	74.98	65.40	62.99	58.80	52.18	42.60	65.98	75.20
26	51.39	50.00	n/a	n/a	n/a	n/a	n/a	n/a	51.39	56.52	51.39	56.58	51.39	65.00	51.39	54.45
42	n/a	n/a	n/a	n/a	65.55	76.82	65.55	87.40	n/a	n/a	70.15	76.36	65.55	78.20	n/a	n/a
43	65.55	49.68	65.55	51.52	65.55	51.52	n/a	n/a	n/a	n/a	70.15	87.36	62.10	82.80	n/a	n/a

Firm	Wage value	Ave wage	Wage value	Ave wage	Wage value	Ave wage	Wage value	Ave wage	Wage value	Ave wage	Wage value	Ave wage	Wage value	Ave wage	Wage value	Ave wage
	Link	Link	Lock-stitch	Lock-stitch	Over-lock	Over-lock	Press first	Press first	Press final	Press final	Stole attach	Stole attach	Seam cover	Seam cover	Tab	Tab
10	53.53	70.00	53.53	60.00	53.53	55.00	62.16	65.00	62.16	65.00	n/a	n/a	57.6	64.00	n/a	60.00
13	n/a	n/a	88.40	87.20	77.60	74.00	n/a	n/a	88.40	89.60	n/a	n/a	n/a	n/a	57.60	62.80
14	64.87	51.10	64.87	65.10	70.91	63.42	61.73	61.77	70.91	63.27	64.87	56.29	61.73	55.38	n/a	n/a
15	60.12	65.85	55.53	55.91	55.53	51.77	74.93	92.97	74.93	93.68	52.45	67.92	47.18	49.70	48.25	58.31
16	69.37	88.02	58.83	61.51	58.83	72.67	63.34	68.32	63.34	68.99	56.25	54.41	n/a	n/a	56.25	59.72
17	n/a	n/a	n/a	n/a	n/a	n/a	65.46	75.18	91.01	58.41	n/a	n/a	n/a	n/a	68.57	57.20
18	n/a	n/a	n/a	n/a	69.00	51.06	n/a	n/a	74.75	77.74	63.25	61.35	63.25	63.88	63.25	68.94
21	n/a	n/a	51.60	49.72	59.34	63.42	64.58	84.49	64.58	84.34	59.34	72.99	n/a	n/a	55.20	80.68
22	n/a	n/a	67.00	75.20	67.00	60.40	n/a	n/a	82.00	103.60	n/a	n/a	n/a	n/a	54.70	48.00
23	n/a	n/a	74.98	102.4	n/a	n/a	62.99	58.20	62.99	58.20	n/a	n/a	n/a	n/a	62.99	60.80
26	51.39	71.63	51.39	57.29	51.39	51.39	61.24	69.80	61.24	74.80	n/a	n/a	n/a	n/a	51.39	39.29
42	n/a	n/a	n/a	n/a	70.15	74.06	70.15	101.20	70.15	101.20	n/a	n/a	65.55	59.34	65.55	71.30
43	n/a	n/a	70.15	69.00	70.15	57.50	70.15	101.20	70.15	87.40	n/a	n/a	65.55	52.90	n/a	n/a

Note: Average wages are calculated after omitting the top and bottom 10%. Identification of the firms was withheld from the members of LDHMA.

Source: Leicester & District Hosiery Manufacturers' Association Limited – Wages Survey August 1980

The NUHKW and gender

The NUHKW was trapped in a long-standing historic tradition. As a craft union, it was important to work for the well-being of existing members, an issue particularly relevant to the countermen. The 1964 Conference supported this position:

> ... the [countering] committee gave consideration to the position where a Company introduced a new method of countering, and after deliberations the Committee recommended to the National Executive Committee that:
>
> - Where men were doing Countering and there was work available they should retain their jobs or be offered alternative employment.
>
> - Where an employer took on female labour, it should be understood that this female labour would be the first to become redundant if there was a shortage of work.

The National Executive Committee[26] accepted this recommendation, thereby supporting the gender divide. The exclusive use of men to perform this task (countering), which had been superseded by new technology, was no longer a viable option. This position was accepted by one full time union representative,[27] although he supported his members:

> People held on too long and refused to change. The countermen were a case in point. It was an all male preserve in the 1960s. In Hinckley they had their own union. They served a six year apprenticeship. Every hose was individually paired. The employers thought they could put women on to it. They [the men] weren't having that. So the firms shipped them out to Ashby and the villages. Now tights are not even examined.[28]

Systems of piecework and rate setting

Traditional negotiated piecerates

The hosiery and knitwear industry has traditionally been a 'piecework industry' with the vast majority of factory operatives being paid and motivated by piecework in its various forms and both men and women had to work hard to earn a living.[29]

---

[26] The NUHKW conference report 1964 p. 9.
[27] Interview with Jack Matlock, formerly an official with NUHKW, 25 May 2001.
[28] Interview with Jack Matlock, formerly an official with NUHKW, 25 May 2001.
[29] Wells (1972), p. 68 notes that payment by piecework, a feature of the modern

Betty Anderson, a partner in the small family-owned babywear firm A. O. Anderson at Market Harborough, described the system for the payment of direct operatives at her firm. All knitting, both on the hand-flat and power-flat machines, was done on hourly time rates. All lockstitching, overlocking and other forms of machining and hand operations were done on some form of piecework. Gradually, a 'list' was established for a simple plain standard garment. There were rates of pennies and fractions of a penny per dozen garments for performing each operation. There were also additions for extra work such as matching stripes and applying extra buttons on cardigans. Because annual rises were given in percentage terms it was necessary every time there was a rise, to uplift hundreds of different pence rates, all on the same day, at the beginning of the pay week. The piecerates were normally 'fixed' by a mixture of experience and negotiation. A. O. Anderson's management tried to set the piecerates to reflect the work content in the garments and at the same time to give a 'reasonable' wage. This did not always happen. At one time there was a problem getting overlockers to make up babies' knitted bootees. The operatives did not like them but the management felt that the piecerate was fair. A notice board was set up which showed that each person had a fair share of 'bad'[30] work: 'One girl would not start hers until she had had a good cry first.'[31]

Later, the pence piecework rates were converted to minutes, (estimated times) and only the 'pence per minute rate' was altered at rise times, after that wage calculation was much simplified.[32] A. O. Anderson Ltd could not use these times for production planning purposes because the target times did not accurately represent the work content and there were large differences in the apparent performance of the operatives.

Straight proportional measured work

The direct labour force in most of Courtaulds' manufacturing units was controlled by using 'measured work' standards. Standard times were issued for each different operation, and were paid at a cash value for each minute earned. The 'standard times' for machine knitting were calculated from the machine's speeds. Standard times for hand-controlled operations were from time studies, synthesis and analytical estimating. The system was relatively simple to understand. Payment was in direct proportion to output, with no bonus enhancements for higher levels of production (or extra penalties for lower levels). The firm operated guaranteed

---

industry, can be traced back to the early days of the trade.

[30] In many factories extremes of colour such as bright white or black were considered to be 'bad work' and were shared amongst the operatives.

[31] Interview Betty Anderson 20 January 2001.

[32] Wage calculations in £.s. d. and small fractions of a penny were very difficult.

hourly rates below which a worker could not drop, and these were in line with union agreements,[33] or later as a national weekly minimum wage. These 'fall back rates' were relatively low. Instead of being perceived by the slower, the less skilled or less motivated workers as a benefit, the fall back rates were often seen as the point below which disciplinary procedures for under-performance were commenced.

Measured day-work

The piecework system, and the perceived lack of a reasonable guaranteed working week, were always contentious issues but were to some extent tolerated. Because the industry was seasonal, and workers were often laid off when work was short, the union fought a long campaign against short-time working. Jack Matlock commented:

> In the industry generally ... when there was a shortage of work, people were laid off for a couple of days. One of the reasons [this was accepted] may have been that when they were at work [on piecework] in the 60s 70s and 80s they earned sufficient... that they accepted the indignity of signing on the dole. ... if they had been on an hourly rate there would have been all hell let loose. There was some good money to be earned.[34]

The traditional piecework system had long been under attack, and the lack of security of earnings contributed to the perception of the factory operatives as being of low status. John Fry of Courtaulds' competitor Corah explained:

> It surely cannot be right that a man who has worked for a company for thirty years and is possibly earning £40 per week can be sent home without pay at a few days notice; is never given an increase in reward in a spontaneous and voluntary manner but only when forced to do so by trade union negotiations; and finally on retirement after forty years is given no pension. If one thinks deeply enough about this fundamental problem one might come to the conclusion that the root cause is not the trade unions or the people at all but the way in which the industry treats its people. But is it not possible that the industry has become a prisoner of a system which enables us to think we are treating our people well when in fact we are treating them badly. The system to which I refer is of course the piecework system which makes all of the people nothing

---

[33] The agreed minimum rates were far below many of the individual factory agreements. NUHKW conference report, 1962 p. 130.

[34] Interview Jack Matlock, 24 May 2001.

but casual labourers. They get no pay unless they are working, and if it is anticipated that there is a lack of forward work it is possible by suspending the guaranteed week to send them off home without earnings except for the humiliation of the dole.[35]

In an attempt to redress this situation Corah introduced in January 1974 a 'measured day-work' system with in-built guarantees of an annual wage. Workers were placed in wage bands based on their performance. Movement up the scale, as a result of a consistently higher performance, was a relatively simple administrative matter; by contrast, the movement down was more complicated. Problems occurred, because there were complex appeals procedures that had to be gone through before workers could be placed in a lower grade: 'Once you got involved with half a room being on appeals it clogged itself up.'[36]

Despite the apparent improvement in the status of the shop floor workers, which this scheme was designed to engender, it still depended on workers performing to measured time standards, over which there were a large number of disputes.

Corah had introduced their progressive, but expensive, payment package at a time when the industry was enjoying a period of prosperity. It was a luxury that it could not sustain when profits fell during the downturn in trade and around 1988, in an abrupt reversal, the firm indicated to the union that they wished to change the payment system as it had lost its usefulness and they were losing money quite heavily. Very shortly afterwards Corah came under the control of Charterhouse plc and in December 1988 the firm (Corah) gave notice that it would be introducing individual plant bargaining. In June 1990, it abandoned the annual guaranteed wage at a time of short time working and the payment scheme, heralded as being in advance of all others in the industry, suffered an ignominious end. [37]

Gender and payment

Gender inequality was rife within the payment system. Not only were jobs segregated into men's jobs and women's jobs, men were paid more highly than women. However, at the 1976 NUHKW conference, this anomaly was fully exposed. The Northern District put forward a motion requesting the national executive to commission an outside body to undertake a job evaluation scheme throughout the whole industry. The National Executive speaker actually opposed

---

[35] John Fry, Deputy Chairman and joint MD of N. Corah (St Margaret) Ltd, speaking to the Hinckley Textile Society in February 1972.
[36] Interview with Jack Matlock, formerly an official with NUHKW 25 May 2001.
[37] For a description of the system see Westwood, *All Day Every Day* (Pluto Press, London 1984), p. 58.

the resolution in overt terms, thereby acknowledging the payment system to be an injustice:

> Our present wages structure is not formed of principle, it is based historically on an economic fact of what the market will bear. ... The point I want to get across to you is this: what would you do with that information and knowledge? Logically [if for example rib knitting was shown to be less skilled than making-up] we would have to get the [making-up] machinist up to the knitter, or bring the knitter down to the machinist. ... If we implemented job evaluation strictly ...the wages system in this industry would become absolutely chaotic. ... So the truth of the position is – if we had a job evaluation exercise what we would end up with ... is giving half of our members an increase and the other half a reduction. [The Resolution was rejected.][38]

Payment for the factory workers was not fully based on the evaluation of skill or effort – the wage structures within firms were marred by the historic and entrenched division of jobs by gender. This situation held true across the industry, not only for the large number of small firms but also for the large employers such as Courtaulds and Nottingham Manufacturing Company.

By the time this was openly recognised as being morally wrong it was economically impossible to change and the NUHKW had no alternative but to support it because even the lower wages of the women were far above those in the Far East. Had the wages of women been increased and the wages of men been cut and balanced, the consequences for the recruitment and retention of men, mainly knitters, would have been catastrophic. Honeyman concluded from a similar situation in the Leeds Clothing industry:

> The strategy was both socially iniquitous and economically short-sighted. The long-run cost was that the industry was unable to move upmarket or adopt flexible production and working practices because of an inadequate pool of skilled labour. From the early 1960s such an approach was no longer viable in the face of very low-wage competition from the Far East.[39]

Honeyman's view has full merit but otherwise the analysis does not hold true for the hosiery and knitwear industry. In contrast to the Leeds clothing industry, the decline of the hosiery and knitwear industry was accompanied by job losses, not a shortage of skilled workers, and the UK industry was able to produce high

---

[38] NUHKW conference report, 1976 p. 147.
[39] Honeyman, p. 248.

quality goods for the fashion stores of the world, any loss of up-market sales was due mainly to price competition from low-cost suppliers.

Honeyman also draws attention to the lack of technological improvement in the different types of sewing machines operated by women in the Leeds clothing industry:

> It is argued that the rapid diffusion of the sewing-machine in the second half of the nineteenth century created a pool of cheap female labour which came to personify the low-skill, labour-intensive nature of the industry. There was subsequently less technical innovation in the (female) sewing room than in any other area of the production process. This can be understood in terms of the industry's overall strategy to contain costs and specifically to maintain its dependence on low-cost labour.[40]

The situation in the hosiery and knitwear industry does not correspond with Honeyman's analysis of the industry about which she was writing. The reason for the lack of investment in the hosiery and knitwear industries sewing technology was that there was no fundamental improvement in the sewing machine from the time of its invention. Honeyman also comments in the context of the Leeds clothing industry:

> Work Study and PBR [payment by results] amounted to a disciplinary system that provided a means to maintain low wages and increasing productivity through labour exploitation rather than through investments in technology or human capital.[41]

However, in the hosiery and knitwear industry the wages paid and the available technology were separate issues. Had faster machines been available to this industry they would certainly have been available on the world market, lowering the global unit-costs of the products. However it is very unlikely that the employers, in the hard pressed UK hosiery and knitwear industry, would have passed the benefits on to the employees. It is more likely that the savings would have been used to reduce the price to the customers.

Teamwork and quick response

In the 1990s, several of the Courtaulds' manufacturing units, particularly those committed to M&S production, introduced changes to their payment systems. A

---

[40] Honeyman, p. 5.
[41] Honeyman, p. 150.

teamwork scheme was set up to satisfy the 'just in time' demands of the customer, rather than as a cost saving exercise or a means to improve operator performances.[42] In the underwear business, the way to success was seen to be supplying M&S with large orders produced in low labour-cost countries by Courtaulds' own factories. These orders were supplemented with supplies of urgently required merchandise made in the UK on a new teamwork system. Banks of machines were set up in a horseshoe shaped layout. At Bolsover, Courtaulds' largest underwear making-up factory, there were typically 14 machines for 7 operators in a team, who moved around the production line operating the machines standing up, producing about two garments at a time. This involved all operations after cutting, including final packing, and all operatives were competent to operate every different type of machine in the line. Significant advantages were the reduction of costly work in progress to almost nil, and the ability to start despatching on the same day that an individually designed product layout was set up. There was no examination stage in the process, but standards were checked through a statistically based quality sampling system. A fixed basic wage was paid, with an efficiency bonus which became effective from a relatively low performance. Disadvantages were that floor space and the machinery requirements doubled and at the same time a lower operator performance was achieved because the workers had to make frequent movements between machines. A further disadvantage, from the management viewpoint, was that if the workers decided that they were having a 'bad day' and were unlikely to achieve a good bonus, they 'could take it easy' for the remainder of that day on basic pay. Some workers were also aggrieved when they were held back by the slower workers in their team.[43]

Not only was it difficult to integrate slow workers into team working, it was also difficult to accommodate part time workers and the physically disabled because there was a need to maintain balanced teams at all times. It became very difficult, if not impossible, to make the ergonomic adjustments necessary to enable a disabled worker to share a wide variety of machines with a team of workers in full health.[44]

Payment by results in any of the above forms tended to engender complacency, with the management failing to confront some workers who were content to set themselves low levels of performance. For some people, such as single parents, there was little incentive to earn above a predetermined level, which could even be below the guaranteed minimum rate, because they could lose state benefits or tax relief. These problems became more acute when the National Minimum

---

[42] This system operated at lower performances than 'straight proportional individual piecework' and cost more per unit of production.

[43] Kelvin Simpson, administrator in Courtaulds underwear factory, Bolsover. Interview 12 October 2000.

[44] It would even be difficult to use a worker who was abnormally short or tall.

Wage was introduced in 1999.

Rate fixing problems

Problems associated with rate fixing or setting production targets were endemic in the industry.[45] Within almost every factory there was a perception that some rates were 'good' and some were 'bad', however, this perception was very prevalent in hand controlled jobs. Jack Matlock described the role of the trade union:

> In the smaller firms price fixing was always a matter of negotiation ... 60% of the district secretary's work was concerned with [firms] cutting back these piecerates ... however [well] things were arranged ... things drifted and there was a cry [from the employer] to get it back again.[46]

Even in the medium sized and large firms problems still occurred. From the mid-1960s the rates were mainly based on time studies, the most consistent method available. Later, 'pre-determined motion time systems' were introduced, which did not depend on estimating, timing or negotiation. These systems were refined and developed from time studies in an attempt to gain total consistency, and were commercially available by the 1980s. Debating a motion that 'Pre-determined Motion Time Systems are not in the best interests of our membership', a delegate to the 1986 NUHKW conference said:

> If you are not negotiating piecerates in your factory, the Unions role is marginalised. If your members do not see you to be active in doing things like this, it brings discredit on the Union. We get blamed for low rates, people have arguments with us on the shop floor, people might even leave the Union, all because of these systems and these processes. We need to get to grips with the situation because, from what we gather, firms are now wanting to introduce GSD (Garment Standard Data) at a rate which they have not done in the past.[47] [48]

---

[45] R. J. Gigli (a consultant to the textile industry), in an address to the Nottingham & District Hosiery Manufacturers' Association, January 1948, described rate fixing as '... guessology ... opinion and bartering'.
[46] Interview with Jack Matlock, 25 May 2001.
[47] NUHKW conference report, 1986, p. 233.
[48] In practice it became more difficult for the Union to achieve wage drift in excess of the annual award.

Despite a formal agreement that time study would be the basis for setting piecerates or standard times, the NUHKW clung to the notion that everything was negotiable, not only the standard wage value, but also the individual times allowed for each element of the task. This was a deliberate and long running attempt by the trade union to de-stabilise the payment system. Because of union pressure some target times were increased, and therefore became 'loose'. The 'loosest' or 'best' times inevitably became the rate against which to judge all others. Within the industry, managers perceived this to be a deliberate ploy to increase wages over and above the annual pay settlement and to achieve wage-drift outside of the national agreements.

Pay rates were also affected by the long tradition that the introduction of new machinery should be used as a bargaining point for improved payment. Because these deals had frequently been associated with the introduction of faster knitting machinery, the effect had mainly benefited men and further increased the gender divide. In practice, it did not necessarily require more skill or greater effort to run faster knitting machines and this type of negotiation could, and did, lead to resentment from other workers who could not benefit.

In the 1950s, there had been several agreements specifying the standard workload for knitting, but in practice these proved impractical. As late as 1962, much thought and discussion centred on the possibility of introducing standard workloads for knitting, combined with a standard hourly wage rate. Following the demise of fully-fashioned hosiery, with its fairly limited range of knitting machines, the notion of a standard work load for any form of knitting was no longer feasible. It had proved impossible to reach agreement on the issue. The new and more complex range of machinery required varied levels of 'back up' workers, such as additional work movers and assistants, workers were also employed to thread up and continuously service the machines with yarn, and automatic pneumatic removal of work became common. These were all issues that led to complexity in fixing pay rates.[49]

The problem of applying a standard wage value to hand controlled operations was equally complex considering the range of differing types of machinery that had become available over the years. These included cutting, sewing, pressing and packing and some machines would need to be used in combination and would need differing levels of skill for their operation. To introduce a standard wage it would also have been necessary to install the same rates of pay in outlying areas as applied in central Leicester and Nottingham, where the highly competitive labour situation had led to higher payment, and it is inconceivable that the Leicester and Nottingham workers would have accepted lower earnings.

---

[49] Singleton p. 87 cites universal wage lists as being a bar to progress in the Lancashire spinning industry.

Benefits and working conditions

The union fought hard for improved fringe benefits, but failed to achieve for the factory workers the status that was standard in many other industries and for most white-collar workers. One trade union official said:

> I suppose the one thing we failed to achieve was a decent pension scheme for the factory floor. I think it is true to say that most members of staff, at least in the bigger firms, were able to join a pension scheme. Some Courtaulds' people did [join]…but the vast majority of the people in the industry never had a pension.[50]

The call for a pension scheme for the shop floor workers featured in several conference motions. Courtaulds, and their competitors Corah and Coats Viyella all allowed shop floor workers to participate in company schemes which were partly subsidised by the employer. The schemes were not compulsory and surprisingly had met with a remarkably low take-up rate in the factories. At the 1997 KFAT conference a delegate remarked: 'There are companies in CV [Coats Viyella] with 400 employees with only two or three in the pension scheme.'[51]

The Courtaulds experience was similar. Information was given in a most explicit manner, and videos were produced to explain the scheme but, for legal reasons, personnel managers were not free to actually advise people to take up the scheme in preference to any other method of pension provision:

> We could tell people what was available to them but we were not allowed to say that Courtaulds' scheme was the best. There was a very low take up in most areas and this type of pension was new for factory workers. Many were not confident they could keep up the payments.[52]

Courtaulds' shop floor workers conditions eventually included a share-option scheme on equal terms with the staff and by the mid-1980s the conditions of employment for Courtaulds, Corah and Coats Viyella shop floor workers were far in advance of the NJIC negotiated conditions for the rest of the industry.

---

[50] Interview Jack Matlock 24 May 2001.
[51] S. Cockayne (North Midlands) KFAT conference report 1997, p. 208.
[52] Interview, Rosemarie Nash-Smith 24 October 2001.

Meridian Haydn Road Nottingham factory. Photo © 2009 Peter Zabulis.

Physical working conditions

Physical working conditions should be judged in the context of light industry standards, but even within that parameter the working conditions varied considerably. Despite the light industrial nature of the work general factory conditions were basic: 'There was an 'us and them' syndrome... The minions worked behind the scenes.'[53]

This attitude was probably encouraged because, until the 1960s, customers were seldom invited to view the factories and therefore the front office conditions were generally made a higher priority than those in the factory. There were some exceptional properties, for example, the Courtaulds' owned Kayser Bondor at Baldock, Meridian at Haydn Road, Nottingham, Bairnswear at Worksop and also the independent Kempton and Corah factories in Leicester. Many others were also maintained to very high standards with good lighting, adequate space to work and good employee amenities.

Many less imposing factories also provided very good working conditions. However, even within Courtaulds there were very variable standards. Before the redevelopment of the Belper factory the prestigious Aristoc stockings were manufactured in a desolate old factory at Langley Mill and the Meridian factory at Ilkeston Junction was in decay. Three 'Dickensian' factories within the Rowley organisation, J F Carnall at St Nicholas Circle, G Ginns in Braunstone Gate and Courtaulds Sock Division Factory in Wanlip Street, all in Leicester, were very rundown and were closed in the 1970s. However, throughout the industry, there were many late Victorian buildings, some of which were very well maintained

---

[53] Interview, Rosemarie Nash-Smith, 6 February 2001.

The dilapidated Meridian factory at Ilkeston Junction. Photo courtesy of the author.

and still in use at the start of the twenty-first century. The M&S ethos affected working conditions in the industry and when the post-war boom period was over, its demands extended as far as specifying the required standards of housekeeping in their supplier's factories. M&S staff saw the suppliers' premises as extensions of their own business, and commented on such issues as the condition of the toilets, rest rooms and the canteen menu.

The impact of health and safety legislation and the resulting claims

New health and safety legislation in 1974 brought a new awareness of the necessity for change in many work places, and highlighted the need for adequate lighting, ventilation, heating and safe working conditions. Later, the control of dangerous chemicals was also covered by new legislation. The trade union was active in pursuing accident and injury claims on behalf of the members and the number of claims rose substantially relative to the numbers employed. This trend was in the context of the increasing publicity given to health and safety issues and there was an increasingly litigious attitude, encouraged by the high level of commitment given to the issue by the worker's representatives. The General President of the NUHKW noted:

We had one factory in the Southern district, ... where I think they had more compensatory cases on file, in operation and concluded than in the rest of the union put together. And they employed only 150 to 200 people. It was one of the best developed factories in the trade, and one of the cleanest.[54]

The number of claims on behalf of members who sustained accidents at work became progressively greater relative to the size of the membership and the trade union successfully concluded an increasing number.

Table 6.11 *Accident claims*

Year	Cases	Membership
1969	67	50,609
1974	123	71,711
1978	322	72,858
1988–89	904*	c.83,207
1995–96	1,020*	c.72,858

Source: NUHKW & KFAT Conference reports
*For two years

Significantly, in the two years for 1995–96 there were 1,020 successful claims, however, information is available to show that of 15 settlements over £10,000, only one was in the traditional hosiery and knitwear industry and the remaining claimants were shoe trade workers.

Courtaulds' employer representation and wage bargaining

By the late 1990s Courtaulds was becoming inhibited by the system of industry-wide negotiations, which were partly designed to protect the weaker members of the employers' organisation. John Harrison, Director of the Knitting Industries Federation (KIF) explained:

We were much influenced, as a democratic body, by the weaker and smaller members. It was the big boys [Courtaulds and Coats Viyella] who led the way towards new concepts in negotiations which set the way towards a new pace in national bargaining.[55]

---

[54] General President NUHKW conference report 1978, p. 307.
[55] Interview John Harrison, retired General Secretary of Knitting Industries Federation, 9 July 1999.

Ultimately, this led the way to plant bargaining as distinct from industry-wide bargaining. Courtaulds set the pace by reaching agreement over issues of working conditions more rapidly than the National Hosiery Manufacturers' Federation, which was held back by the need to represent hundreds of small firms.[56] Issues such as bereavement leave and parental leave were easier to settle with the big manufacturers than with the small firms.

From the mid-1960s,[57] Courtaulds had operated its Group Industrial Relations Department that provided expertise to businesses needing support when attempting to tackle specific industrial relations and productivity problems. Courtaulds' employees were represented by both the hosiery and the tailoring unions and it would therefore have been difficult or perhaps impossible, from a management and a union viewpoint, to resolve some issues within the constraints of an industry-wide agreement and some productivity deals at individual factories were concluded on the basis of pay settlements above the national agreements, which caused embarrassment and problems for the KIF.[58]

In common with most industries, annual negotiations were held to settle the wage increase for the forthcoming year. In addition to the pay claim the union regularly requested improvements in the payment for waiting time, improved payment for working on an unfamiliar job, reduced hours and the introduction of a sick pay scheme.[59]

As members of the KIF, Courtaulds implemented the annual industry-wide pay agreements until 1970, when it moved to a Courtaulds group agreement separate from the rest of the industry.[60] In 1987, the company gave notice that it would negotiate on an individual plant basis for the forthcoming pay round. This was in line with the general policy of making chief executives progressively more responsible for their own unit's profits.[61]

Courtaulds soon broke away from the KIF. As a multi-site and multi-product conglomerate Courtaulds found its links with the rest of the industry to be a constraint on the way it ran its business. Units needed to respond in a flexible way to pressures that confronted them such as a shortage or surplus of labour in their operating areas. This applied particularly to the annual 'pay round' negotiations. It became impossible to reconcile the policy of making executives responsible for their own profits with industry-wide pay settlements, and it was

---

[56] Interview John Harrison 9 July 1999.
[57] Courtaulds operated a Labour Relations Department at Coventry from 1938.
[58] For a short period Courtaulds left the KIF.
[59] Other issues included a guaranteed year, guaranteed week, and guaranteed hourly rate, maternity pay and time off with pay for cervical smear tests.
[60] From the First World War until 1967 annual pay rises were given in proportion to the alteration in the cost of living. Wells, p. 212.
[61] Refer to Devolution of control in Chapter 5.

equally difficult for the KIF to represent the smaller firms that were unable or unwilling to introduce pay settlements agreed on behalf of the whole industry.

The trade union was placed in a difficult position attempting to deal with pay negotiations. There were specific problems at individual factories that could not be resolved by a 'broad brush' approach across the large number of small and dispersed factories. Courtaulds proposed an unwieldy 21 negotiating centres, but this was eventually reduced to eight. However, there were covert upper negotiating limits imposed on the chief executives by Courtaulds' head office, although in exceptional circumstances these could be exceeded.[62] Courtaulds was operating across a wide spectrum of clothing manufacturing, and justified the need for individual negotiations on the grounds that it was difficult to make a different pay settlement with more than one union, for example the NUHKW and the TGWU.[63] For factories working geographically close together, this situation could also cause problems for the unions involved. The trade unionists were more experienced at negotiating than the individual factory managers, but the biggest problem was the lack of continuity within the management. Some workers found themselves negotiating with different management representatives, year-on-year.

Staff salaries

Throughout the industry, with very few exceptions, staff salaries were a confidential matter between the employer and employee. Although supervisors were said to earn little more than their subordinates and some were paid less,[64] they were usually of staff status. Their conditions varied from firm to firm but would almost certainly include a guaranteed fixed weekly wage, sometimes with overtime premiums, pay for holidays and some sick pay advantages.

Staff and worker relations

Sallie Westwood's thinly disguised description of factory organisation at Courtaulds' competitor, Corah Ltd, in the early 1980s, could equally well have applied to almost every factory in the industry and certainly to most, if not all of Courtaulds.[65] The pay system affected the whole factory control. The workers' output targets and earnings depended on it. The supervisors were required to keep the flow of work going so that their department's targets could be met and accountants were dependent on it to monitor profits and overhead recovery rates.

---

[62] Information provided by a source involved in the negotiations.
[63] Tailors and Garment Workers Union.
[64] Information from Dr J. B. Smith 14 September 2001.
[65] Westwood, *All Day, Every Day* (Pluto Press 1984).

There was also a continual challenge by the workers who claimed that the targets were unfair. It was in this atmosphere that the supervisors worked. They were in an ambiguous position as part of the management team. They suffered criticism from the shop floor workers below and from middle management above, whilst they carried the day to day problems of discipline, quality and organisation of the production. The job needed great strength of character, and carried stress that was seldom adequately rewarded in financial terms.[66]

Sallie Westwood throws light on the position of the female making-up employees – 'the girls'. They were required to work very hard all day making-up part of a garment such as side seams or button holes, every day, every week. They were never required to make up the whole thing. There was however some attempt at individuality:

The machines would be adorned with pictures of family members, a favourite dog, a current heartthrob or a picture from a card or magazine which was usually a sweet and sentimental study of children.[67]

There were lighter moments, the celebration of birthdays, engagements and marriages. There were also sad moments such as when a worker was bereaved or suffered some calamity. All these events were shared together by the workers and the supervisors who, despite their frequent conflicts, understood each other's problems more than was commonly appreciated.

Recruitment and training

During World War Two the hosiery and knitwear industry suffered from the loss of workers to other trades and the armed forces, and subsequently their failure to return in peacetime. Due to competition for labour from other industries this loss was particularly felt in the industry's traditional centres in Leicester and Nottingham.

Being perceived to offer poor career prospects and poor pay, the industry suffered a continual shortage of skilled workers and was unable to attract the best recruits. Short time working, multiple redundancies, falling wages and the emergence of 'sweat-shops' affected its image. 'Off the job' training was almost non-existent in the vast majority of factories, and very few firms ran training schools for shop floor workers. However, with a few exceptions, there was a low level of unemployment, particularly in the Midlands where there was competition amongst employers for that labour which was available. This was a serious problem for firms across the whole industry, particularly in the period up to 1974.

Despite the long running shortage of skilled workers there was seldom a shortage of raw recruits. The industry could be regarded as an employer of last

---

[66] For an interesting overview of the supervisor's position read Westwood, pp. 25–38.
[67] Westwood, p.21.

resort and bright young people were often discouraged by their school careers advisers from taking up factory work. Careful selection of youngsters, many of whom were academic underachievers, was important because both training costs and labour turnover rates were high.[68]

In small and medium sized firms the most usual form of training for direct operatives was the system where a learner was shown the basic elements of the task by watching an experienced worker. The learner gained basic skills using waste or surplus materials. This system was officially described as 'training by exposure' but was often irreverently described as 'sitting next to Nellie'.

Courtaulds and its competitors Coats Viyella and Corah had been in the forefront of operative training for many years and produced high quality trainees. The Corah experience was particularly costly. The firm ran a training school, using skilled training staff and highly developed training programmes. At the end of the training period these workers were then able to enter the labour market and work for Corah's competitors, a situation which Corah was powerless to stop. Other firms that suffered similarly were Wolsey, Rowley, and their competitor Kempton.

In response to the shortage of skilled workers, the Industry Training Act 1964 authorised the setting up of Training Boards to redress the problem. The Knitting, Lace & Net Industry Training Board was established in March 1966. The duties of the Board were:

> To ensure an adequate supply of properly trained men and women at all levels of the industry. To secure an improvement in the quality and efficiency of industrial training [and] To share the cost of training more evenly between firms.[69]

The Training Board Scheme, funded by a compulsory levy, met with considerable antipathy from the manufacturers. The Board operated a system of rebates, and the easiest way for the larger firms to recoup training levies was to employ a training officer and fulfill the bureaucratic needs of the Board. The Board did highlight the need for training, and having established the levy it was only reasonable for firms to do their utmost to recoup some cost wherever possible. During the period of the Board's existence training was put on a more formal basis, but whatever the legacy of the Board the formality and onerous record keeping it introduced was abandoned with its demise.

---

[68] The formal educational qualifications required were often very low or non-existent. Dexterity, discipline and the ability to learn and accept instructions were highly regarded.

[69] KLNITB newsletter October 1966.

Sweatshops and low-wage competition

There had always been some level of exploitation of vulnerable workers in the industry. In the 1970s rumours abounded that some 'Asian'[70] firms were paying far below the prevailing rates in the industry, particularly penalising those with a poor command of the English language, many of whom were unable to gain employment in the established local firms. In fairness, many firms in the Asian sector were very good employers but were unfairly regarded as a threat to the traditional firms on the grounds that the wages paid were far below those generally prevailing in the industry.[71] By the 1990s Leicester had become known as the 'Sweatshop Capital of Britain'.[72] Some Asian firms paid only around half of the legal national minimum wage and frequently counterfeited well known brand names.[73] It is certain that most of these firms were suffering badly from the downturn in the trade. The vast majority could not be described, in the strictest sense, as hosiery and knitwear manufacturers, but could more aptly be described as 'allied trade' firms. Although language problems had largely disappeared by the 1990s, the shortage of work in better establishments still allowed these firms to recruit workers who were unable to obtain better jobs. In April 1999, the government introduced the national minimum wage at a rate of £3.60 per hour. The union set up a campaign to highlight the problem of the low-paid workers in the industry using the slogan '£3.60 or more or they're breaking the law.' The Union cooperated with an Asian Women's Centre in Belgrave, Leicester and the Low Pay Campaign of Leicester City Council in an attempt to make the campaign effective. After extensive advertising, a public meeting was held on 7 June 1999; which was followed by confidential 'surgeries'.

> At the meeting, workers spoke out about how employers are trying to get around paying the minimum wage. Indeed their pay slips recorded £3.60. However, rather than recording their correct number of hours worked, which was anything between 40 and 54 hours per week, they recorded 20 hours per week.[74]

---

[70] 'Asian firms', generally describes firms set up and run by people of Indian descent, many of whom were former business people who fled from Uganda in the early 1970s. The description does not refer to Asia in the strictest sense. There were many good employers in this sector. From the Asia Business Directories of 1990 and 1994 it is possible to identify approximately 70 businesses in this industry but by the late 1990s most of these were general clothing manufacturers.

[71] Information from N. B. Ashcroft 25 February 1999, former Managing Director, Driver Group.

[72] B. S. Morris Lecture, The Secular Hall Leicester 17 January 1999.

[73] Information from KFAT union official B. S. Morris 17 January 1999.

[74] Ms C. Parmar (Community Organizer) 1999 KFAT conference report p. 183.

Outworkers and part timers

Home working was a feature of the industry from its early days and it remained so, to a limited extent, even in the declining years of the industry at the end of the twentieth century with some branches of major firms such as Courtaulds and Coats Viyella regularly employing outworkers on tasks that offered no continuity of employment, such as hand finishing, some sewing machine operations, and the rectification of minor faults. It remained a method of employment in Courtaulds throughout its time in this industry.[75] Outworkers provided a source of flexible labour that cushioned firms from the effects of peaks and troughs in demand and outworkers were commonly perceived to be liable to exploitation although that was not necessarily so, particularly in the unionised factories of the larger manufacturers.

After the introduction of the factory system in the mid-nineteenth century, outworkers were still employed to produce goods in their own homes. These workers provided a casual source of labour that could supplement production levels when required, frequently at lower wages than those in the factories, with almost no social obligations on the part of the firm, or rights for the workers. Many of these workers were former factory employees who were supplementing their family income whilst unable to go out to work for family reasons. Even when the industry was relatively buoyant, in the mid-1970s, activists described outworking as a threat to their jobs, claiming that workers were suffering short time working due to work being 'sent out'. One was very vocal on the subject:

> ... I would like to see some positive action taken with regard to the deplorable malpractice that is eating away at our industry like a malignant cancer.[76]

> ... we had this problem ... when I became the factory trade union representative. I used rather harsh methods to outlaw the pirates, because they are pirates who use outworkers, and to me the outworkers who work at the rates prevailing in the factories are pirates and scabs as well. They are the enemies of the people who are trying to keep up the rates and the enemies of the people in the factories.[77]

---

[75] Some outworkers would be responsible for fetching and returning their own work but in the latter years the firms would have a van which speeded up the process. Speed was essential because outworkers were often used when urgent orders had to be met or the factory workers had become 'out of balance'.
[76] Mrs S. Allen (Hinckley District) NUHKW Conference report, 1976, p. 157.
[77] D. Tennant (Scottish District) NUHKW Conference report, 1976, p. 157.

In 1985 it was alleged that there were 4,000 homeworkers in Leicester[78] (although it was not specifically claimed that they were all part of the hosiery industry). The Leicester Outwork Campaign urged that the unions should seek to achieve employee status for homeworkers, and that rates of pay should be the same for homeworkers as for in-factory operatives doing the same work and should also redress other differentials such as the lack of sick pay, holiday pay and maternity and paternity pay.

Part time working was almost totally the province of women. In 1999, KFAT stated that nearly one in ten jobs in their sector was part time, and of these nine-tenths were for women. The bulk of these were paid on a pro-rata basis to full time workers. Discrimination over non-wage benefits, such as sick pay, was considered rare in unionised companies, but there was concern that this practice was more frequent in non-unionised firms, particularly in sweatshops:

> Although we are unable to quantify the extent of the problem, we are concerned that some unscrupulous employers are taking on part time workers for just enough hours to keep their wages below the national insurance threshold. Clearly, the individual workers do not build up their national insurance contributions, and the employers save money. It is our belief that this practice is quite common within those companies we describe as sweatshops. (Indeed, this avoidance of national insurance contributions is compounded by some unscrupulous employers paying cash in hand).[79]

Employment of part time workers was perceived by the employers' organisation (KIF) to be fraught with problems. When adequate work was available, it was preferable to employ full time workers. The large majority of part time operatives were sewing machinists, and it was an advantage to keep the sewing machines fully occupied during the working day. Unfortunately, there was difficulty in attracting part time workers for work in the afternoons. Administrative costs were increased, and in some cases the machines needed frequent adjustments to suit the ergonomic needs of different workers. As some sections of the industry moved towards team-working, there was a need to create balanced teams and a constant need to train and retrain the multi-skilled workers: 'This cost would be increased considerably if part time workers were to be employed.'[80] These arguments would seem to apply in large measure to disabled workers also.

---

[78] *Leicester Mercury* 8 March 1985.
[79] KFAT Evidence to the House of Commons Select Committee on Education and Employment, prepared 30 March 1999.
[80] KIF Evidence to the House of Commons Select Committee on Education and Employment, prepared 30 March 1999.

Management and technical staff

Charlotte Erickson's book,[81] which was published shortly before the events around which this book is mainly concerned, is a comparison of the entrepreneurs of the steel and hosiery industries. Although her research related to the Nottingham part of the trade, she might easily have been describing Leicester, the other major centre. Erickson does not attempt to judge the effectiveness of the hereditary manager relative to the professional and salaried manager[82] but it is clear that there were very effective founder managers and hereditary leaders, as well as very effective professional managers. There were also some unsuccessful managers in the ranks of both the professionals and managers who inherited their positions. The 1960s was a period of massive change. Erickson had rightly foreseen further development of the limited company. This hastened changes in the senior management role and the recruitment and qualifications required for this type of position. However, she did not forecast the actions of the larger players in the clothing industry such as Courtaulds and Coats Viyella that were to take control of much of the hosiery and knitwear industry.

Changes in the structure of the industry inevitably meant that the position of many owner-managers weakened. This was due to the increase in joint stock ownership, the absorption of firms by the predatory multinationals and the business failure of others. With the industry becoming dominated by Courtaulds, Coats Viyella and Nottingham Manufacturing Company, the relative status of the factory managers was much lower than that of the original owners. Even those owner managers that survived the takeover of their firms were in a lower decision making position than previously and were salaried rather than enjoying the profits (or suffering the losses) of their business.

Courtaulds' management void

Courtaulds' acquisitions ranged from the very small to some of the largest in the industry, some had been run by salaried administrative managers and some by owners or shareholders. These managers fell into two groups, those that retired, resigned or were dismissed and those that were offered and accepted salaried positions.

There had been no traditional clearly defined route to top management. Very prominent was the inheritance route or via the foundation of a new firm. Of the salaried remainder, there seems to have been a mixture including former accountants, sales staff and outside appointments. There seems very little evidence

---

[81] Erickson, *British Industrialists: Steel and Hosiery 1850–1950* (CUP, London, 1959).
[82] Erickson, p. 138.

of technically qualified staff from within the knitting industry attaining top management status, a fact emphasised in Erickson's work.

The retirements, resignations and dismissals associated with the acquisition policy caused a management void that had to be filled. For legal and taxation reasons, some of the acquired firms remained separate legal entities, some for several years.[83] At the very least, it was necessary for Courtaulds to provide at least two senior staff, not necessarily full time, preferably with some knowledge of the textile industry, one of whom was familiar with Courtaulds' accounting system. This problem was difficult to deal with because there were much larger acquisitions in other fields that were also demanding attention at the same time.[84] Courtaulds had little choice other than to use existing managers because they had little or no existing surplus staff with an innate understanding of the problems of the industry. Ironically, some that worked in ailing firms before acquisition were able to sustain a long career in their new environment. It was certainly not a deliberate policy to displace the previous higher management from the new acquisitions, although in some cases this was inevitable. However, Courtaulds had to provide new top management for much of this untidy mixture of single and multi-product firms and many of the vacancies were filled by research staff from Courtaulds' laboratories at Coventry. As Knight wrote:

> In the rapid development of the post–1962 period, the most abundant source of talent for management training proved to be the research division. … With a research department of about 300 graduates and an annual recruitment of about sixty, about forty a year move out of research into management jobs or jobs with a management potential: this has a further advantage of constantly replenishing the pool of talent in a research team.[85]

Unfortunately, most of these were more familiar with the problems of the large-scale chemical engineering industry than of a fashion-orientated manufacturing industry. However, they were certainly comfortable working in the context of a large-scale enterprise employing large amounts of capital on new projects which few managers in the hosiery and knitwear industry were.

---

[83] Some firms also still had minority shareholders that had not sold out to Courtaulds.

[84] For example – International Paint, James Nelson, Fras Hinde, Derby and Midland Mills, Symington, Clutsom Penn, Northgate, Morton Sundour Fabrics, Susan Small, Victor Marks, Barracks Printing, Premier Dyeing, Spray and Burgass, Joseph Sutherland, Samuel Heap, Thomas & Arthur Wardle, Moygashel and Fletcher, Lancashire Cotton Corporation, Fine Spinners & Doublers, Hayshaw, Ashton Brothers.

[85] Knight (1974), p. 83.

In 1952, Courtaulds' Chairman John Hanbury-Williams proudly wrote about the working ambience within the firm:

There has been a Gentlemen's Club atmosphere in the Boardroom, and I believe it is true to say that over the years this has spread to all the Departments of our business. It is in fact part of the goodwill of the Company which we must safeguard.[86]

The Courtaulds culture of the 'Gentlemen's Club' that was evident among the higher levels of employees at Hanover Square was not transferred to the acquisitions. There was no single cause for this, but a 'Courtaulds Man'[87] being placed in this new environment would without doubt have felt very uncomfortable. The 'Gentlemen's Club' feeling was certainly not transferred from Coventry and London to the garment manufacturing units. Immediately a firm was acquired, any prestige car such as a Rolls Royce was sold off and signs of opulence, such as grand directors' dining rooms, were cut back. Any loyalty to the parent company that may have existed in the minds of the employees transferred from Coventry to the garment companies was vastly diluted by working with a much larger proportion of employees who did not join Courtaulds by choice, and may indeed have not seen the acquisition of their firm in any favourable light. The fact that Courtaulds' infusion of cash saved many firms from ruin did not automatically mean that the employees had to love Courtaulds and its ethos, and in many cases the culture of the original firms was quite long lasting and recognisable.

In line with the policy of vertical trading, one very senior executive, John Grew, was appointed with specific instructions to maximise the use of Courtaulds' Celon in the Hosiery Group, but in other sectors the needs of a fashion industry demanded more freedom of action.

Never before had the industry seen such an influx of highly educated staff. The accepted wisdom in the trade was that these 'chemists from Coventry' ruined several of Courtaulds' acquisitions, but on further examination this can be viewed in a much more charitable light. Several of these people were placed in a situation in which they were doomed to failure particularly when they moved into acquisitions that were bordering on collapse and in need of experienced new managers. Of the larger acquisitions, Ballito, Brettle, F,C&W, KB, and Morley fell into that category. The appointment of staff from the parent company did not improve the situation of these firms, mainly because, by the time their loss-making divisions were eliminated, their remaining

---

[86] Coleman vol. 3 (1980), p. 24.

[87] The notion of the 'Company Man' is explored in Sampson, *Company Man: Rise and Fall Of Corporate Life* (Harper Collins, London 1995).

constituent parts were prime targets for splitting up and tacking on to more successful businesses.[88]

Background of the chairmen

The two Chairmen who were responsible for assembling Courtaulds' stake in the garment industries, Kearton and Knight, were both from working class backgrounds and crossed the hurdle between a working class upbringing and a high executive position in British industry and commerce.

Continuity of top management

Both Kearton and Knight had successful wartime occupations. Kearton had joined the firm as head of the Chemical Engineering Department after a period with the Atomic Energy Authority and Knight joined after service as a lieutenant colonel in the Control Commission.

Knight worked closely with Kearton and was an established figure in the firm's hierarchy at the time of Kearton's departure and a suitable candidate to take on the combined role of chairman and chief executive. Christopher Hogg was known to Kearton as a member of the Industrial Reorganization Corporation when Kearton was chairman of that organisation and he later worked for Courtaulds with Kearton. Martin Taylor also had a history of continuity, having been previously known to Hogg as a financial journalist and had been employed by the firm since 1982. Finally, John Eccles had been a non-executive director of Courtaulds Textiles plc prior to his appointment to the chairmanship in 1985 and had therefore worked alongside both Hogg and Taylor.

It was in education and intellect where a common factor can be found. The five chairmen in this study came from diverse backgrounds, working class, middle class and affluent. They did not share a common background in pre-university education with both the state and public school sectors being represented. It is at the intellectual level that they appear to converge, all being graduates of top universities and highly capable people, but while it may be invidious to draw comparisons, Kearton and Taylor have been considered intellectually outstanding.

A comfortable family background for Hogg and personal wealth for Eccles may have been an advantage in their formative years, but their shareholdings, in common with the others being discussed, were modest relative to the overall size of Courtaulds and had no influence on their appointment.

---

[88] For example, Contour Hosiery had no input of Courtaulds' central staff. The firm was split up and its constituent parts, which were relatively small and self sufficient, were allocated to larger and more specialized parts of the group in an almost immediate reshuffle.

Table 6.12 *Courtaulds Ltd chairmen*

Chairman	Family status	School	University
Kearton. Lord	Working class	State School	Oxford
Knight. Sir Arthur	Working class	State School	LSE

Sources: The Guardian. The Times. Who's Who. The Royal Society

Table 6.13 *Courtaulds Ltd and first chairman of Courtaulds Textiles plc*

Chairman	Family status	School	University
Hogg. Sir Christopher	Affluent	Marlborough	Oxford

Sources: Who's Who. The Observer

Table 6.14 *Courtaulds textiles plc chairmen*

Chairman	Family status	School	University
Taylor. Martin	Middle class	Eton (scholarship)	Oxford
Eccles. Lord (Non-Exec)	Affluent	Winchester	Oxford

Sources: Who's Who. Management Today

Stanworth and Giddens' research published in 1974 shows that only a very small proportion of the chairmen in their study of chairmanships were from a working class background. They explained:

> Of our total population (460 chairmanships), there are no more than five cases in which chairmen can be definitely identified as working class by social origin ... The poor boy who has succeeded in becoming the chairman of one of Britain's largest companies is rare indeed.[89]

---

[89] Stanworth and Giddens (eds), *Elites and Power in British Society* (CUP, London 1974) Chapter 5, pp. 83–86.

Table 6.15 *Social origins of UK company chairmen*

	Working class (%)	Middle class (%)	Upper class (%)	Unknown (%)	Total nos. individuals
Clearing banks	-	3	74	23	74
Merchant banks	-	-	89	11	38
Miscellaneous manufacture	1	13	59	27	161
Breweries	2	11	75	12	55
Iron and steel	2	11	55	32	41
Railways	-	11	86	3	37
Shipping	-	10	67	23	21
Oil	-	13	47	40	14
Retail	-	32	21	47	19
Mean	1	10	66	23	460

Sources: Stanworth and Giddens *Elites and Power in British Society*

The value of effective middle management

Some examples will serve to explain the value of effective middle management. Bairnswear was, from a top-level management viewpoint, in an equally serious situation to some of the firms mentioned above, having lost its previous managing director shortly after the firm was acquired by Courtaulds. By contrast, this firm did manage to retain some measure of its previous identity. This was almost certainly due to fortuitous factors: the popularity of cut and sewn knitwear in the 1960s in which the firm specialised, the growth of the chain stores, which a large supplier was ideally placed to serve, and the strength of its middle management. Immediately on acquisition, three staff experienced in the wider textile industry were appointed by Courtaulds, replacing the previous top management, Jack Willock from Coventry[90] research laboratories, H. J. Coast, an accountant and E. B. Thomas, who was familiar with the spinning industry.[91] Shortly afterwards Bill Dale, a skilled administrator, joined them on a secondment. The more successful Aristoc and Prew-Smith were faced with the retirement of founding and long-serving managers, but these firms had middle level managers able to provide continuity. Meridian, Wolsey, Lyle & Scott, Rowley and Blounts were allowed to continue substantially unchanged with a minimal input of central staff.

---

[90] J. Willock was appointed Vice Chairman and Managing Director.
[91] Bairnswear had its own spinning and hand knitting wool subsidiary.

Professional staff

With the development of the large firms such as Courtaulds, Coats Viyella and Corah, the role of the chief executive and the managers of large sections of these groups became almost exclusively non-technical. These firms were able to employ specialist staff in fields such as accountancy, personnel management, work study and information technology, many of whom were later promoted to higher management positions. Professional training was not perceived to be the responsibility of the technical colleges as this was provided by the appropriate professional bodies. Within Courtaulds, particularly in the Courtaulds Textiles plc era, vacancies in these fields were frequently filled with qualified people from outside the firm, as these were seen to be transferable skills.

Technical training

The technical skills needed in the industry were taught by the colleges of technology and later by the polytechnics and universities. Formal certificated training followed two main paths: technical and technologist. In the 1960s, technical courses were offered to fifteen-year-old trainees, which did not require particularly high entry qualifications. The main technical colleges offering this type of course were at Hinckley, Leicester, Derby, and Nottingham and by studying on a day-release scheme it was possible to obtain a City & Guilds Full Technological Certificate within five or six years.

For the technologist, as distinct from the technician, full time education would lead to OND, HND and the ATI[92] qualification (which was nominally of degree standard but not recognised as such) but it was not possible to transfer from the technical path to the technological path because the entry qualifications for this were much higher. Recruitment was widespread for both types of course and attracted local and overseas students. There were also universities that offered technologist-type courses leading to BA qualification and research degrees. Over a number of years, the day release courses were in decline due to lack of demand and well respected specialist training centres, such as the section at Hinckley College that concentrated on hosiery machine courses, were closed and the polytechnics no longer provided part time education in this field.

Designers

Changing retail trading patterns led to an increasing demand for good designers. From the mid-1960s, the role of the designer became much more important.

---

[92] Ordinary National Diploma, Higher National Diploma and Associate of the Textile Institute.

For chain store suppliers, it was necessary for designers to be competent in face-to-face contact with the clients. In all sectors of the industry, it was necessary to react to colour trends and general coordination of the product ranges. In the knitwear field, the swing from fully-fashioned to cut and sewn styles was fundamental and led to a need for specialist design capabilities. It was no longer a matter of changing the colour or the type of yarn from which a 'classic' garment was made. Particularly at the time when the mini-skirt was in vogue, fine-gauge hosiery firms with specialist machines were at a distinct advantage and could take advantage of design skill in a way not possible before. UK firms were faced with a Europe-wide domestic market and the more sophisticated buying procedures employed by the UK chain-stores, and from the mid-1960s the role of the designer became a fundamental element of success for many firms.

A long-standing traditional technical education centre, the Nottingham College of Technology, was heavily involved in design teaching but eventually it amalgamated with the local College of Art and Design and later was absorbed into Trent University. The University began to concentrate on garment design, using mainly bought-in woven fabrics. However, at the end of the twentieth century, using a reduced range of specialist machinery, it was able to combine the design and technology functions within a knitwear course and was still able to maintain a limited amount of up-to-date machinery. These courses were very design orientated and marketing techniques were included.

The number of overseas students also declined because indigenous universities and colleges had been set up, with Hong Kong having one of the leading universities of textiles in the world and at the turn of the century, training to a high level was also available in Australia, Pakistan, India, and Bangladesh.

Human resources management

Human resources management, formerly known as 'personnel management' was a well established function in the larger and more prestigious of Courtaulds' acquisitions before they were taken over.[93] Firms such as Meridian, Bairnswear and Wolsey and KB had long recognised the need for professional management in this function and by the early 1970s, the individual businesses were beginning to employ professional practitioners in this field. Despite the fragmented nature of Courtaulds' hosiery and knitwear activities, this was an area of management in which there was a large measure of cohesion across the group as it also was in accountancy and finance.

With the formation of Courtaulds Textiles plc in 1990, the tradition of having a main board director responsible for personnel and industrial relations was

---

[93] Courtaulds set up a personnel department in 1945, responsible to a main board director. Coleman vol. 3 (1980), p. 297.

continued. There were regular meetings of the personnel managers who operated identical selection procedures and record-keeping systems. This was due in large measure to the increasing pressure of industrial relations legislation that took effect in the 1980s and the need to maintain a united position when dealing with a single trade union for most of the employees.

Contracts of employment remained standard across the garment companies within the four groups of employees: factory operatives and manual workers paid a standard weekly wage (SWW); Group B which covered clerical administrative and supervisory workers; Group A which included junior managers up to assistant divisional chief executive status; and senior executive which included divisional chief executives and above. The function of the recruitment of staff up to the level of assistant divisional chief executive was the responsibility of the divisional chief executive, with the aid of the division's personnel staff, but appointment of divisional chief executives was solely the responsibility of the Group Chief Executive.

Career progress

Historically, career progress had been difficult in the industry, because the top jobs were traditionally reserved for (male) members of the owning family, or at least major shareholders. In the large firms, such as Courtaulds and Coats Viyella, the lower-level prospective managers were inhibited because there was very little upward mobility and vacancies were often filled by staff that would otherwise have been redundant at other branches of the organisation. It was a matter of concern right across the organisation when redundancies were proposed that these be kept to a minimum; not only was there a moral obligation involved, but there were also legal and public relations implications.

By 1994, Courtaulds recognised the need to redress a shortage of lower-level managers within the industry and new training programmes were put in place. The industry did not match the salary expectations or career aspirations of most young graduates, and therefore special training schemes were set up in an attempt to develop the existing management. Around this time Sampson wrote: 'The traditional company man with his confidence in annual increments and a growing pension is as extinct as an eighteenth century clergyman.'[94]

There was therefore a move to recognise potential managers within the firm and to recruit non-graduates from outside.

With the closure of factories, many managers were lost to the industry.[95]

---

[94] Sampson (1995), p. 307.

[95] The group structure was evolved by closing units for which there was perceived to be no hope of a viable future. Fragmented firms such as Contour Hosiery were split up and parts allocated to more stable management groupings. Where there was commonality these tended to gravitate together. Where there was commonality in both sales and production

Staff numbers were reduced by natural wastage, the grouping together of manufacturing units, and ultimately by redundancy.

Notes to Chapter 6

Table 6.16 *Courtaulds – Group reporting system and numbers employed*

Management group	Employees	
1975		
Hosiery	4337	
Bairnswear/Rowley	4533	
Meridian	5317	
Wolsey/Lyle & Scott	4088	18275
1976 Sock division formed partly from Wolsey and partly from Rowley factories		
Hosiery	3954	
Bairnswear/Rowley	4191	
Meridian	5650	
Wolsey/Lyle & Scott	3634	
CKL sock division	835	
CKL financial services	51	18315
1977		
Hosiery	3291	
Bairnswear/Rowley	3706	
Meridian	5788	
Wolsey/Lyle & Scott	3684	
CKL sock division	818	
CKL financial services	62	17349
1978 Part of sock division transferred back to Wolsey, part to Rowley		
Hosiery	3040	
Bairnswear/Rowley	3588	
Meridian	5370	
Wolsey/Lyle & Scott	3676	
Rowley sock division	392	
CKL financial services	62	16128

this trend was almost certain. Gradually more successful management teams swallowed others.

1979 Rowley separated from Bairnswear		
Hosiery	2948	
Bairnswear	2702	
Meridian	5324	
Wolsey/Lyle & Scott	3195	
Rowley & sock division	1254	
Financial services	57	15480
1980 With reorganisation of the reporting system the hosiery division continued to report separately but all the Courtaulds Knitwear Ltd companies reported together		
Hosiery	2746	
Courtaulds Knitwear	10597	13343
1981		
Hosiery	2160	
Courtaulds Knitwear	10179	12339
1982		
Hosiery	1987	
Courtaulds Knitwear	10292	12279
1983		
Hosiery	1774	
Courtaulds Knitwear	9677	11451
1984 April the firm started the process of forming the **Brand** and **Contract** groups		
Contract		
Courtaulds apparel	7052	
Foundationwear	1971	
Meridian knitwear	2777	
Meridian others	3195	
Rowley	1117	
Brand		
Wolsey	853	
Lyle & Scott	1281	
Courtaulds hosiery	1667	
Kilsyth hosiery	97	20010
1984 December the clothing companies reported as Courtaulds Clothing		
Contract apparel	15812	
Courtaulds hosiery	1548	

Lyle & Scott knitwear	667	
Kilsyth hosiery	96	
Wolsey	842	18965
1985 Courtaulds Clothing reported in two divisions		
Contract apparel	16708	
Brands group	4705	21413
1986		
Contract apparel	15178	
Brands group	4817	19995
1987		
Contract apparel	15653	
Brands group	4637	20290
1988		
Contract apparel	13878	
Brands group	4981	18859
1989		
Contract apparel	12269	
Brands group	4358	16627

Source: Acordis Ltd

Notes:
These figures are an indication of the employment in Courtaulds hosiery, knitwear and knitted underwear factories. The figures are overstated because leisurewear and some other products are included.
Commencing in 1980 with the formation of Courtaulds Knitwear Ltd the group consolidated together all knitwear, sock and underwear figures.
During 1984 figures were issued that give some indication of the labour force of the various management groups but from then all apparel and foundation-wear is included together.
The 1988 increase in Brands reflects the acquisition of Corah sock activities.

SEVEN

Changing Markets

BACK IN 1903 Marks & Spencer was operating a chain of 36 bazaars and shops but six decades later was the highly respected and leading retailer, a landmark on the UK high street and central to the aspirations and fortunes of Courtaulds. M&S was dedicated to the ethos of service and quality and for many years made it a policy to buy most of its merchandise from UK manufacturers. Retail competition was always strong but from the 1970s competition on the high streets became increasingly fierce – the close proximity of the multiple stores allowed customers to walk from one store to another and compare quality and prices. However, other stores such as BHS and Littlewoods were beginning to pay more attention to quality, and at the same time competing on price by taking advantage of the availability of cheaper goods produced in the Far East and North Africa. Although M&S remained for many years loyal to the UK suppliers, its stores became less competitive in the 1990s, particularly in the basic underwear and commodity lines for which they were the recognised market leaders.

Courtaulds in the supply chain

From its entry into the trade Courtaulds became involved with a wide range of customers and progressively through the 1960s established a comprehensive coverage of the available types of sales outlet. The purchase of F,C&W offered an immediate entry to M&S. Another acquisition, Bairnswear, using its own brand name, supplied childrenswear direct to retail stores. Prestigious brand named products such as Aristoc, Kayser Bondor, Wolsey and Lyle & Scott, were all supplied to the independent trade and department stores. Contacts were therefore established with the whole spectrum of the retailers via the declining wholesalers to the small independent retailers, and directly to the expanding chain stores and other larger outlets.[1]

---

[1] In addition to the chain stores fine-gauge hosiery sales developed very strongly in the supermarkets and chemists. Hosiery and knitwear products were also sold through outlets including mail order, department stores, discount retailers, factory shops, market

Porter comments that: 'In consumer goods and services, a vibrant retail sector has created pressures to innovate. Marks & Spencer, for example has been a major force in the upgrading of British suppliers in food and apparel.'[2] However, when writing about the Leeds tailoring industry Honeyman wrote that the downstream move into retailing '… was an essential part of making the connection between production and consumption.'[3]

These writers were describing two vastly different markets. The chain stores which were Courtaulds' prime sales target, had developed sophisticated marketing techniques and worked with the manufacturers developing an innovative response to their needs. In contrast, the large Leeds tailoring industry had to develop its own high street presence in order to enter the mass market. Therefore Courtaulds was able to enter the mass market without entering into competition and strife with its own customers.

The wholesale trade

Courtaulds was dependent on the wholesale trade as an important link in the supply chain although this link was in serious decline by the mid 1980s. The textile wholesalers performed a vital service for the manufacturers and independent retailers. The function of the wholesaler was to purchase stock in bulk quantities and distribute goods in the smaller quantities that served the needs of the retailers. Specialist wholesalers could carry stylish ranges and respond to fashion changes in a way that was not possible for the general wholesaler.

Wholesalers were an essential link in the export trade, and several of the larger firms had agencies overseas, particularly in the commonwealth countries.[4] It was a high-cost function and many of the wholesalers were based in expensive sites in city centres. From the 1920s, price competition from the high street multiples became a major issue in a way that it had not previously been. The chain stores were buying in huge quantities from the manufacturers at special prices, and wholesalers' selling prices were frequently close to, and in some cases were actually higher, than those in the high street chain stores. In the short term, specialist wholesalers were less affected than the general wholesalers because they had more buying power and expertise in their own product, but eventually all suffered and the wholesale system went into decline.

---

stalls and later, in a small way through the internet.
2   Porter, p. 502.
3   Honeyman, p. 2.
4   British made high-quality goods were in demand in areas such as Malta, Cyprus, Hong Kong and the Bahamas. Another aspect of the export trade was that agents of foreign firms visited the major wholesalers in the UK, and purchased store-sized lots for collation and despatch to their customer. Information from Gwyn Stevenson 22 February 2002.

A feature of successful wholesaling was the need for a link to an established brand name. The long-established wholesalers took a pride in the quality of their goods and the brand formed a type of guarantee.[5] Well known brand names were often promoted and advertised by the wholesalers or the manufacturers and ownership or the exclusive right to use a well known and respected brand name was tremendously advantageous, and it needed constant vigilance to ensure that the brand was not 'pirated' and the quality debased.

Courtaulds and the wholesale distributors

Courtaulds' ill-fated acquisition of many of the major wholesalers was an attempt to complete the firm's links in the UK supply chain although Courtaulds was already aware of the declining number of small retail outlets:

> This venture was part of the continuing effort to strengthen the company's position in relation to the rapidly changing retail scene. It was apparent that the disappearance of small retailers was due in part to the high costs of distribution through traditional wholesale channels, adding typically some 25% to the cost of textile products between the manufacturing stage and their arrival in the hands of the retailer.[6]

Courtaulds entered the specialist wholesale trade with the purchase of Brettles in 1964. It is unclear if this firm was acquired for its wholesaling or manufacturing abilities, or both. Over a period of more than two hundred and fifty years, this firm had developed its image and product range, concentrating solely on its brand name, Brettles.[7] This combined manufacturer-wholesaler had, by 1964, lost its former success in manufacturing and was sourcing much of its merchandise from other firms in the industry. The manufacturing and wholesaling sides of the business were separated under Courtaulds, the wholesale side being placed in the Cook & Watts group of wholesalers. Long after the demise of most of the UK's general and specialist hosiery and knitwear wholesale businesses,[8] George Brettles struggled on into the mid-1990s serving the remaining independent shops and doing some limited export business.

Courtaulds' entry into the fragmented wholesaling sector was understandable in the context of the firm's downstream vertical trading policy, but contrary to the mass production ethos of the fibre producing divisions and the large scale

---

[5] Costs included expensive sites, salaries, representatives' commissions and expenses, stockholding, the cost of providing customer credit and liquidating redundant stock.
[6] Knight (1974), p. 60.
[7] See 'Brettles' in Chapter 3.
[8] Information from Gwyn Stevenson 22 February 2002.

manufacturing ambitions of the downstream clothing manufacturers, including the hosiery and knitwear industry producers.[9]

Courtaulds' expansion into the wider field of wholesaling, with the acquisition of Cook & Watts, Bell Nicholson and Lunt, Bradbury Greatorix, and Wilkinson & Riddell as well as numerous smaller firms, was an attempt to establish a leading presence in wholesaling to the independent trade, which was in decline but still functioning. These wholesalers operated from over forty sites in the UK.

Despite early attempts by these wholesale firms to source supplies from within Courtaulds, the firm's own manufacturers did not cooperate, finding the business an encumbrance whilst they concentrated their efforts on their target customers, the chain stores, and other larger customers, and the wholesalers then had to obtain their merchandise from outside the group. This defeated the purpose of Courtaulds being in the wholesale sector of the trade.

Wholesaling – a problem for Courtaulds

The cost of working capital was always a serious concern for the wholesale trade, and in general wholesaling the departmental buyers frequently had to argue very hard for their perceived share of the money available. However under Courtaulds things became even more difficult when advertising the brand names was reduced as the wholesalers were believed to be soaking up Courtaulds' capital for little return.

Competition between Courtaulds' wholesaling firms soon began to pose problems, and was made worse by competition from the 'direct to retail' specialist producers, such as Wolsey in socks and knitwear and KB in fine-gauge hosiery[10] that bypassed the wholesalers. It proved unhelpful in practice to coordinate selling prices between competing wholesalers, and impossible for the specialist wholesalers who used aggressive special price promotions to develop their business and to clear unfashionable and surplus stocks. In effect these businesses were cannibalising each other's sales and inevitably there were soon calls within Courtaulds for consolidation and rationalisation of the wholesale outlets.

Despite the demise of its wholesalers, Courtaulds was cushioned from the worst financial effects of the closures because many of their acquisitions traded from prime city sites that were sold for development at a time when this type of property was in demand and property prices were high.

---

[9] The 'tied wholesalers' attempts to demand that Courtaulds fibres be used in their products met with poor response particularly from the non-Courtaulds carpet manufacturers.

[10] Courtaulds' specialist manufacturers such as Wolsey supplied small orders to independent shops as did the Hosiery Division, using the Kayser Bondor and Ballito brand names and bypassed the wholesale trade. Ballito packaged hosiery was supplied in small quantities to the 'rack trade' in chemists, garages and other outlets.

Direct to retail

If the fierce competition between Courtaulds-owned wholesalers is considered strange business practice, even more bizarre was the attack from the 'brand name' suppliers, several of which were also Courtaulds-owned and supplied directly to the retail trade including the larger departmental stores. Two prime examples – Byford (Viyella International) and Wolsey (Courtaulds) developed and advertised their own brands extensively from the 1920s. Their merchandise was successfully marketed by sales forces of representatives that called on the better class outfitters, and these were backed up, in later years, by telephone sales people. They had such a strong position in the market that they were able to compete on quality, price and service with the wholesalers, holding this position long after the demise of most of the major wholesalers.

The relationship with Marks & Spencer

From the earliest days of its involvement in the trade, Courtaulds had recognised the advantages of being a major supplier to M&S. The continuity of large orders allowed the factories to plan production without incurring the 'stop-go' problems associated with other customers and it was possible to plan the delivery of materials and organise production in such a way that continuity of manufacturing was more or less assured. There is little to suggest that costs were much lower, if any, than those incurred when supplying other chain stores but M&S gave a degree of certainty that the others did not, and which was mutually beneficial to both parties.

Around 1980, when Richard (later Sir Richard) Greenbury took charge of M&S clothing, it was obvious that the supplier base had become unwieldy and with the consent of the M&S Chairman (Lord Sieff) he set about reducing the number of smaller suppliers. The beneficiaries were Courtaulds and other large firms that were needed to produce, in large volume, the basic lines that were essential to the business: bras, knickers, nightdresses, skirts, knitwear and socks; areas in which Courtaulds was firmly established. Many of the supplier firms had long-standing relationships with M&S and were given up to two years' notice of the change:

> However delicately M&S directors may have thought they were managing the process, some manufacturers, after decades of working with M&S, reacted to what was effectively losing all or part of their livelihood with anger and bitterness.[11]

---

[11] Bevan, *The Rise and fall of Marks & Spencer* (Profile, London 2001), p. 111.

This relationship demanded total commitment on both sides. M&S had phased out hundreds of small suppliers after the post World War Two boom and built up the relationships with the major suppliers, the two sides becoming mutually dependent on each other. The reduction of orders from the high street stores created a profound impact on these smaller suppliers who were unable to quickly switch production to other customers. A downturn in the fortunes of M&S in the late 1990s was bad for their shareholders but for some supplier firms it was catastrophic. Decay in the UK manufacturing sector was inevitable, due largely to the effects of globalisation and the large manufacturers were not immune, but the speed with which M&S lost its market share rocked these manufacturers and was unprecedented:

> Like a marriage, it was for better or worse. When the going was good, the suppliers reaped the benefit and acquired for themselves Rolls-Royce cars, trophy wives and villas in Spain. When the going got tough they were expected to cut their margins and 'make a contribution'. Relationships were based on trust and there was one extra dimension that until the mid 1990s set M&S apart from so many other large companies – top management clearly enjoyed seeing their suppliers prosper with them.[12]

The relationship between M&S and their suppliers, Courtaulds, Coats Viyella, Dawson, Baird, Dewhirst, Claremont, Nottingham Manufacturing and others had become symbiotic. Over a period of years these large firms had, to a large extent, made the M&S business 'their own', and M&S had come to rely on them as the major suppliers. The name of the store itself was a guarantee of quality. M&S had created a reputation for consistently well made and comfortable clothing, in styles that appealed to the buying public, all at reasonable prices, although these selling points were insufficient in themselves to offset the near disaster that met M&S in 1999 and Courtaulds Textiles plc in 1999/2000.[13]

Decline by sector

Whilst it is clear that improved productivity and faster machinery had some downward effect on employment, statistics are available that show the far more devastating effect of imports. All sectors were eventually hit by import penetration but fine-gauge hosiery manufacturers also suffered badly from a decline in retail demand for their products.

---

[12] Bevan, p. 104.
[13] Refer to Chapter 9.

Fine-gauge hosiery manufacturing in decline

Table 7.1 *All full length women's stockings – million pairs*

Year	1962/3	1963/4	1964/5	1965/6	1966/7
Production	319.6	370.6	398.6	427.0	457.9

Source: Board of Trade Business Monitor Series

In the trading climate of higher living standards, the stockings industry enjoyed considerable progress throughout the 1960s. In this period fully-fashioned stockings[14] fell from favour at the upper end of the market; circular knitted stockings became more fashionable, and with the popularity of short skirts, tights began to take over the market.

Table 7.2 *All full length women's stockings, tights and pantyhose – million pairs*

Year	1967	1968	1969	1970	1971	1972	1973
Production	456.7	466.0	434.8	468.0	541.2	582.5	567.3

Source: Board of Trade Business Monitor Series
Note: Figures for 1966 contain one estimated quarter.

The second half of the 1960s and the early years of the 1970s were good years for fine-gauge hosiery, with production reaching its first high point in 1973. However, in this period Courtaulds seems to have lost its way, and failed to make the progress that could have been expected from a large multinational firm.

Table 7.3 *All full length women's stockings and tights. Synthetic fine-gauge – million pairs*

Year	1974	1975	1976	1977	1978	1979	1980	1981
Production	485.2	492.8	474.6	453.3	466.2	463.1	464.6	453.3
Exports	31.2	40.2	67.3	67.5	54.3	49.8	40.4	33.6
Imports	95.5	85.9	88.7	82.6	101.4	116.4	112.5	154.8
Apparent UK market	549.5	538.5	496.0	468.4	513.3	529.7	536.7	574.5

---

[14] By this time nylon had become established as the main yarn and stockings were widely referred to as 'nylons'.

Year	1982	1983	1984	1985	1986	1987	1988	1989
Production	457.9	489.1	465.6	507.5	513.0	521.2	541.4	566.1
Exports	41.6	31.2	33.7	36.9	30.9	33.9	26.4	33.1
Imports	162.2	154.9	174.3	174.1	187.3	182.3	142.7	131.0
Apparent UK Market	578.5	612.8	606.2	644.7	669.4	669.6	657.7	664.0
Year	1990	1991	1992	1993	1994	1995	1996	1997
Production	497.1	472.6	433.4	395.1	387.8	350.9	359.0	340.2
Exports	22.0	15.9	22.5	22.3	26.5	21.7	17.1	17.8
Imports	90.5	104.4	76.7	118.5	103.3	91.7	84.1	90.9
Apparent UK Market	565.6	561.1	487.6	491.3	464.6	420.9	426.0	413.3
Year	1998	1999	2000	2001	2002	2003		
Production	311.1	267.5	245.5	196.4	192.0	124.1		
Exports	14.4	12.4	16.3	14.4	11.4	6.1		
Imports	92.8	96.7	100.3	95.8	89.6	89.5		
Apparent UK Market	389.5	351.8	329.5	277.8	270.2	207.5		

Source: Knitstats

The market reached its peak in the late 1980s after a period of rising production during which Pretty Polly,[15] which later became a Sara Lee subsidiary, captured a large share of the trade through grocery outlets, whilst the upper end of the trade was held by the chain stores:

Brian McMeekin of Pretty Polly foresaw that the economies of scale of highly-automated production would soon imply two or three major producers in each national market with 10 or 15 others as specialists in particular fashion lines or other corners of the market.[16]

His forecast proved correct. Courtaulds, under Kearton, had used Booton, its own 'in-house' machine supplier that was brought into the group as part of the acquisition of Contour in 1968. This machine builder was technologically far behind the Italian manufacturers of the day, and by investing in faster machines

---

[15] Part of the Tilling Group.
[16] See Chapman (2002) and Birley *European Entrepreneurship: Emerging Growth Companies* (EFER Cranfield 1989), p. 56. It was more probable that economies of scale were achieved through the economies gained by good organisation and effective advertising.

McMeekin was able to set his firm on the path to outstanding success and a marketing triumph.

McMeekin recognised the immense potential in the supermarket trade and concentrated on this market using a heavily advertised Pretty Polly brand, 'Galaxy by Pretty Polly'. Unlike Courtaulds, Pretty Polly was fully committed to the policy of low selling prices which was to become a feature of the supermarket trade. From 1976 Pretty Polly utilised a sales force of 100 to service the supermarkets:

> The outcome of this endeavour was to reverse the dominance of the supermarkets 'own label' within five years, which is against the overall trends in British retail trading. Spontaneous brand awareness of the 'big four' chain store brands declined significantly in this period. It was this gamble, more than any other single development at the company, that raised Pretty Polly to the No.1 position in the British industry.[17]

Courtaulds Hosiery, in contrast, abhorred price competition, preferring to develop its business whenever possible on a reputation for service and reliability. McMeekin recognised that tights had to cater for two markets, the day-to-day mass produced product ideally served by the supermarkets and the higher fashion higher price trade of the up-market high street stores and department stores. McMeekin chose the former and left the latter, which was a much smaller share of the market, to others. Courtaulds attacked the chain store 'own label' business and the high class department stores using the Kayser Bondor and the Aristoc labels. By the time Courtaulds and others tried to establish themselves in the low-price sector Pretty Polly had already become well established and Courtaulds never succeeded in displacing them.

The general trend for women to wear casual clothes (including jeans and trousers) on almost all occasions caused a massive reduction in tights production. Exports were stagnant and imports saw very little change, although they took a larger portion of the smaller market. However, in the first few years of the 1980s, Courtaulds suffered more than most and lost ground to its competitors. By 1985 Pretty Polly was well established as the market leader with Courtaulds Hosiery second and Adria third.[18]

Throughout the 1990s the market declined, production was on a downward trend, exports were flat and imports made no impact. The salient factor throughout most of the post-World War Two period was the rise and fall in demand for what was more a commodity than a high fashion product.

The distribution of women's hosiery is unique among the products of the

---

[17] See Chapman (2002), Birley, p. 64.
[18] Refer to Table 4.1.

hosiery and knitwear industry, because the tendency to treat the product as a simple commodity worked in favour of the grocery outlets that took the biggest share of this market at 34%,[19] which compared favourably with the 26% share held by the variety stores.

Knitwear manufacturing in decline

Table 7.4 *Men's, women's and children's knitwear excluding dresses – million pieces*

Year	1963	1964	1965	1966	1967	1968
Production	87.8	92.0	97.6	97.0	90.6	107.4
Year	1969	1970	1971	1972	1973	1974
Production	108.6	111.2	135.0	138.5	150.1	144.0

Source: Board of Trade Business Monitor Series

The knitwear industry was comprised of two separate strands, fully-fashioned and cut and sewn. Knitwear manufacturing benefited from the trend towards informal clothing that decimated the formalwear industry. The highest production in this sector was attained around 1974, which coincided with the time of highest employment in the industry.

Courtaulds had entered the knitwear industry through a series of major acquisitions. These brought into the group several well-known brand names such as Bairnswear, Meridian, Ballito, Morley, Wolsey and Lyle & Scott. Most of these brands were sold to the public through the independent retailers. However Wolsey and Lyle & Scott, both predominantly menswear suppliers, survived successfully in the department store trade, and also, much later, under different ownership.

By the mid-1970s the fully-fashioned type garment was fast losing favour, and the cut and sewn technology, which offered a wider choice of styles and patterns, became more popular.

---

[19] Mintel Underwear retailing 2001.

Table 7.5 *Knitwear – million pieces*

Year	1975	1976	1977	1978	1979	1980	1981	1982	1983
Production	133.3	139.6	139.3	137.1	125.0	109.1	105.9	106.1	101.3
Exports	15.1	19.5	22.1	19.0	18.7	21.4	22.1	21.9	21.2
Imports	66.0	70.9	70.0	68.6	68.7	67.2	73.8	68.2	63.7
Apparent UK market	184.2	191.0	187.2	186.7	175.0	154.9	157.6	152.4	143.8

Year	1984	1985	1986	1987	1988	1989	1990	1991	1992
Production	99.5	94.0	93.5	96.5	89.1	80.3	57.7	54.6	52.2
Exports	22.7	24.7	25.0	26.8	24.2	20.3	22.1	27.3	33.4
Imports	64.4	58.2	78.6	81.8	83.9	88.9	83.2	98.6	116.3
Apparent UK market	141.2	127.5	147.1	151.5	148.8	148.9	118.8	125.9	135.1

Source: Knitstats
Note: Categories unchanged from Table 7.4.

Despite Courtaulds' long-term ambition to become the top knitwear M&S supplier the company had made slow progress towards this. Profitability was low, and the bulk of the business was in the hands of Nottingham Manufacturing Company (controlled by the entrepreneurial Djanogly family) with 52%. Courtaulds had 12.5% and Corah had slipped to only 5%.[20]

The knitwear sector seems to have been affected more than others by the world recession around 1990. In stringent times clothing sales seem to suffer quite quickly and this applies particularly to men's clothing. Imports remained steady for many years, but from the mid-1980s they became a progressive threat to UK production.

Table 7.6 *Knitwear – sweaters, jumpers, pullovers, cardigans turtle, polo, and roll neck styles – million pieces*

Year	1993	1994	1995	1996	1997	1998	1999	2000
Production	82.4	94.0	93.9	83.6	80.1	68.7	61.9	58.5
Exports	32.6	40.3	40.7	42.4	44.7	45.0	40.3	38.0
Imports	137.7	142.5	135.8	161.5	167.7	171.6	184.6	200.4
Apparent UK market	187.5	196.2	189.0	202.7	203.1	195.3	206.2	220.9

Source: Knitstats

---

[20] See Table 4.3.

CHANGING MARKETS

Meridian produced 'long johns' as this newspaper advert shows, as did Morley and Wolsey.

Despite the trend towards more casual dressing in the workplace, knitwear became a small segment of the women's market as casual tops became more popular. By value, in 2000 knitwear sales were only 2.8% of the total of the market, with tops at 22.6% and casual jackets 9.3%.[21]

Unfortunately, the figures in Table 7.5 do not run seamlessly into Table 7.6 due to a different categorisation of styles. However, the indications are that the biggest factor affecting production was a rise in imports, rather than the reduction in the size of the market. The way that the export sales held up in the 1990s was due in part to the high regard with which high class knitwear,

---

[21] Mintel Womenswear Mainstream Marketing 2000.

particularly Scottish knitwear, was held in the export markets. However, by the turn of the century, Courtaulds' knitwear manufacturing capacity in the UK was minimal.

Knitted underwear manufacturing in decline

Table 7.7 *Knitted underwear – million pieces*

Year	1964	1965	1966	1967	1968	1969
Production	213.4	218.3	205.6	198.0	218.0	216.9

Source: Board of Trade Business Monitor Series
Note: The statistics for this sector of the industry are less reliable than for other products but they do indicate a peak in production at an earlier stage than for other products.

Courtaulds' underwear manufacturing branches included some of the biggest in the industry. Foister, Clay & Ward and Prew-Smith were heavily committed to M&S, Meridian and Morley to wholesale, and Wolsey and Lyle & Scott to 'direct to retail' trading. The brand name Morley (heavy underwear) was in long term decline, but Wolsey X front and Lyle & Scott Y front were particularly well known in the privately owned retail outfitters as well as the larger department stores.

Table 7.8 *Knitted underwear – million pieces*

Year	1970	1971–4	1975	1976	1977
Production	209.1	N/A	197.9	195.4	196.1

Source: Board of Trade Business Monitor Series
Note: Statistics for exports and imports are not in a form compatible with production and it is therefore not possible to calculate a meaningful figure for the overall size of the market.

Knitted underwear can be disregarded as a high fashion product, and is likely to be bought to replace garments discarded as a matter of need, as can be the case with the lower price range of women's tights. The knitted underwear trade was highly price competitive and susceptible to import penetration. The need to produce colour-coordinated garments in technically advanced materials was not very important in the 1970s and style changes were introduced very gradually, with some garments, such as vests and pants, remaining fundamentally the same over many years.

Table 7.9 *Knitted underwear – T-shirts, vests etc. – million pieces*

Year	1978	1979	1980	1981	1982	1983	1984	1985
Production	N/A	180.6	169.5	157.6	155.6	150.1	146.1	105.1
Exports	N/A	33.8	38.0	44.8	44.7	43.4	44.5	46.2
Imports	N/A	115.5	126.1	155.3	156.0	159.2	185.4	177.6
Apparent UK market	N/A	262.3	257.6	268.1	266.9	265.9	287.0	236.5

Source: Knitstats

Note: Exports include the export of some previously imported goods.

Courtaulds, as a major player in the knitted underwear sector, had to respond to a price war in the high street, and in 1981 commenced a joint venture in Portugal, through Rowley group, to supply children's knitted underwear to Mothercare. This venture was undertaken with the full agreement of all the major chain stores, and this eventually led to the firm making cheaper goods available to the high street stores, although at this stage M&S, with its 'buy British' policy, did not avail itself of this facility.

Table 7.10 *Knitted underwear – million pieces*

Year	1986	1987	1988	1989	1990	1991	1992
Production	N/A	N/A	111.0	115.7	N/A	N/A	N/A
Exports	N/A	N/A	66.8	63.8	63.95	70.5	77.7
Imports	N/A	N/A	310.9	274.6	270.4	400.9	431.9
Apparent UK market	N/A	N/A	355.1	326.5	N/A	N/A	N/A

Source: Knitstats

Knitted underwear remained price sensitive and the need to produce colour-coordinated ranges in specialist materials put the UK industry in deeper trouble. Despite the scarcity of the statistics, it is clear that the impact of low-cost imports was devastating for the UK producers, although much of the import of finished garments was under the control of the major British manufacturing companies.

Table 7.11 *Knitted underwear shirts, vests, briefs slips etc. – million pieces*

Year	1993	1994	1995	1996	1997	1998	1999	2000
Production	177.8	203.5	171.5	170.0	159.2	133.2	114.6	92.1
Exports	100.2	118.2	127.2	135.2	108.6	106.9	100.5	N/A
Imports	466.5	451.5	531.5	572.4	576.7	600.2	664.3	N/A
Apparent UK market	544.1	536.8	575.8	607.2	627.3	626.5	678.4	N/A

Source: Knitstats

Note: Includes garments produced from knitted fabric in the garment industry. Figures from 1999 are provisional and liable to revision.

Eventually M&S was forced to take part in the price war in the high street, and Courtaulds set up manufacturing capacity in Sri Lanka largely dedicated to its needs. This ultimately led to the total loss of Courtaulds' UK knitted underwear production.

Figures for the distribution of knitted underwear are difficult to isolate, but figures for men's underwear and women's lingerie in total suggest that 34%–36% was sold through variety stores,[22] of which M&S was by far the biggest.

Sock manufacturing in decline

Table 7.12 *Socks – million pairs (excluding fine-gauge)*

Year	1963	1964	1965	1966	1967	1968
Production	160.2	164.9	171.4	180.8	153.5	162.2

Year	1969	1970	1971	1972	1973	1974
Production	173.4	179.1	188.2	182.0	203.1	205.2

Source: Board of Trade Business Monitor Series

Following the post-war shortage of merchandise, the industry made steady progress and production increased for several years beyond 1974/5 which was the high point of employment in the industry as a whole. This was in contrast to the much earlier slow down in the knitted underwear industry.

It is interesting to note that the sales arm of Wolsey,[23] a good quality

---

[22] Mintel Underwear retailing 2001.
[23] Wolsey had a distinct selling advantage at the 'top end' of the retail trade in the

specialist supplier, was able to carry on selling branded socks, using the trade names Wolsey and Cardinal and continued to do so after a management buyout, when the manufacturing side (by then called Courtaulds Socks) was concentrating on M&S and the major chain stores. Outside of Courtaulds, the Byford brand name was sold by Viyella International at around the same time whilst still a going concern, but the business was much smaller than in the heyday of the top quality retail outfitters.

Table 7.13 *Socks – million pairs (excluding fine-gauge)*

Year	1975	1976	1977	1978	1979	1980	1981	1982
Production	224.1	236.4	246.5	255.0	255.1	232.0	226.8	242.6
Exports	33.3	40.3	47.9	40.4	44.3	39.1	33.6	31.8
Imports	9.0	14.1	13.2	19.4	24.5	23.2	31.1	38.1
Apparent UK market	199.8	210.2	211.8	234.0	235.3	216.1	224.3	248.9

Year	1983	1984	1985	1986	1987	1988	1989	1990
Production	237.0	240.3	242.7	256.8	251.7	258.9	258.3	251.3
Exports	29.8	30.4	38.0	32.1	34.4	31.0	37.4	41.5
Imports	49.7	50.4	45.4	60.4	66.2	91.9	100.5	90.6
Apparent UK market	256.9	260.3	250.1	285.1	283.5	319.8	321.4	300.4

Year	1991	1992	1993	1994	1995	1996	1997	1998
Production	247.1	252.8	291.4	286.4	285.2	294.2	282.6	207.0
Exports	47.9	48.6	33.2	53.0	62.5	51.6	46.3	36.8
Imports	119.4	190.0	174.1	158.5	178.4	218.6	239.9	226.6
Apparent UK market	318.6	394.2	432.3	391.9	401.1	461.2	476.2	396.8

Year	1999	2000	2001	2002	2003			
Production	172.8	143.5	152.8	126.2	116.6			
Exports	34.7	29.5	34.1	113.2	47.5			
Imports	278.8	333.7	353.9	411.4	473.2			
Apparent UK market	416.9	447.7	472.6	424.4	542.3			

Source: Knitstats
Note: Figures for 2003 are provisional and liable to revision.

UK, and also in export markets, being possessors of the Royal Warrant.

The sock market was progressively attacked by imports. Imports were relatively low in the early 1980s and were largely absorbed by the increasing size of the market, but in the 1990s import penetration became a serious threat to UK production.

Courtaulds was slow getting into their target M&S business that was dominated by Coats Viyella (Simpson, Wright and Lowe) and Corah. It was not until 1988, with the acquisition of Corah Sock Division, that Courtaulds took a major share of the business, and by this time the industry had reached its peak.

Socks can be treated as a commodity, and are frequently bought by women for men. However, the grocery outlets had not cornered such a large share of this market as they had for women's hosiery. The variety stores had by 2000 around 31% of the market, with clothing chains 28% and grocers only 11%.[24]

---

[24] Mintel Underwear retailing 2000.

EIGHT

The Changing Supply Chain

THE HOSIERY AND KNITWEAR INDUSTRY supplied garments from geographically widespread factories through a diverse supply chain to thousands of retail stores throughout this country and to export markets. The early historical reasons for industrial location had long gone. It was no longer vital to locate the manufacturing units close to the sources of raw material[1] and it was unnecessary to locate production facilities near the end users, even if that had been possible, because modern transport facilities were available to move large quantities of raw materials to the factories and the finished goods rapidly to their destinations.

Government policy and labour shortages

Two factors that first affected the geography of the industry after World War Two were the shortage of labour in the established centres of the industry[2] and the government policy of encouraging, by the provision of grants, the move of industry to 'assisted areas' in the mainland and Northern Ireland.

It is interesting to compare the experiences of competitors Corah and Courtaulds, two firms that were affected in quite different ways by the post-war business environment. Corah, later a competitor of Courtaulds and a long-established Leicester based M&S supplier, was hit particularly hard by the shortage of workers in Leicester after the war. Small businesses had fewer problems than the larger firms as they could expand using a single floor in a disused factory or perhaps an old chapel, workshop or garage. The larger firm would probably need purpose-built property. For this it would need a licence to expand and under the government's 'Distribution of Industry' policy this might not have been sanctioned near existing premises or even in the same town. Some

---

[1] A detailed explanation for the early location of the industry in the Midlands is given in Wells (1972), Chapter 3.
[2] Even if labour had been available planning permission for new buildings was severely restricted.

businesses had to expand outside congested areas many miles from their main sites.

That problem was pressing for Corah in the late 1940s. In response to the enormous sales potential of this firm, a large and efficient branch was set up in Brigg in 1946, followed by factories at Oakham, Aberbargoed, Scunthorpe, Rochdale, Sutton-in-Ashfield, Birmingham, Barnsley and Bolton-upon-Dearne. Corah also expanded by acquiring several existing firms of which the most significant were Fosse Knitwear (Leicester), Iway Fashions (Burbage), Reliance Hosiery (Halifax) and the former Byford factory at Immingham.

Corah, with its multi-product tradition of manufacturing, maintained its central organisation in Leicester, including its design, sales and technical departments. Wages were high in Leicester so the knitting, dyeing and finishing departments, which required low levels of labour relative to a large floor space, were retained at Leicester. Despite some of the outlying factories employing several hundred people, they were actually treated as satellite units, receiving cut work from Leicester for making-up and returning it to the central warehouse for packing and despatch, but the acquisitions which came later were smaller and autonomous to a much greater extent.

The Geography of Courtaulds' hosiery and knitwear factories in the UK

In contrast to Corah, Courtaulds was unable to achieve control of the geographical spread of its manufacturing units. Courtaulds had no traditional base in the industry. Courtaulds' drive for expansion in the 1960s was achieved by acquiring existing businesses, each with existing customers. The three early acquisitions, F,C&W, Meridian and Bairnswear were already multi-product and multi-location firms. The last two were in direct competition for labour within a short distance of each other in the north of Nottingham but this was never a problem Corah faced because it set up factories in carefully selected areas of low employment.

Indirectly, Courtaulds acquisition of the hosiery and knitwear firms was influenced by the government grants system. Over a six year period, during which the overall investment in new assets was £258 million, grants to Courtaulds had contributed £62 million. As Courtaulds was committed to rapid expansion across a wide field of activities, the £62 million government grant must have enhanced the size of the overall expansion activity. However, in general Courtaulds developed the capital-intensive parts of the business in designated development areas, but the hosiery and knitwear branches were, with a few exceptions, acquisitions in the trades' traditional areas. Therefore, while a large amount of government aid was received it was not as a result of 'ring fenced' expansion specifically in the hosiery and knitwear industry in which opportunities for the firm to benefit from investment and re-location grants were few. It is not possible to know if Courtaulds would have expanded in a similar way if Government aid had not been available for other activities. It did, however, free up capital which benefited the whole range of Courtaulds' activities.

Although some new hosiery and knitwear plants were set up, such as Rowley's highly efficient factory at Lincoln, establishing new factories was not an important feature of Courtaulds' activities in the industry as most expansion at new sites was put in hand by the acquired firms in their pre-takeover existence.

Other than in Northern Ireland,[3] the firm did not attract much in the way of government grants specifically for expansion in the hosiery and knitwear industry. In total contrast, in some other fields such as chemical engineering capital-intensive production plants were set up from scratch. However, within the wider textiles sector there were takeovers of existing firms, but new starts were enormously significant. This applied particularly to the jersey knitting sector[4] (which was separate from the traditional hosiery and knitwear industry and does not form part of this study), in which Courtaulds was definitely helped to achieve its overall expansion plans by taking advantage of government incentives.

By 1973, Courtaulds' conglomerate operated at some 400 sites in the UK of which about 250 were in assisted areas. Courtaulds' total UK employment across the whole conglomerate was 122,000, of which 80,000 was in assisted areas.[5] The firm's employment within the hosiery and knitwear industry at that time was around 20,000. Within this industry some Courtaulds' regional establishments were in what was described as 'Special Areas'.

---

[3] In Northern Ireland the government incentives were the greatest and at one time Courtaulds employment there reached 10,000 which was more than that of Harland & Wolff, until then the largest employer. Knight in F. Cairncross, *Changing perceptions of Economic Policy* (Metheun 1981), p.121.

[4] Exquisite Knitwear was set up after the acquisition of a small business in Kings Road, Chelsea and around the years 1968–1970 new branches were set up in France, USA, Canada, Jersey, Northern Ireland (2) and the North of England (2).

[5] Cairncross, pp. 121–22.

Table 8.1 *Courtaulds hosiery and knitwear factories in 'Special Areas'*

Area	Establishment
Scotland	Lyle & Scott and Queen of Scots Knitwear at Hawick, Jedburgh and Kelso
Welsh Development and Special Development Area	Kayser Bondor at Dowlais
Northern Ireland	Courtaulds Hosiery at Carrickfergus
Notts-Derby Intermediate Area	Aristoc and Morley at Kirkby-in-Ashfield and Heanor
North Midlands Derelict Land Clearance Area	Brettle, Aristoc, Meridian and Wolsey at Belper, Bolsover, Calverton and Ilkeston

Note: Most of these were long-established sites and were in existence before these firms were acquired by Courtaulds. The exception was the short-lived Carrickfergus fine-gauge hosiery factory. Courtaulds set up plants in Northern Ireland and South Wales for the production of fine-gauge hosiery and benefited from the grants that were available.

Courtaulds did not influence the geographic spread

When existing units needed a boost to their capacity Courtaulds generally achieved this by acquiring already-established small enterprises close to existing factories. Courtaulds' early acquisitions were mainly made with their ability to use the firm's yarn as a main consideration. Most of the larger sites were acquired as going concerns during the successful trading period for the industry from the early 1960s that peaked around 1974–1975, and the geographical implications were of little importance. It was only the very small satellite factories that were acquired with location and the availability of labour as a main concern. The exception to this was the rapid expansion of the seamless stockings industry in Northern Ireland, which was set up as a new enterprise near the site of the Celon processing site. This expansion was a deliberate attempt by Courtaulds to create an outlet for Celon from the Carrickfergus processing site. However, this short-lived venture in Northern Ireland proved to be ill-judged and contributed to overcapacity in the market, and was closed within a few years.[6] There was no real geographical significance to putting the stockings factory close to the yarn processing mill because yarn is an easily transported product; it was simply a fact that there was surplus land, adequate labour for recruitment, and government grants[7] were available to attract employment to that area. In evidence to the

---

[6] Courtaulds failed to anticipate the effect of over-capacity in the fine-gauge hosiery industry which resulted in falling prices.

[7] Investment grants were exceptionally high in Northern Ireland.

Parliamentary Expenditure Committee (Trade and Industry sub-Committee), Arthur Knight explained:

> ... that once you are established on a particular site there are tremendous advantages in going on expanding on that site. Certainly, once you are on a site like Carrickfergus in Northern Ireland there is every incentive in taking advantage of the built-in facilities [such as surplus land and available labour] which you have got.[8]

The industry manages decline

As the industry went into decline, within multi-site businesses the closure procedure generally followed a common pattern with small units being closed first. However should there be a choice the furthest factory from the main site would generally be closed first and in this manner Courtaulds, in line with much of the industry, shrank back to the traditional manufacturing areas.

Small firms, multi-location firms and conglomerates

Small firms, typically those that were family owned, tended to operate on a single site, producing a single product. They were therefore most vulnerable to the danger of a downturn in trade which was always a possibility in a fashion led industry. Multi-product firms were somewhat cushioned from that threat. In the labour intensive clothing industry there was little or no merit in operating as a single product or single site firm, and economies of scale were mainly illusory, but the large multi-location firm was better placed and could react to events in a more flexible way. This was particularly important when there was a downturn in trade or a change in fashion. If a peripheral site could be closed it was sometimes possible to limit the damage by transferring work to other sites allowing them to remain viable. Sometimes it was possible to retrain and redeploy workers, and Courtaulds took this course of action on several occasions and with its large number of sites, many of which were small in relation to the overall size of the firm, it was able to benefit from this flexibility. The UK manufacturing divisions of conglomerates, such as Courtaulds and Coats Viyella, by reason of their fragmented manufacturing sites, were sheltered (in the short term) from the risk of total closure resulting from a change in fashion or a downturn in trade that might cause the loss of a few factories.

In contrast Corah's system did not provide security or the same level of safety. Corah's sites were dedicated almost exclusively to M&S and the closure of any one of these could have a seriously damaging effect on the whole firm.

---

[8] Parliamentary Expenditure sub-committee, paragraph 1668. 28 February 1973.

As has already been noted, Corah maintained the central Leicester site as an administrative headquarters and a centre for knitting, cutting and dyeing and finishing. This meant that even their largest factories were actually satellite units dependant on the main site at Leicester, and when they were closed the central staff levels could be reduced, but it was almost impossible to vacate large and expensive 'central' premises in Leicester and reduce costs in proportion to the size of the closure. For Corah, unlike Courtaulds and Coats Viyella, an orderly retreat was not therefore possible.

Employment in the regions

Table 8.2 *Employment in the industry ('000s)*

	North	Yorkshire Humberside	East Midlands	East Anglia	South East	South West	West Midlands	North West	Wales	Scotland	Northern Ireland
1970	3.2	4.1	78.4		8.7		3.1	10.1	2.9	18.6	5.9
1977	2.7	6.0	70.0	0.1	4.0	0.4	2.7	6.0	1.4	15.3	4.2
1987	2.4	4.5	52.6	0.2	1.9	0.5	2.5	3.7	1.0	13.0	2.6
1993	0.9	1.0	31.3		0.7		1.0	2.0	0.2	8.6	1.9

Source: Business Monitor series. Report on the census of production.

Statistics showing the shrinking back to the traditional centres of the industry are sparse and of doubtful reliability, but Table 8.2 shows that in the period from 1970 to 1993 employment in the industry's main locations, the East Midlands and Scotland, continued to dominate. The East Midlands and Scotland fell away by 60% and 54% respectively, but other areas were affected even more seriously. Employment in the clothing industry in Lincolnshire was dominated almost exclusively by Corah and to a much smaller extent by Courtaulds (Rowley), and many workers found it difficult to find alternative work after the closure of their factories in the area.[9] Less hardship was caused in the South East as there was a shortage of workers in more high-technology industries, and throughout the period the peripheral areas suffered from a withdrawal to the two main areas: With UK factories having little or no competitive advantage over the low-cost foreign producers the only hope for employment was that the manufacturers could slow the decline.

---

[9] Ironically the Rowley factory was hit hard by the opening of Courtaulds' own factory in Portugal that could produce more cheaply.

Liberalisation of world trade and globalisation

Having survived the Napoleonic wars, two world wars and several depressions, the greatest set-back and the cause of the UK industry's almost terminal decline was the liberalisation and globalisation of world trade that hit the hosiery and knitwear industry particularly hard from the mid-1970s, an issue that is absolutely salient to any study of decline in the industry.

The Multi-Fibre Arrangement

Before the First World War there had been increasing trade and capital flow across the world but between the wars there was a move towards protectionist policies, however after World War Two, in contrast to the 1930s, the industry was never able to gain strong government support in the form of import barriers or tariffs that its lobbyists demanded. In common with other sectors of the clothing industry the trade suffered increasing competition from suppliers in low labour-cost countries. International trade liberalisation was somewhat controlled from the 1950s under the General Agreement on Tariffs and Trade (GATT). In 1959 the problem of disruptive imports from low-cost countries was raised by the USA and in 1961 a 'Short Term Arrangement' was introduced. A 'Long Term Agreement' was reached in 1962 and after a series of revisions was extended until 1974 when it was superseded by the Multi-Fibre Arrangement (MFA).[10] The industry peaked, in terms of employment, around that time, but from then was in decline.

The UK industry was therefore squeezed between the Far East low-cost suppliers and the warring multiple stores on the UK high street. With the increase in global trading, the industry suffered intense price competition from low-cost countries, initially Hong Kong, Taiwan and Korea, producers that had wiped out the UK knitted glove industry that was already suffering competition from leather and woven fabric gloves which were more fashionable.[11]

Courtaulds' executives seemed aloof from the problem at that time, perhaps deluded that the firm could hold back the tide of imports and be immune to the consequences of the MFA. They therefore did not exploit the firm's size and status to lead the lobby against increasing imports. That would have been somewhat insincere because Courtaulds was already importing merchandise to supplement its own production at that time.

The purpose of the MFA was said to be to encourage the progressive

---

[10] Official reports are available, notably, Silberston, (HMSO) Department of Trade and Industry (1984 and 1989).

[11] Information from John Harrison, Director of the Knitting Industries Federation 9 July 1999.

liberalisation of trade while at the same time, by restricting the annually increasing rate of imports, protecting the existing markets and individual products from disruptive surges in imports. Under the Uruguay round of GATT negotiations which were concluded in 1991, it was finally agreed that the MFA would be phased out by 2005.

It was therefore against a gradual but relentless lowering of protection against low-cost import penetration that the hosiery and knitwear industry operated from the Second World War and was heading for almost terminal decline from the mid-1970s.

Low-cost competition

By the end of the twentieth century the industry had become truly global and the UK had become an inhospitable home base for the manufacture of hosiery and knitwear. The industry was dependent on foreign machinery, technological expertise and supplies of raw materials, for all of which it was necessary to compete on a world market, but by far the most telling cost was labour.

Even when the industry was at its peak in the mid-1970s, it was clear that there was a threat from the emerging nations in the form of low-cost imports. Intense competitive price pressure on the high street stores was passed back to their suppliers who were then forced to seek low-cost labour sites in a bid to remain competitive as an alternative to extinction. Porter notes:

> No nation can be competitive in (and a net exporter of) everything. A nation's pool of human and other resources is necessarily limited. The ideal is that these resources be deployed in the most productive uses possible. The export success of those industries with a competitive advantage will push up the costs of labor, inputs, and capital in the nation, making other industries uncompetitive. In Germany, Sweden and Switzerland, for example, this process has led to a contraction of the apparel industry to those firms in specialized segments that can support very high wages.[12]

Fröbel, Heinrichs and Kreye[13] identified three prerequisites as decisive in the increasing transfer of manufacturing to the low-cost areas; first the inexhaustible supply of cheap and renewable labour, second, the division and sub-division of low skilled tasks into short and quickly learned elements, and third, the development of rapid forms of transport and communication. The first two were

---

[12] Porter, p. 7. Experience later showed that UK retailers at the 'top end' of the market also sourced garments from low-cost countries.

[13] Fröbel, Heinrichs and Kreye, *The new international division of Labour* (CUP 1980).

historically available and communications and transport were developing rapidly.

Since the 1970s, there has been a significant development in the transport and communications industries. Air freight, containerisation, and the ability to move bulk cargoes over long distances has developed rapidly and there has been significant improvement in communications, first of all the telex and then fax, followed by e-mail and video links.

De-skilling for the specific purpose of transferring jobs abroad has not been necessary. In the clothing industries the number of low-skilled or quickly learned jobs far out-numbers those for skilled workers. In these low-skilled jobs the ability to divide labour into small subdivisions made the industry vulnerable to attack from 'third world' countries. The industry has a long history of the division of labour from complex assemblies into small elements. With the introduction of the factory system in the 1850s there was a flood of workers from the land and the rural economies into the industry. As an aid to rapid training and the effective use of the rudimentary machines then available, the tasks were broken down into small elements that were easily learned. As technology developed this system continued unabated.[14]

Taken together, these factors have created a world market for labour in which the employees in the UK hosiery and knitwear firms have become unable to compete, and when considering the site for a new factory, decisions are now made on a global basis. It should not be overlooked that the developing countries are also competing with each other and are therefore unable to demand significantly higher wages for their workers. It is therefore arguable that the developing countries have a vested interest in maintaining low wages.

Comparative costs for the hosiery and knitwear industry are sparse[15] but in 1988, for the related spinning and woven fabric industry, wages in the Western World far exceeded those of the countries that eventually became important suppliers after Japan, Hong Kong and others had ceased to be competitive.[16]

---

[14] Even in the teamwork production lines described in Chapter 6 (Teamwork and quick response) the elements of work were very small.

[15] Dr J. B. Smith in a personal communication informed the writer that on a visit to Hong Kong in 1989 he was told that overlockers, the main making up operatives, were paid approximately £150 per week in Leicester, £75 per week in Hong Kong, and £2 per week in The People's Republic of China.

[16] Porter, p. 3. Porter suggests that Japan, which has suffered labour shortages, has succeeded internationally in many industries by automating away much of the labour content. However, this did not apply to the hosiery and knitwear industry in which automation equipment would not have been exclusively supplied to or retained by the Japanese industry.

Table 8.3 *Woven fabric costs*

	Average cost per operator hour (USD)	Ratio to US cost (%)	Days per operator year	Mill operating days per year
USA	9.42	100	260	305
UK	8.43	90	229	248
PR of China	0.27	3	306	306
Indonesia	0.22	2	290	348
Pakistan	0.40	4	287	333
Sri Lanka	0.30	3	292	343
Thailand	0.66	7	290	353

Source: Trela and Whalley (1989)
Note: An example of hosiery and knitwear costs is not available.

After various adjustments the average supply prices of quota restricted textiles and clothing for five of the above countries for 1984/1985 were around 50% of the USA prices.

Table 8.4 *Textile and Clothing supply prices*

	Adjusted for differences in labour productivity and product quality (USD)
USA	1.00
Indonesia	0.52
Pakistan	0.55
Thailand	0.60

Source: Trela and Whalley (1989)

With competitive advantage removed there was no way to compete.[17] Rapid transport and information technologies were available to all, including the 'emerging economies'.

---

[17] Porter commented that '... Britain lacks national competitive advantage in ... most areas of textiles/apparel...' Porter (2000), p. 494.

The industry's response

The industry was slow to grasp the benefits of off-shore production and failed, at an early stage, to use its UK design, quality, capital and expertise in the development of cheaper manufacturing plants abroad. From the 1970s, both Courtaulds and Coats Viyella invested in low-cost manufacturing countries. This enabled them to supplement their own UK production with lower priced goods whilst relieving the chain stores of the organisational problems and risk associated with importing on their own account.[18] Some developments were joint ventures with other firms, either local or trans-national, some were in collaboration with the government concerned. The quota restrictions against competing nations such as Hong Kong led manufacturers in those places to move their supplier base into very low-wage countries such as Bangladesh, situated outside of the quota areas. It was this era of intense price competition that presaged the moves offshore and was the reason for the Marks & Spencer policy decisions of the late 1990s, which encouraged their suppliers to produce abroad. This was a late and crisis driven response to falling profits and intense pressure from other chain stores.

Figure 8.1

UK BRAND OPERATOR DIRECT TO RETAIL

Figure 8.2

UK BASED MULTINATIONAL CONTRACT SUPPLIER

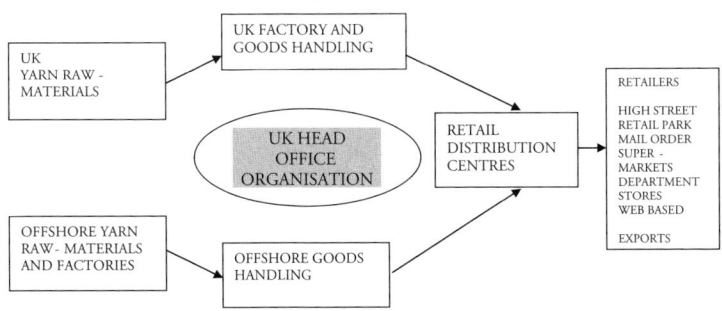

---

[18] Information from John Harrison, Secretary of the Knitting Industries Federation, 9 July 1999.

Supply chains

Three distinct methods of trading used by the UK clothing industry were discussed in the previous chapter: the old established traditional distribution through wholesalers; the UK brand operator that bypassed the wholesale trade and the most recent system, the UK based multinational contract supplier. These changes to the structure of the industry have developed gradually with no clearly distinct cut-off point when one replaced the other; indeed, elements of the much earlier forms of trading still existed at the end of the twentieth century.

Traditional supply chain

Using the traditional supply chain, from the clothing manufacturers to the retail trade via the wholesale trade, was essential to Courtaulds in the early 1960s. At that time the private retailers were still selling a considerable quantity of merchandise and almost every small town and large village seemed to support a clothing shop of some sort and in the larger towns and cities they still existed in considerable numbers. In the late 1960s the multiple traders had not decimated the small shops in the way that was seen in later decades. Therefore it was essential to Kearton's plan to secure every possible outlet for the firm's merchandise, including the wholesaling route, even if this had no long term future.

Courtaulds owned many of the well known wholesalers including Cook & Watts, Bradbury Greatorex, and Wilkinson, Riddell & Larkins Limited. These operated in major towns and cities from over forty sites, and several were operating in close competition. Although these wholesale traders had tried for many years to boycott manufacturers that dealt with the chain stores, by the mid to late 1960s they clearly recognised their own vulnerable position and were also aware that they could no longer offer orders that would fill the available manufacturing capacity.

The inability of the troubled wholesalers to give out economic sized orders to the manufacturers was a serious issue by the late 1960s. Many orders the wholesalers were getting from their customers were smaller than those accepted by the 'direct to retail' brand manufacturers who were getting higher prices for their own merchandise. It was believed with justification by the manufacturers that accepting and processing such small orders from the wholesalers was doing much of their work for them. Mike Deacon, warehouse manager at Rowley described the situation at that time:

> When I first went to Rowleys we were doing wholesale and we used to have loads of stock and men packing it into little parcels and sending

it through the post. No wonder it [Rowley's wholesale business] didn't survive. They were living in the past; we had to move with the times. Sometimes the number of samples of a style sent to the wholesaler at the beginning of the season exceeded the total year's sales of that item.

The UK brand operator 'direct to retail'

When Courtaulds entered the clothing industry there were many manufacturers that had freed themselves from the constraints of the wholesale system by dealing directly with the retailers, particularly the department stores and the thousands of independent retailers and outfitters still to be found in the towns and cities of the UK. Around this time heavy brand advertising, which inferred a guarantee of quality, reduced the sales expertise and product knowledge required by the wholesalers and retailers. However, the manufacturers' main incentive to bypass the wholesale trade was the tendency for wholesalers to order in small quantities, thereby passing the responsibility for stockholding back to the manufacturers, but by far the most serious threat to the 'brand' came from the private labels of the chain stores.[19]

The UK based multinational contract supplier

In response to the need for lower prices, the contract suppliers developed sales and design teams that utilised a range of manufacturing units both in the UK and overseas.

The development of the logistics of moving the vast range of goods to the retailers did not follow an orderly pattern. The handling systems for the multiples went through a series of changes. During the 1970s it was common for the manufacturers to pack their products, label and despatch them to the individual chain store branches. Later as the stores set up their own distribution centres it was quite usual for the manufacturers to continue to pick, pack and label merchandise but this was mainly distributed by transport firms contracted to the chain stores, with only export and mail order goods being sent in bulk. When eventually hanging garments on rails for transport became a favoured method it was still common for these to be bar coded by the manufacturer for each individual store.

In the 1970s the large multi-product manufacturers had a real advantage over the smaller suppliers because they could pack a mixture of goods together and minimise the handling involved. In the 1980s there was a move by the stores to standardise distribution, and road transport was organised on a massive scale

---

[19] Wells (1936), pp. 217–223.

by specialist carriers such as Tibbett & Britten, Exel Logistics and Christian Salveson. This was the era of the large retail distribution centres owned by the stores.

By the end of the century the offshore supply line was gaining rapidly at the expense of the UK supply line although the central distribution warehouse systems, from which final despatch to the retail stores took place, remained intact. Most large manufacturers, including most of the M&S suppliers, largely abandoned their UK manufacturing sites, but the biggest, including Coats Viyella and Courtaulds, still forwarded imported goods alongside locally processed merchandise through their own warehouses. Tesco, the leading grocer, was very well organised and could receive bulk clothing supplies from the factories and distribute the necessary quantities to their stores using their own systems, storage and handling equipment. For goods that were purchased from the low-cost areas a new breed of firms' sub-contractors, the offshore goods handlers, came into play and these checked garments, rectified minor faults, pressed them when necessary and hung them on hangers ready for the distribution centres to forward to the stores.

Cluster groupings

The hosiery and knitwear industry differs from general apparel manufacturing because all operations including the knitting of fabric, making-up and packaging are normally carried out by the manufacturers.[20] In Figure 8.2 the industry is seen to be placed between the spinning industry and the warehousing and distribution organisations. These distributors may, in the case of the larger firms, be owned either by the manufacturer or be part of the chain store's dedicated distribution network. However, in either case they will almost certainly handle a range of products from the clothing industries and possibly even non-clothing items.[21]

---

[20] In contrast, dressmakers and tailors purchase fabric from weavers or their agents. However, tailoring firms that created a vertical structure downstream forming a retail chain were a feature of that industry, examples were Montague Burton, Hepworths, Fifty Shilling Tailors, Alexandre and Weaver to Wearer. Honeyman (2000), pp. 53–72.

[21] For example: tailored garments, furnishings, automotive products and medical supplies.

THE CHANGING SUPPLY CHAIN

Figure 8.3

UK CLUSTER CHART

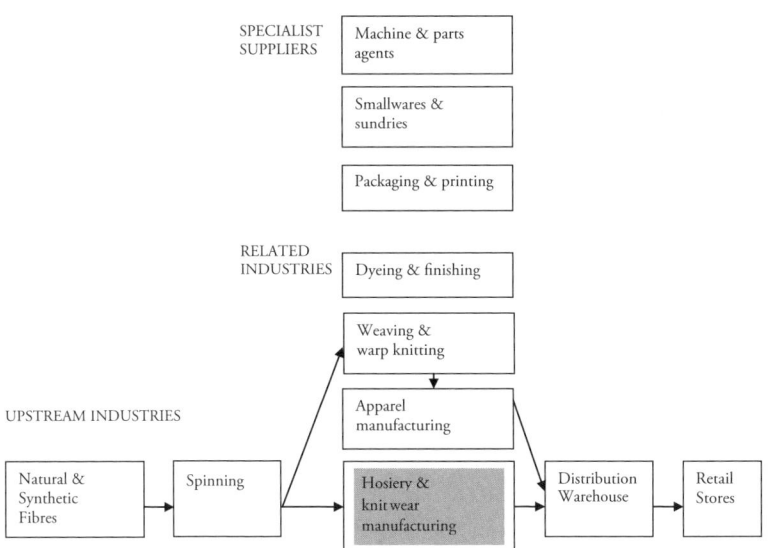

Knitting machine industry

The knitting machine building firms are mainly based in Switzerland, Germany, Italy, Japan, America and the Czech Republic and research and development for this machinery is carried out by the machine builders' own staff. Sewing machines are also imported, particularly from Japan. Courtaulds Textile Research Unit at Spondon, Derbyshire did make a ground-breaking contribution to knitting technology with the invention of the 'presser foot' attachment. This improved the ability of flat machines to produce complicated patterns. The real breakthrough was the ability to produce shaped panels, a feature which had previously been exclusive to the fully-fashioned machine, but even Courtaulds with its large resources did not have the ability to develop this exclusively for its own factories and the patent was licensed to Dubied, the Swiss machine builder and the machines were distributed worldwide.

Leicester had long been a centre of machine building for the trade and famous firms such as Wildt Mellor Bromley employed thousands of workers producing high quality machines after the Second World War. At the end of the twentieth century there were only four small hosiery and knitwear machine building firms still operating in the UK, Camber International, Monk Cotton, Bentley Group and Monarch that erected machines from American made parts and these few firms faced a very uncertain future and what limited future could be foreseen was likely to be outside the UK hosiery and knitwear industry.[22]

Not only is the ability to launch new machines onto the market outside the control of the knitting industry,[23] the same applies to knitting yarn, the basic material from which the merchandise is made. Courtaulds was heavily committed to research into fibres and spinning in collaboration with its garment factories, but what remained of Courtaulds' supply chain was broken in 1990 when Courtaulds Textiles plc was demerged from Courtaulds plc, the fibre production and spinning side of the company. With the closure of the firm's spinning mills any sense of formal collaboration *up-stream* was finally lost.

Clear advantage on the demand side

It is important to differentiate between corporate survival and survival of the industry. What remains therefore is a small UK manufacturing industry with no technical or capital advantage over its foreign competitors and a serious labour-cost disadvantage. From a corporate point of view, the loss of the UK manufacturing industry does not automatically mean a total loss of control to foreign manufacturers. The UK firms may have lost their competitive advantages in manufacturing, but clear advantages remain on the demand side, particularly their closeness to the customer, and their understanding of the design requirements of the UK market and distribution systems of the UK multiple retailers. These are intellectual advantages that it has proved almost impossible for foreign competitors to replicate. As Porter comments,

> … pressures from buyers to improve products are most acutely felt in the home market, where proximity and cultural similarity make for clearer communications. The importance of the home market goes beyond greater attention, however. Firms are better able to perceive, understand, and act on buyer needs in their home market and tend to be more confident in doing so. Understanding needs requires access to buyers, open communication between them and a firm's top technical and managerial personnel, and an intuitive grasp of buyers' circumstances. This is hard enough with home buyers. It is extremely difficult to achieve, in practice, with foreign buyers because of distance from headquarters and because the firm is not truly an insider with full acceptance and access.[24]

---

[22] Textile History 30 (2), 1999, pp. 207–233.
[23] *Knitting International* February 1982 p. 84.
[24] For a comprehensive discussion of demand conditions see Porter (2000), pp. 86–87.

Porter's argument has a serious weakness however. He failed to take into account the full impact of globalisation as it became manifest in this industry. As things evolved various functions such as production, design and distribution and sales were able to function in isolation. It became perfectly feasible for a firm to employ sales and design staff of any nationality and culture and situate them far from the manufacturing units but close to the customer. This was particularly practical as English, the language of commerce, films, popular music and the web became the worldwide means of communication.

Having lost the bulk of their manufacturing capacity (which continued to decline), trading possibilities still remained for those firms with dedicated or partly owned foreign manufacturing subsidiaries, including Courtaulds. They were particularly well placed to control the stages of the supply chain such as distribution and design, and the logistics of supply. They were also able to understand the needs and requirements of the sophisticated technical specifications imposed by firms such as M&S in a way that was not easily open to foreign firms.

Dangers remained on the horizon for the major firms such as Courtaulds, Coats Viyella and Dewhirst. As these firms spread their manufacturing abroad their expertise could be easily acquired by their competitors simply by employing staff previously employed by them. It must not be overlooked that firms such as Sara Lee Courtaulds were able several years later to form a bridge between the demanding and critical UK customers and the off-shore factories and integrate them into the supply chain in the way that the retail firms demanded, not only regarding quality and price but also adhering to their complex organisational and logistical systems.

Upstream industries

The globalisation of trade and the decline of the industry (and other associated garment trades) weakened the natural and synthetic fibres and the spinning industry in the UK. With two distinct supply chains available to the UK contract clothing suppliers, (refer back to Figure 8.1) a growing proportion of the larger orders were processed by way of the offshore route and correspondingly larger amounts of yarn and other supplies were also bought in offshore low-cost countries. By the end of the twentieth century the amount of yarn manufactured in the UK was small – China having become an almost overwhelming force in the industry as it supplied its massive domestic garment industries. However the remaining suppliers in the UK and other EEC countries became very responsive to the needs of the garment industry and had no choice but to supply small orders that they might previously have considered uneconomic, although some extra cost was involved.[25]

---

[25] Information supplied by Ian Wykes, purchasing manager, Courtaulds Sock

Specialist suppliers

The UK cluster of knitting machine builders that once enjoyed a worldwide reputation for their high quality products was almost non-existent by the 1990s.[26] This was due much more to the lack of technical advancement than to trading conditions[27] but the knitting industry was hardly affected because those few knitting firms that were still able to buy new or good second-hand machines were served by well organised agents and representatives in the UK. Overseas knitting firms were able to purchase new machinery from, amongst other places, Japan, Italy and the United States. At the same time the Far East producers were also able to purchase modern second-hand machinery at advantageous prices from areas such as the UK, where the trade was in decline.

The garment industries consume large amounts of 'smallwares' such as zips, buttons, sewing thread, Velcro, tape and elastic, and the local distributors of these items were also badly affected by the downturn in trade. However they responded in a positive manner by sourcing their supplies mainly from the Far East in bulk lots and supplying smaller quantities to the remaining firms in the garment trades. In practice this had a positive effect because these firms became faster reacting and prices were, in many cases, lower in 2000 than in 1995.[28]

There remained a market for locally produced printed products, such as labels and packaging, but for the remaining small manufacturing firms the supply of special labels was usually negotiated by the end users such as the chain stores. However, large quantities of packaging materials such as polythene bags were being imported in bulk by specialist firms and sold-on in smaller lots to a variety of industries. The manufacturers that survived, in the downsized hosiery and knitwear industry, suffered little as a direct result of the problems encountered by their specialist suppliers who, by the year 2000, were generally accepting small and complex orders for raw materials that would have been shunned only a few years previously.

Dyeing and finishing

Traditionally most dyeing of fine-gauge hosiery has been done 'in-house' by the hosiery firms, a situation that remained unchanged, but the dyeing of socks had been replaced almost totally with the availability of 'pre-dyed' yarn and the same applied in knitwear production, most significantly following the introduction

---

Division 30 April 2003.

[26] Well known machine builders included Wildt, Mellor Bromley and Stibbe Monk and Kirkland.

[27] Chapman (2002), pp. 220–21.

[28] Information supplied by David Hill Proprietor of Brit Fashions 25 April 2003.

of the Neochrome process in which colour was introduced into acrylic yarn at the manufacturing stage. Therefore the contraction of the dyeing industry in those trades had more to do with improved technology than globalisation, government policy or the 'high street' war between the large retailers. In knitted underwear manufacturing the fabric dyeing processes had no economic future in the UK following the movement of knitting and making-up to areas of low-cost production.

High Street and multiple retail outlets cluster

The businesses that dominate the retail scene are the high street stores spread across the main towns of the UK. These are often situated close together, even in the same shopping mall. The intense price competition these have placed on each other and the remainder of the retail trade has triggered off the movement of manufacturing from the UK to low-cost countries. The supermarket chains such as Tesco and Asda have added new intensity to this competition but mainly concentrate their offering on the lower price sector of the industry.

Warehousing and distribution

So far, low-cost importing was not undertaken on a large scale by the chain stores. This remained in the domain of the former manufacturers. This had several distinct advantages for the retailers who were relieved of the responsibility for design and development, quality control, organisation and the vital area of finance, and complex organisation problems were avoided because many distribution warehouses were owned and controlled by the suppliers or specialist logistics firms.

Perspectives

Courtaulds remained a large supplier to the multiple retail stores and maintained a large design and warehousing presence in the UK. The firm was able to interpret and develop the customers' design ideas and take care of manufacturing and distribution to the stores, but with the increase in offshore processing the firm actually owned much less of the supply chain. However, in the warehousing and distribution stages it remained strong, particularly for the M&S business.

The supply chain was in a fluid and constant state of change but Kearton's policy, the concept of vertical trading – complete from yarn manufacturing to delivery of finished goods to the retailers – was well and truly dead. There was also an ever present danger that the chain stores might accept the risks involved and decide to deal directly and on a large scale with the Far East suppliers.

NINE

Courtaulds Textiles plc 1990–2000

Problems from the 1980s

COURTAULDS SUFFERED a run of low profits from 1979 and in consequence cash for reinvestment became severely restricted during the depressed trading conditions of the early 1980s.

By 1983 the main knitwear competitor, Nottingham Manufacturing Company, had built up a massive lead and invested heavily in new machinery and design services.[1]

Following a decade of low investment in hosiery and knitwear machinery, it became necessary to re-invest heavily during the late 1980s and early 1990s in order to bring the plant and equipment up to the standards of the competition. Heavy investment had taken place much earlier under Kearton, but that was in a period when the industry was expanding. In contrast this new investment took place when the long term decline in the fortunes of the industry was already an established fact. Towards the end of the 1980s, advancing technology had made shaped knitwear panel manufacturing a viable reality within the cut and sewn sector.[2] The machines cost £80,000 each, plus the additional cost of Computer Aided Design technology (CAD), and this investment was beyond any but the most well financed and confident firms such as Courtaulds.

Large investments were also made in the fine-gauge tights business and a major reorganisation of the firm's manufacturing capacity was completed in 1993. This was one of the largest projects undertaken by Courtaulds Textiles plc around that time and brought the factory buildings and plant up to the most efficient levels, probably surpassing Pretty Polly, then a market leader. Elsewhere in the group investment fell away, particularly in the non-M&S manufacturing units.

---

[1] Refer to Chapter 4.
[2] Refer to 'Technology' Shaped Garment Panels in Chapter 4.

When making a case for new capital investment, non-M&S businesses had little influence with the board and it became almost impossible for them to obtain capital for new equipment and some units did not even apply, even though almost new machinery was on the market at knock down prices.[3]

The conglomerate had become unwieldy by 1985 and Hogg, in a major restructuring, separated the firm into more manageable sections under Alan Nightingale. In May 1987 Martin Taylor was put in charge, still under Nightingale and following Nightingale's retirement in 1988 Taylor became head of the Textiles group which included within its garment section the hosiery and knitwear sector.

Martin Taylor was a strong advocate of international expansion and movement towards a more up-market business and he recognised the danger in remaining committed to the mid-market UK high street chains, and in particular M&S, with its established policy of selling large quantities of UK produced clothing. With a move into unfamiliar territory he was responsible in 1988[4] for the purchase of a stretch fabrics firm in the USA and in 1989 of a high class fashion firm in France.[5]

Those two businesses were unconnected to the hosiery and knitwear industry. The exception had been the opportunistic acquisition in 1988 of the Corah Sock Division, an important part of the M&S supply chain, which was threatened by the failure of its parent company. Although acquiring any clothing business in the UK or Western Europe might seem perverse and risky and contrary to the firm's own policy, the sock division was to prove highly successful for a decade. Despite having at its disposal considerable research and evidence of the decline of the UK industry, the firm pressed ahead. This was justified on the grounds that it would create for Courtaulds a leading position in the M&S supply chain for socks and was welcomed by the still very successful M&S as a means of safeguarding their supplies. In practice it did operate successfully in that role, and Courtaulds picked up a large socks order book in the process. The UK investment in Corah was impressive by hosiery and knitwear standards[6] but it is important to recognise the relatively small scale nature of the hosiery and knitwear business when compared to Fabrics and Garments. Just prior to the breakup of the conglomerate the overall contribution to Courtaulds' turnover by this industry has been estimated at around 4–5% in 1989, and after demerger still only around 11%. The hosiery and knitwear production still remained an essential ingredient of Courtaulds' merchandise-offering to M&S and the major chain stores, but Kearton's small scale businesses had disappeared and the concept of vertical trading had collapsed. Martin Taylor commented:

---

[3] Information from J. D. Floyd, 19 December 2001.
[4] Liberty.
[5] Georges Rech.
[6] The acquisition of Corah cost £7.1 million.

The policy of vertical integration, long abandoned by my own company, always appeals to people in difficult times when customers are hard to come by and unreasonable – wouldn't it be nice if you simply owned your own customers?[7]

The prospects for the industry

Prospects for the UK industry were poor. The two influential reports, Silberston on the Multi-Fibre Arrangement[8] and Courtaulds' own report 'CTG 2000' both signalled that in all sectors of the textile trade there would be a slow erosion of the UK manufacturers' market share and that there would be increasing imports from the newly emerging countries. The new information technology was already forecast to be the means of fast communication across the world. It was also forecast that the leading trading centre in the Far East, Hong Kong, was also likely to use very low labour-cost factories in emerging countries.

Confidence in M&S

Confidence in M&S was long standing. As far back as the time when Kearton was still chairman of Courtaulds, Marcus Sieff, then Chairman of M&S, had a declared policy of encouraging UK production and supporting the UK textile industry. M&S had a long record of stability, expansion, improving profits and loyalty to its UK suppliers. It was seen that developing ever-closer relationships with large suppliers at the expense of a host of smaller ones[9] was the route M&S would follow, and that Courtaulds could benefit from taking a major role in the process. The longstanding relationship with M&S was to be deepened even further. Following the retirement of Sir Arthur Knight, the new chairman Christopher Hogg had set out to establish an even closer relationship between Courtaulds and M&S, the core customer. However, for Courtaulds to achieve Hogg's ambition it was necessary for the firm to embrace the M&S ethos that involved a close working relationship that might have been anathema to Kearton and perhaps to a slightly lesser extent to Knight.[10] It should also be remembered that Kearton had operated in a period when the market for clothing was slightly less fierce and certainly less complicated.

---

[7] Taylor, *The Mather Lecture*. October 1989.
[8] See Silberston, (HMSO 1989).
[9] In the post World War Two period there was a shortage of merchandise. M&S was prepared to purchase from small manufacturers. Betty Anderson, a partner in a firm that employed less than fifty workers, informed the writer that in the late 1950s her firm supplied children's garments to M&S, BHS, and C&A. Interview 20 April 1999.
[10] However, a source close to Kearton informed the writer that he saw the M&S directors on a fairly regular basis and visited one of their stores most weekends.

M&S Stores are a feature of the UK High Street. © Alex Atkin

The degree to which M&S influenced working conditions is considered elsewhere in this book, but the new relationship involved opening the factories to M&S staff that saw the manufacturing units as an extension of their own business, particularly in such matters as quality control. Such was the relationship that even major issues such as the establishment of new factories and heavy capital expenditure were undertaken on the strength of a verbal understanding. Bevan describes the relationship between M&S and its suppliers:

> It was often said that Marks & Spencer was Britain's biggest manufacturer without owning any factories and that its suppliers were retailers with no shops. For decades this symbiotic relationship provided low prices and flexibility for M&S and security for the supplier.[11]

This relationship was based on trust. There was no contract other than the current order to supply a quantity of goods. Despite the apparent lack of a formal long-term agreement or binding contract with M&S, Hogg appears to have had every justification for pursuing his policy. There was little or no alternative for a firm that operated on the scale of Courtaulds in the UK market. M&S had been floated in 1927 and by 1935 its pre-tax profits exceeded £1 million. There followed an almost continuous and spectacular growth and around the time Hogg had become chairman of Courtaulds, M&S profits had

---

[11] Bevan, p. 103.

increased to £303.4 million and showed every sign of continuing to rise, which they did, reaching around £900 million in the mid-1990s.[12] By 1998, the profit was £1,168 million.

Demerger 1990

Hogg believed that overall shareholder value would be increased if the firm were split up and the chemicals and industrial side of the business, with effective management, be made to perform more effectively. At the same time he believed that the textiles side, which was still manufacturing mainly in the UK, was strong enough to continue effectively in an independent form whilst it moved into the global economy. Christopher Hogg called a meeting one Sunday morning in October 1989 to which the senior executives or representatives of all the Courtaulds businesses were summoned. It was then that he announced the demerger plans for the conglomerate which would be separated into two publicly quoted companies: Courtaulds plc[13] and Courtaulds Textiles plc.

It is not clear when the idea was first mooted among the directors that Courtaulds might be split up but the division of the company in January 1990 formalised what had been a reality for several years: the firm had operated as two separate arms; a chemicals and industrial part and a textiles and clothing part.

The firm had originated as a silk throwing and weaving enterprise, but from the commencement of the twentieth century until the late 1950s the chemicals, fibres and industrial side of the business had become overwhelmingly more important. However, as the firm undertook its series of acquisitions and new ventures, particularly between 1955 and 1975, these again changed the whole character and balance of the business. When announcing the demerger in 1989 Hogg described the existing situation as he saw it:

> [the firm was] …going downstream into chemicals and downstream into textiles and the fact that they were in two different directions, and the fact that they were going towards the customer but really entering worlds with really different characteristics from the upstream fibres world, caused the firm an enormous amount of trouble.[14]

---

[12] These profits were in the context of high inflation in the 1970s and early 1980s.

[13] In July 1998 Courtaulds plc was acquired by Akzo Nobel. Courtaulds' leading positions in high-tech paints and coatings and fibres complemented those of Akzo Nobel. In October of that year Akzo Nobel formed a new business 'Acordis' from its fibre business and those of the former Courtaulds plc. Shortly afterwards Acordis was sold.

[14] Video tape. Christopher Hogg speaking at the demerger conference 19 October 1989.

The two strands of the business also differed in their focus and in their size and scope. The chemicals and industrial side was driven by technology and was fundamentally an international business. In contrast the textile side needed to be responsive to fashion and to the requirements of the UK multiple retail trade.[15]

In reality, Courtaulds had become a mixture of a wide range of different businesses producing an inadequate return on investment and the whole business had no real competitive edge. It is now very difficult to determine in any detail the level of profitability of the many businesses within the various sectors of the group prior to the demerger, but in broad terms textiles was very much smaller and less profitable than the chemical and industrial business and much more labour intensive.

Table 9.1 *Relative size of the new sectors*

1990	Textiles	Chemical industrial
Turnover	£980m	£1,743m
Operating profit	£50m	£142m
Employees	31,000	22,000

Source: Courtaulds Accounts

Most of the hosiery and knitwear firms (and other garment firms) had been acquired during the 1960s, many for around their asset value. However, to turn these into effective enterprises, remain competitive and stay in business it had been necessary to invest large sums of money, but during the 1980s there seems to have been some reversal of fortunes. As Hogg stated:

> [textiles was] ... fundamentally cash producing and having been so all through the 1980s regardless of the problems it was having in trading terms. You could argue, if you were a Courtaulds textiles manager, that you have seen, over the last five years a lot of your cash-flow going into Courtaulds chemicals. There is a benefit, and the benefit for the Textiles in their autonomy is that they now have management to their cash flow and can make choices in their own domain. The corollary of that is that Chemicals has got to look to its own resources and its own choices without thinking that there is another source sitting there when it wants to do things which are disproportionate to its means.[16]

---

[15] The use of information technology was soon to have a profound impact. The functions of sales, design and despatch remained close to the customer but production could then function on a global basis.

[16] Christopher Hogg speaking at the demerger conference 19 October 1989.

Martin Taylor – Chief Executive of Courtaulds Textiles plc 1990 – 1994; Chairman 1993–1994. Photo from Courtaulds Textiles Annual Report and Accounts, 1992.

With the demerger of Courtaulds Textiles plc from the remainder of the group, the yarn processing mills became separated from the garment producing firms with whom they no longer had common ownership. Any pressure on the clothing factories to favour Courtaulds' fibre products was long gone and in the context of the new organisation all loyalty to the downstream concept was lost, the power of the final user being paramount. It is not possible to accurately quote the amount of inter-company trading, but by 1994 it was less than 4%.[17]

Management – The main board

With the splitting up of the conglomerate it was necessary to reorganise the two boards but Christopher Hogg remained chairman of both companies with Martin Taylor becoming the chief executive of Courtaulds Textiles plc, both of whom were established and recognised figures in the city.

---

[17] Courtaulds Textiles Accounts 1994.

Structure of Courtaulds Textiles plc

Courtaulds Textiles plc was set up with a leaner top management structure than had been the case before the demerger. Taylor was then able to carry the process of devolution much further than had previously been possible. Taylor was scathing in his comments about the role of head offices in large firms, arguing that: 'Unit autonomy certainly frustrated the most poisonous and deadening habits of head offices, but it left them with an identity crisis.'[18]

He believed that the head office had a role to play as the financial controller, particularly for garment producing companies, but that the fast reaction to the needs of the business, and the ability to take the many urgent decisions that had to be made on a daily basis in a fashion led industry should be devolved as far as possible, unhindered by a bureaucratic head office. In practice the firm remained complex and still functioned as a loose multidivisional organisation but with a much larger element of devolved control.

Continuing decline

Although there was a wave of optimism at the demerger, the problems faced by the textiles and clothing industries in the developed world were getting worse as time passed and Courtaulds was not immune to these problems, being fundamentally a UK based sales and manufacturing company.

Strict control of cash flow and careful usage of capital had long been enforced in the manufacturing units. A target for the generation of cash had been set at 12% of capital employed for each business prior to demerger. However, by 1993 it was recognised that there was then less scope for this strategy and the firm was looking for profits growth based on the restructuring of acquisitions and investment that had already taken place. A significant boost to the cash position was obtained when the firm took a much criticised cash return from the pension fund.[19]

Taylor became chairman in addition to chief executive in 1993, a year that saw the first sales growth since demerger. Taylor left within a few months to become Chief Executive of Barclays Bank although this proved an unhappy appointment.[20] He later became Chairman of W H Smith Group and held several other directorships.

---

[18] Taylor, *The Mather Lecture*, October 1989.
[19] £19.4 million in 1993.
[20] The *Andrew Davidson Interview* in Management Today March 2002 explains clashes of personality. Taylor criticised the quality of Barclays board but '... *others see it differently ... and put the blame solely on Taylor's manner...*' Personality clashes were not particularly noticeable at Courtaulds, however.

Noel Jervis – Chief Executive of Courtaulds Textiles plc 1994–1996. Photo from Courtaulds Textiles Annual Report and Accounts, 1992.

Noel Jervis as chief executive under Christopher Hogg

Christopher Hogg resumed the chairmanship of Courtaulds Textiles plc until the appointment of John Eccles. Noel Jervis stepped up to the position of chief executive to replace Taylor in January 1994. Jervis was a long serving employee who had previously been finance director of the Textiles Division and was one of a trio that formulated Courtaulds' forecast of its prospects up to the year 2000; the CTG 2000 (Courtaulds Textile Group 2000) report.

Table 9.2 *Financial data 1990–1999 (£000,000)*

	1990*	1991	1992	1993	1994	1995	1996	1997	1998	1999
Turnover	983.8	922.0	889.6	923.1	1,053.2	1,120.0	1,006.5	911.5	893.0	900.1
Pre-tax profit	40.3	42.2	39.1	38.8	47.3	36.5	0.4	38.4	25.1	10.1
Profit retained	8.3	5.0	16.8	15.1	19.1	10.3	(21.1)	11.5	0.2	2.0

Source: Courtaulds Textiles Accounts
Note: *15 months

By the time Jervis became chief executive the UK hosiery and knitwear sector of the firm seems to have been overlooked in the policy direction set out in the CTG 2000 report some ten years earlier, which not only recognised the inevitable decay of UK clothing manufacturing but required a bigger emphasis on global manufacturing and distribution.

Table 9.3 *Strategic Development 1985 to 1994*

Businesses bought		Businesses sold	
Liberty Fabrics/United Elastic	USA	Samuel Courtauld	UK
Georges Rech	FR	Bentley Smith	UK
Desseilles	FR	Distributors	UK
Laces & Textiles	UK	Symington NZ	NZ
Corah Socks	UK	Design Archives	UK
Penn Sedespa	PS	Wolsey Greece	GRC
Chelco	MOR	DMF	FR
Galler	PS/PGL	Treforest	UK
Broderies Deschamps	FR	John Hampden Press	UK
Gold-Zac	FER/Phil	Courtaulds Wollens	UK
Dentelles Calaisiennes	FR	S African Fabrics	SA
Gorgetex/Sotexa (*WELL*)	FR	Thiollier	FR
Bear Brand	UK	Slane	IR
Total sales	£375m	Total sales	£85m

Source: Hurd Memorial Lecture

As a result of the CTG 2000 report the fabrics, lace and textiles businesses had been considerably internationalised. In contrast, in the clothing businesses there had been no real transformation of the UK business. Most of the changes had been a reaction to events. As fashions changed or declined, businesses were put together and their names changed. This was simply a way of managing or even disguising the inevitable reduction of UK capacity, rather than being an implementation of forward policy.

The son of 1st Viscount Eccles, John Eccles was appointed to the board of Courtaulds Textiles plc in 1992 and became Chairman of Courtaulds Textiles plc in 1995. He was educated at Winchester and Magdalen College, Oxford and held a large portfolio of directorships in industry, finance, public service and the arts.

Lord Eccles – Chairman of Courtaulds Textiles plc 1995–2000. Photo from Courtaulds Textiles Annual Report and Accounts, 1996.

The final decline

In 1994, Noel Jervis said in his Hurd Memorial Lecture,

> ...what has been the [gain] value to the shareholder? On day 1 nothing: Four years later, an out performance of the FT index by over 60% ...So far so good, ... the current share price can only be built on a great deal of promise and expectation of better things yet to come, together with the supposition that we have a sound management team to tackle these challenges successfully.[21]

Jervis's spirited defence of the Courtaulds Textiles plc was well timed, 1994 was Courtaulds Textiles plc's best year. In the run up to the demerger some £20 million in exceptional costs had been loaded onto the firm as a result of previous closures and these were eliminated by the financial year 1994, reflecting that much 'dead wood' had been cut out.[22] Around 1994 there were signs of

---

[21] Noel Jervis, The Cyril Hurd Memorial Lecture 1994.
[22] Textilnet 11 March 2002.

improvement in the UK economy. Sales, profits, and profits retained were the highest for any year since the formation of Courtaulds Textiles plc with sales of £91 million resulting from the businesses acquired in that year, but this improvement was to be short lived.

European mainland expansion

Early in 1994 the firm announced the acquisition from Hartstone plc of the 'Well' brand name with its French hosiery manufacturing plant and its small Sutton-in-Ashfield business that used the Bear Brand name.[23] They were bought for £59.4 million cash, the stated purpose being to provide an entry into the clothing trade in Mainland Europe, and Well did indeed provide a boost to takings and a short term uplift in profits. In France the hypermarkets were gaining a large share of the tights market and purchasing a popular brand name and a high volume producer was perceived by Courtaulds Textiles plc to be a good means of entry into the mainland European market. The board probably saw tights as a product with relatively low labour-costs and believed the firm's expertise in fine-gauge knitting would take a long time to replicate in the emerging textile manufacturing countries. Therefore owning Well brand was an opportunity to internationalise the market for the firm's garments and compete with Dim,[24] a highly successful brand in Mainland Europe.

Up to this time there had been no thrust to sell hosiery and knitwear in the rest of the world and there was a need to redress this. The firm was lacking an international platform for distribution and sales of clothing to the retail trade. Courtaulds Textiles plc had a highly developed UK skill base in design, manufacturing, sourcing, sales and distribution that served the multiple stores and particularly M&S and it was envisaged that this could be replicated in Mainland Europe. There was no UK chain operating in Mainland Europe on the scale of M&S so the acquisition of Well was seen as a way to enter a supply chain that was suited to the needs of a very different retail culture, starting with France and based on an existing organisation. The opportunities for sales in the fragmented retail markets in China and India were considered poor at that time and did not fit well with the firm's available skills. Courtaulds had concentrated on fabrics and the need for a European merchandising and sales organisation for hosiery, lingerie, socks, knitwear and knitted underwear had not been addressed and consequently the clothing businesses did not have any international selling outlets.

---

[23] The Gogetex/Sotexa (Well) acquisition included a small factory at Sutton-in-Ashfield and ownership of the Bear Brand trademark. See Table 9.3.

[24] Dim was owned by Sara Lee Corporation. Sara Lee also owned Filadoro (Italy) Sans (Spain) and Pretty Polly (UK).

Despite Courtaulds plc having local knowledge, established expertise in fabrics and lace manufacturing, and sales outlets for these products in France, the Well acquisition was never a success. There was no real integration using UK sourcing skills, and the hoped for transfer of UK products into the French hypermarkets and supermarkets never materialised.

Only a firm with access to large amounts of capital could have acted in this way. Under Kearton, Courtaulds had operated in a climate of expansion with increasing markets for the products of its garment industries. That was a period when a 'big is beautiful' strategy was generally accepted as the way forward for British Industry. In contrast, the moves to increase the firm's UK and Mainland European manufacturing stake in the industry, in the late 1980s and the 1990s took place with full knowledge of the CTG 2000 report that had highlighted the high cost of manufacturing in Western Europe and nothing had occurred since its publication to cast any doubt whatsoever on its findings. The Well failure can be partly explained because its high cost manufacturing arm had to be purchased alongside the sales, distribution, and brand name enterprise as part of the overall deal. French manufacturing caused severe problems. Courtaulds found that the local trade unions were uncooperative and new working practices that would have involved some loss of jobs but made the product more competitive were not implemented. This had severe repercussions for the firm and the management persisted with local manufacturing partly because French culture and law made closure very expensive.

1995 started well, but the UK trade was to be hit heavily by one of those factors to which the fashion industries are susceptible – unfavourable weather. Due to abnormally warm weather, between mid-June and mid-November the sales of socks, knitwear, hosiery, nightwear, slips and leisurewear were all adversely affected. Bad news followed when in the later part of the year there was a tendency towards de-stocking in France and the USA. Therefore, despite a slightly higher turnover, manufacturers selling prices were significantly lower than the previous year. So after the promising start to 1995 the long term downturn was soon firmly resumed. In 1995 there were costs of setting up factories in China and Thailand, and 1996 trading conditions were bad for the whole trade. Inevitably, Noel Jervis was tainted by the poor results feeding through from the 1994 Well acquisition.

During 1996, five businesses closed and ten were sold and after a series of mill closures the firm finally ceased spinning yarn.[25] The Well Business had consumed a large amount of money over the previous few years and had performed badly during a period of weak demand, suffering further stock reductions in the French hypermarket sector.

---

[25] George Courtauld 1 had entered the silk business as an apprentice in 1755.

Colin Dyer Chief Executive Courtaulds Textiles plc 1996–2000. Photo from Courtaulds Textiles Annual Report and Accounts, 1996.

Colin Dyer as Chief Executive

Midway through 1996, in a period of falling profits, Noel Jervis was replaced by Colin Dyer, the executive formerly in charge of the clothing division. Dyer was recruited to Courtaulds in 1982 from McKinsey Management Consultants. He was also a non-executive director of Northern Foods. During 1997 the slow down in profits of the previous two years was halted, but the company never again achieved the 1994 profit, and the general trend towards lower turnover continued.

Problems loomed when in 1996 M&S featured in Granada Television's *World in Action* television programme. This claimed that one of its suppliers had used child labour in a Moroccan factory and had labelled garments manufactured there 'Made in the UK' an accusation that was vigorously denied. M&S won a libel action[26] on the grounds that it had not known about this false labelling but from then on there was some doubt about the absolute integrity of the firm. Despite increasing profits, there were signs that the customers were less satisfied. Staff levels on the shop floor were lower, and stores were not stocked with the full range of sizes and colours. A mixture of a poor press, bad trading conditions

---

[26] Bevan, p.178.

for clothing, an unfortunate choice of grey as a predominant colour statement for autumn 1998,[27] and an uncompetitive pricing structure, led to lost sales on a massive scale.

High Street retailing had become an increasingly more expensive business. Extravagant stores in high cost locations, extended hours with premium pay rates, electronic supply chain technology, and increased advertising all contributed to an improved shopping experience.[28] This all had to be paid for and M&S increased the mark-up on the cost prices and pressure was put on suppliers selling prices but the UK clothing industries could not absorb this and the shopper could not benefit without cheaper goods from offshore and inevitably there were factory closures.

Claremont

During October 1998, encouraged by M&S boss Richard Greenbury, with whom Hogg had a good working relationship, the firm took over Claremont, a formalwear, lingerie and tailoring manufacturer. This acquisition cost £11.7 million and carried with it a debt of £42.1 million. Annual turnover for troubled Claremont was estimated at £160 million but the acquisition was too late in the financial year to have any significant effect on that years accounts.

By this time, Courtaulds Textiles plc had manufacturing capacity in Morocco, Sri Lanka, Turkey and Tunisia and was about to open a factory in Mexico. These moves were estimated to raise the offshore garment stitching capacity of the firm to 50%.

In the light of the successful acquisition of Corah Sock Division a decade earlier, the relationship with M&S had became even closer and that successful experience probably encouraged the belief that the acquisition of Claremont Textiles plc would provide a lucrative opening into the tailoring departments of the M&S supply chain. However, Claremont brought with it a debt that burdened the rest of the firm. Claremont was on the verge of bankruptcy, but the formalwear side of this business employed very skilled workers and did give Courtaulds an entry into the M&S business that it would otherwise have been almost impossible to achieve. However, part of this business was lingerie manufacturing with a turnover of £40 million per annum. Courtaulds was already overexposed to this sector and this part of the business was unsustainable. Courtaulds needed to close eight factories with a loss of over a thousand jobs, incurring heavy reorganisation costs.

---

[27] Whilst grey may not necessarily have been a bad choice the vast areas of grey on the large sales floors lent a depressing look to the stores.

[28] M&S was also suffering increasing pressure from Matalan and Next and also from other chain stores that tended towards lower 'mark ups'.

Courtaulds Textiles plc in disarray

Pre-exceptional results had been poor under Jervis but Colin Dyer fared no better. Despite acquiring several large firms, turnover was falling and margins and cash flow worsened, and in the years 1997–99 earnings per share, after exceptional charges, declined from 26.4p to 7.2p. Altogether, 1999 was a dreadful year for shares in the textile sector. Bevan wrote:

> By the end of the year the stock-market value of the 'mid-market player' Storehouse [including BHS and Mothercare] had fallen 61% to £226m; Arcadia, the old Burton group, was down by half to £168m; Debenhams was down 47% to 714m and M&S was 40% lower at £7bn, a pale shadow of the £19bn valuation achieved in the heady days of October 1997 when M&S was by far and away Britain's top retailer by market value.[29]

During the year ending December 1999 Courtaulds Textiles plc gained a small increase in turnover, but profits were the second worst since its formation in 1990. Despite inflation, sales for the whole period were down. Profits were in decline and after taxation and dividends had been paid the amount of profit retained was totally inadequate to support a substantial investment programme.

M&S, on whom the firm's confidence had been placed for several decades, was in serious trouble. Profits slipped: for 1998 a record £1,168 million, for 1999 a disastrous £628.4 million, and for 2000 £557.2 million, with worse to follow.

Taking an overall view of the decade of Courtaulds Textiles plc's existence, results were catastrophic. In six of the subsequent nine years, the restructuring costs, mainly resulting from closures and redundancies, were an enormous burden. In 1998, they were £11 million, in 1999 £17.5 million and in 2000 the directors estimated that the restructuring costs for the current year and 2001 would be £40 million.[30] An interim dividend was paid in October 1999, but there was no final dividend and a profit warning was issued that November.

Takeover bid

Things could not continue as they were. In February 2000 Courtaulds Textiles plc was the subject of a takeover bid from Sara Lee Corporation, the US foods and consumer goods group. Courtaulds Textiles plc shares had recently reached a low of 55p, but risen to 62.5p shortly before the Sara Lee offer of 100p was

---

[29] Bevan, p. 211.
[30] Courtaulds Textiles plc Accounts.

announced. This valued the firm at £103.8 million, only one third of the value of the shares two years previously.

Even when the takeover bid was in progress the firm continued to divest itself of several businesses and announce large scale redundancies. It is not possible to know if the board as it was first constituted by people of the stature of Sir Christopher Hogg and Martin Taylor would have acted any differently, but the end result would probably have not been very much different. Possibly, due to the slightly milder business climate, Taylor and Hogg were able to project their own image and that of the firm in a way that later directors were unable to equal. What is certain is that one of the major acquisitions that caused serious problems (Well brand) was organised during their management and the timing of their exit from the company proved to be well judged.

Sara Lee gains control

Due to the disastrous forays into the French hosiery and lingerie market (Well) and UK formal-wear (Claremont) the stability of the firm was shaken. At this time the firm needed a period of calm but circumstances did not favour the firm or the clothing industry. Particularly serious was the loss of shareholder market value, reduced sales to M&S, and the pressure of rapidly advancing globalisation in the late 1990s.

In March 2000 Courtaulds Textiles plc claimed that the firm was worth 240p per share, but the directors finally recommended acceptance of 145p[31] per share which sealed its final demise. There were no counter offers as the remaining major clothing firms were all suffering a similar fate. Sara Lee Corporation gained control in May 2000 and Courtaulds Textiles plc ceased to be listed on the stock exchange. Following the takeover, the new owners announced their intention to sell the Well[32] business, the International Fabrics Division, Zorbit, Lyle & Scott, Georges Rech and Christie, the home furnishing group.

Attempts to accurately isolate the fortunes of Courtaulds Textiles plc hosiery and knitwear interests from the rest of the firm's products are fraught with problems but there are indications that despite the declining profits, the firm had regained its leading M&S sales position lost to other firms in the 1980s. It

---

[31] The shares had been traded as low as 62.5p in the week prior to the bid which was only one third of the price two years earlier. Textile sector shares were hit by the unpopularity of this sector of the market and the flight of investment into the 'high technology' shares that were popular at that time.

[32] This was to keep within the European Commission's opinion that the combined sales of Well and Dim in the French hosiery market would have been 45–55% by volume and 60–70% by value and was therefore incompatible with the aims of the European Commission.

should be recognised, however, that much of the increase came because many competitors had suffered a worse fate and were no longer in the market.

Post script

Sara Lee bought Courtaulds Textiles plc with unfortunate or miscalculated timing as Marks & Spencer was suffering a run of awful profits[33] with worse to follow. UK clothing manufacturing was in freefall, with factories closing at an alarming rate.

Sara Lee was a mixed conglomerate with wide ranging interests including bakery, beverages, meats, body care, air fresheners, detergents, shoe polish and branded clothing including the famous USA names 'L'Eggs' in hosiery and 'Haynes' and 'Playtex' in underwear. Sara Lee had highly developed skills in branded clothing sales and the takeover would bring with it two well known Courtaulds' intimate apparel brands, 'Gossard', 'Berlei' and in the hosiery trade, 'Aristoc'.[34] These were well established but did not have the cachet of the more modern and highly promoted sports or glamour brands and as far back as 1985 it had been recognised that they had an ageing customer profile. Aristoc in particular was operating in a market that was declining at an alarming rate and this increased Sara Lee's exposure to further decline in that market. In socks and knitwear Courtaulds had already sold a main brand 'Wolsey' in a management buyout in 1996 and this became an outstanding success under its new management, mainly because of its close trading connection with the rapidly developing discount store Matalan and the abandonment of its involvement in manufacturing.

For the takeover to be successful it would be necessary for Sara Lee to break new ground in some way, possibly by increasing sales of the remaining Courtaulds Textiles plc brands and creating a big market for merchandise from its American factories, and by using Courtaulds Textiles plc's undoubted distribution and service skills as an entry for Sara Lee brands into the UK high street stores.

Despite all the well documented problems affecting the clothing supply chain in the western world it seems most likely that Sara Lee believed it could operate in the chain stores market in a way that Courtaulds Textiles plc had not. Unfortunately for brand operators, at that time the major UK chain stores did not generally sell suppliers' brands that were in competition with their own. M&S, the main target customer, already had an established and highly

---

[33] M&S pre-tax profits. 1998 £1,168 million, 1999 £628.4 million, 2000 £557.2 million, 2001 £480.9 million.

[34] Aristoc and Well (a continental brand) were managed together, as were Gossard and Berlei.

regarded leading brand (M&S) in lingerie and underwear and to convince the store buyers that introduction of a new main brand would increase sales and widen the customer base, without diluting existing sales of its own brand would be enormously difficult.[35] At the same time M&S and the other chain stores could not risk a situation where they might be selling suppliers brands that were available to their competitors and enter a price war on the high street.[36]

At the time of the takeover John H Brian, Chairman and Chief Executive of Sara Lee, had described Courtaulds Textiles as having declining sales, falling profits, falling margins, declining earnings per share and worsening book gearing[37] and yet despite this still saw the firm as a likely asset.

Sara Lee did little to transform the businesses it acquired from Courtaulds Textiles plc and faced the same problems that would have beset them if they had remained under Courtaulds ownership. At the time of the Sara Lee takeover, Courtaulds Textiles plc was already in advanced negotiations for the sale of Lyle & Scott which was operating at the higher end of the market dealing with golf wear suppliers and retailers such as Harrods and Galeries Lafayette, a market unlikely to appeal to Sara Lee. Outside the knitwear industry there were plans to sell Christie, Zorbit and Georges Rech Fashions and around, or soon after the takeover, all this was put into effect. This was followed in 2001 by the sale of Penn Nyla fabrics to Dogi, and the closure of the Sara Lee Pretty Polly hosiery factory and the former Courtaulds Sock Division factory at Abbey Meadows Leicester in 2003.

New Policy under Brenda C. Barnes

In 2005 Sara Lee had new leadership and policy under President and Chief Operating Officer Brenda C. Barnes under whom it was refocused to concentrate on its core business, selling off its clothing interests to concentrate on its food, beverages and household and bodycare products. In 2006 Sara Lee sold its Courtaulds Division for an undisclosed sum that was widely reported to be a 'give away' price.

This left Sara Lee with a share in the highly successful Sri Lanka factories that were heavily involved in making M&S merchandise but they were also left with a seriously large £260 million pension deficit.

---

[35] M&S did sell some goods under Sara Lee's minor brand name Ego Boost.

[36] The introduction of Per Una left M&S in a difficult position because it was highly successful but the 2004 deal in which this brand became M&S owned redressed the situation.

[37] Sara Lee offer letter 2 March 2000.

TEN

Epilogue

Few who worked in the hosiery and knitwear industry in the 1960s would have imagined the changes that would take place over the next three decades or so. Why should not the industry continue to provide a good living for thousands of workers in the way that it had for several centuries in the UK, most significantly in the East Midlands?

Courtaulds was reshaped by its leadership, first of all by Kearton and followed by Knight and others as it responded to evolving circumstances. But our present judgments of their actions can only be made with the benefit and luxury of hindsight. We should therefore be careful that in our analysis of their actions we take into account the approaching changes in communications, technology, and global political thinking of which Kearton and Knight in particular were not then fully aware.

It is inescapable that Kearton understood that the UK hosiery and knitwear industry had been strongly protected by tariff barriers since the 1930s and in global terms the industry remained uncompetitive. It was also clear that the industry faced an uncertain future. There had been a period of a few years after the Second World War when there was a general shortage of merchandise in the UK, but it soon became clear that the era of free trade brought in by the GATT (General Agreement on Tariffs and Trade) would expose the UK clothing industries to severe competition.

Kearton was under intense pressure as the firm needed sales to bolster its falling profits as existing products began to lose favour. He was driven by the need for high volume sales for the chemicals plants producing a new generation of fibres that had not yet been fully developed for launch onto the manmade fibres market. These plants were dependent on high levels of plant utilisation if they were to compete with the large and efficient American suppliers.

Courtaulds' expansion into the hosiery and knitwear industry resulted from Kearton's strategic vision – that vertical trading would safeguard Courtaulds' manmade fibre producing plants, for without a wide customer base for its fibres the firm could not survive. Part of his policy was to enter the spinning and clothing industries, and thereby try to establish a captive market for the firm's fibres, and this policy had much merit in the case of nylon, in which there was little differentiation between the products of the various suppliers, but overall the range of yarns available was highly susceptible to the vagaries of the fashion trades.

Leadership and Corporate Governance

Kearton was from a culture of big enterprises, having previously worked for ICI and the British Government; he was also a strong believer in the concept of big business. Knight, his successor, came from a similar background and supported him in the repulse of the ICI takeover and subsequently in the expansion of the conglomerate in the 1960s.

Giddens[1] draws attention to a stereotypical image of British industrial and commercial leadership; an upper-class elite group with a 'near monopoly' exerted by public schools and Oxbridge over recruitment to elite positions. Whitley, in the same work, shows a strong relationship between education, kinship, shared directorships and personal wealth. Neither Kearton, the son of a bricklayer nor Knight, the son of a steel hardener who later became a railway porter, fit this social mould or had access to personal wealth. Both attended state schools and received a good university education, Kearton had an exceptional mind, but neither benefited from favourable connections at an early age.

After this relatively short run of chairmen from the working class there was a reversal of the trend, with men from middle class and more affluent backgrounds being at the head of Courtaulds. Public school education then again became the rule.[2] However, the common factor throughout the whole period was higher education, and from this highly educated group Kearton and Taylor were recognised as outstanding scholars.

Charlotte Erickson's work[3] compares the education of the entrepreneurs in the highly capital-intensive steel and the small scale, largely non-technical hosiery and knitwear industries over the hundred years 1850–1950. She describes a hosiery industry that operated under predominantly hereditary ownership, sought talent from within itself, and had almost no technically trained leaders. The highly capital-intensive fibres and chemicals industry and the steel industry shared a common culture of employing educated leaders. However, within a few years of Erickson's work being published, Courtaulds had entered the hosiery and knitwear industry.[4] Had Erickson followed her case study forward

---

[1] Giddens, in Stanworth and Giddens, *Elites and Power in British Society* (CUP, 1974), Preface.

[2] Martin Taylor entered Eton by way of a scholarship.

[3] Erickson, p. 138.

[4] Courtaulds' acquisitions began in 1963.

for fifteen years or so she would have discovered an entirely different scenario. Courtaulds' entry into the clothing trades resulted in the transfer of well educated staff into this industry on a scale not previously known; many replaced those managers who did not survive the acquisition of their firms. However, they found themselves in an unfamiliar industry run on a small scale, servicing a complex range of customers and they were unable to revive many of the ailing firms they were sent to manage.

Kearton's leadership of the resistance to a hostile takeover bid by ICI was in stark contrast to that of his immediate predecessor, who actually favoured merger with ICI, and it was due to Kearton's personal strengths that the bid was resisted. The successful repulse of the takeover and the subsequent departure of the Chairman and his agreed successor soon left the way clear for Kearton to take over the combined roles of chairman and managing director.

Chairman Kearton, who was a very minor shareholder,[5] treated the firm as if it was his personal property. His involvement in the day-to-day activities of the firm went far beyond mere supervision of senior managers; and he was prepared to seek information from however far down the chain of command he saw fit. This was partly necessitated by the lack of an effective formal management structure for the garment industries during the first decade of the expansion and diversification policy.

Because the roles of managing director and chairman were combined, it was possible for Kearton, with his extremely strong personality, to decide major issues on his own. However, it must be recognised that even the largest acquisitions in the hosiery and knitwear and clothing sectors were very small, relative to the size of Courtaulds in total, and therefore many of the individual decisions that appeared strategic to a knitwear manager, were small in the context of Courtaulds' operations as a whole.

In practice, he acted in a style that might have been more appropriate to the owner of a 'Victorian' private company in which all members of the management were responsible to him. Obviously there were decisions that were cleared by the board but the indications are that high level decisions (by clothing industry standards) were being taken personally by him. It is totally clear, however, that the size of the stake in the industry was not pre-planned. Kearton authorised the acquisition of firms that were in difficulties; many were bought at only around their net asset value, and expanded the scope of the firm in a way that, due to changing circumstances, was not open to his successors.

The main historiography is around big business, dominated by an American

---

[5] In 1968 when the acquisitions were nearly complete the 16 directors shareholdings were all quite small: 0–3,000 (7 inc Kearton and Knight with 2,664 each) 3,001–6,000 (4) 6,001–9,000 (1) 9,001–12,000 (2) 12,001–77,000 (2 inc R. A. Butler, son in law of Samuel Courtauld).

influence. This invites a comparison with the problems encountered when bringing together Courtaulds, a big international business and the British hosiery and knitwear industry which was comprised of small operating units. It was inevitable that problems would occur when attempting to assimilate the acquisitions from this untidy and fragmented industry into the main conglomerate. The inability of Courtaulds to create an organisation and structure that could accommodate this uncomfortable mix brings into question the viability of the whole vertical trading concept in the context of the marriage of the fashion industries and the large scale chemicals processing plants.

Other leaders followed Kearton and held joint positions of chairman and managing director,[6] but none exercised them in the same way that he had. All reacted to prevailing circumstances, but Kearton's strategy was put in place when the climate in which the UK manufacturers operated was somewhat more favourable, while his successors were operating in an era of more intense global pressures.

The position that Kearton assumed shortly after the repulse of the ICI takeover bid fits very uncomfortably with the tenets of Charkham,[7] who was in favour of split responsibility rather than the positions of chairman and chief executive being combined in one person. Quail's model of the joint stock company as it evolved towards the commencement of the twentieth century had a clear separation of powers between the directors, who were normally substantial shareholders, and the managers who controlled the business.[8]

Knight's[9] highly credible view, offered in retrospect, was that building a vertical supply chain within the firm was a way to protect the fibre producing plants from damaging competition from foreign firms, whilst at the same time bringing these plants closer to the end user. This was a fast way of understanding the technical and marketing problems[10] that were being met as new fibre products were being developed.

Courtaulds' entry into the hosiery and knitwear industry provided more advantages than simply being an outlet for the firm's products. The industry was a complex link in the supply chain, taking a wide variety of yarns from spinning mills and carrying out all subsequent functions including designing, knitting, garment assembly and packaging as well as warehousing, distribution

---

[6] Christopher Hogg of Courtaulds plc and Martin Taylor of Courtaulds Textiles plc.

[7] The Committee on the Financial Aspects of Corporate Governance (The Cadbury Committee) reported in 1992.

[8] Quail, *'Debates and Speculations The Proprietorial Theory of the Firm and its Consequences'* in Journal of Industrial History, 3(1) (2000).

[9] Knight was deputy chairman of Courtaulds at that time.

[10] See Comment by John Boyes-Watson in 'Proprietary yarn brands' in Chapter 2.

and despatch to the chain stores or other distributors.[11] Therefore, the hosiery and knitwear industry was much closer to the final customer and was responsible for product innovation, styling, and the rapid introduction of new materials to the ultimate customers in a way that the Lancashire weaving and cotton industries (in which Courtaulds was also involved), were not.[12] Therefore, the hosiery and knitwear industry was a quicker channel of sales and marketing intelligence for Courtaulds' fibre producers than their Lancashire spinning and weaving plants.[13]

There were diametrically opposed views of the purpose of the knitting industry. Under Kearton, Courtaulds saw the knitting businesses as a vehicle through which yarn could be pushed downstream into the supply chain, whilst the big retailers saw the knitting firms solely as suppliers of attractive goods with which to stock their shops, a situation in which the retailer must always be the winner.[14] There were two issues that had to be addressed; falling sales of the existing manmade fibre products and development and launching of the new developments such as Celon onto the market. In this context Kearton recognised the importance of the M&S supply chain and he recognised that M&S had the technical knowledge to collaborate with Courtaulds' knitting businesses that provided a link back to the research laboratories. At the same time M&S could provide continuity of orders on a scale that no other customer could match.[15]

---

[11] In retailing Courtaulds owned a department store, McIlroy at Swindon, Contessa (Corsets), three small clothing outlets and a laundry. Courtaulds Textiles plc also owned a large clothing shop at Haydn Road Nottingham. In contrast Coats Viyella was heavily committed to retailing and owned over 300 retail shops trading as *Jaeger, Bellmans* and *Scotch Wool Shop*.

[12] 'Spinning and weaving firms made little contribution to product innovation, since within the constraints of this vertically disintegrated industrial structure they had no direct contact with the views and preferences of the final customer.' Singleton, *Lancashire on the Scrapheap* (OUP Oxford, 1991), p. 5.

[13] Woven fabrics were processed by the apparel industry before being sold to the chain stores.

[14] Firms in the hosiery and knitwear industry were particularly suitable for Kearton's ambitions because these took yarn from the spinning industry and converted it into garments packed and ready for retail sale.

[15] By the 1950s rayon was being overtaken by other fibres, particularly nylon, in which Courtaulds did not have a stake. A massive programme of research and a scramble to acquire cognate industries was set in motion in the 1950s and 1960s.

Organisation and Structure

Kearton left behind some serious organisational problems. As Courtaulds expanded, its structure became more multi-product, multinational and fragmented, and included a number of associate companies that were not fully owned. These complications, plus differences in language, culture and national law, meant that the conglomerate was not naturally suited to central control of all its functions. As Courtaulds expanded it did not take on a straightforward divisional structure. Within the clothing industries the untidy mix of products, small sites, geographical spread and the practice of dedicating production units to specific customers made these trades particularly unsuited to central control. Channon[16] saw the American multidivisional form (M-form) with highly developed central functions as a way to facilitate expansion. However, this style did not suit Courtaulds as a mixed conglomerate.[17] Some functions such as pension administration, the purchase of motor vehicles and the control of legal services in the UK did become centralised. On a worldwide basis the movement of currency, the appointment of lawyers and the allocation of capital were functions of head office because it was felt that these responsibilities were best handled centrally. Quail's description of a large multidivisional global oligopoly, in which functional management is controlled throughout the organisation by a head office setting out the procedures to be followed, and with line management responsible for enforcing compliance in the divisions, bears little resemblance to Courtaulds as it functioned on a worldwide basis. Neither did Kearton develop a divisional structure of that type for the clothing factories, any serious movement towards formal structure being left to his successors. In practice, acquisitions were made without a formal management structure being in place to integrate these into a cohesive entity or make them an integral part of the parent organisation. The full aims and scope of this opportunistic acquisition policy was not known as it progressed, and therefore setting up any central administration would have been a shot in the dark. By the end of the 1960s there were signs of downturn and the acquisition policy ground to a halt. Within a short time the UK industry was in decline and the opportunity for planned integration was probably lost.

Courtaulds' acquisitions retained much of the traditional small scale structure of the industry and many of the features of the traditional system. The larger manufacturing units proved suitable for dealing with M&S; the remaining single and multiple retailers were best served by factories appropriate to their size. Customers demanded suppliers who were able to concentrate on their particular needs and all customers needed to feel that they had a special relationship with their suppliers.

---

[16] Channon (1984).

[17] Any form of organisation that favoured a large central organisation was later shunned whenever possible by Martin Taylor on the formation of Courtaulds textiles plc.

Davis[18] accepted that mergers did offer economies but that these might take some time to come through. However, unlike Courtaulds' acquisition of British Celanese, a rival fibre producer[19] which did offer some opportunity for rationalisation, Courtaulds' expansion into the clothing field was opportunist and unplanned and brought excessive fragmentation to the conglomerate. What Davis fails to address is the problem faced by firms when their existing markets decline and their skills and technologies are not transferable to other types of enterprise. Davis also fails to recognise that established firms may have to diversify to survive. Taking over small independent firms with which large customers refuse to deal may be a justifiable route to take when small customers are still trading.

Organisation under Kearton's successors

Knight, Kearton's successor, was faced with serious challenges. By the early 1970s, it was seen that Kearton's policies, of which he had been a supporter, had many failings. In a change of strategy they were relaxed in favour of a much larger measure of autonomy for the firm's textiles sectors and clothing businesses. At the main board level, running a large conglomerate with a wide portfolio of mixed business types presented difficulties and conflicts[20] that the directors were unable to reconcile.

At divisional level executives had lost the authority and ability to make decisions affecting their own businesses. As Anthony Sampson[21] noted, some employees of major firms became 'cogs in a wheel', simply carrying out the commands of others. While this may not be totally true of Courtaulds' hosiery and knitwear businesses, because few manufacturing functions were controlled from head office, it is certain that managers were in many ways unable to influence issues on which their own success was judged.[22]

Serious attempts to re-organise under Knight and his successors were in response to problems within Courtaulds' chain of command created in Kearton's era and there was a need to put more decision making power in the hands of managers that were being made progressively more responsible for the results of their own enterprise.

---

[18] Davis (1970).
[19] Courtaulds and British Celanese had large overlapping research divisions working in the same field.
[20] Particularly the problem of conflicting demands for investment capital. Also managers thought their profits were being diverted to other less cash producing sections.
[21] Sampson (1995).
[22] For example the availability of capital and certain labour issues and centrally fixed transfer prices for yarn.

During the 1970s attempts were made to form large product-based divisions from a mixture of large, small and medium sized manufacturing units partly to counter the success of the customers in playing off one production unit against another during price negotiations. However, the formation of these divisions met with only limited success. It was found that it was the small scale specialist business units serving a wide range of customers that were most difficult to integrate into these large divisions. Important decisions were needed, often at short notice, and decision-making managers needed to be close to the manufacturing units and in contact with the customers. Products that seemed at first glance to be quite similar presented vastly different challenges in commercial, technical and fashion terms. The multi-product factories presented particular problems for those attempting to build up product based divisions, partly because their managers would have been in the unenviable position of being responsible to more than one divisional chief officer.

Courtaulds never succeeded in instituting a totally effective organisation structure for the clothing factories. The factories still maintained the features of the craft based industry described by Chapman [23] and bore a distinct similarity to many British firms of an earlier era described by Hannah,[24] and by Quail.[25] Although there was some element of 'grouping up', many maintained their own sales organisations, and considering the complexity of the product mix and the number of departments into which the chain stores were divided, this can be readily understood.

Scale and Scope

Courtaulds had a long history of large scale production. The firm was originally a single product (silk fabric) family-owned firm that late in the nineteenth century was suffering decline and falling profits as its major product, black mourning fabric, declined in popularity. Early in the twentieth century the introduction of professional management, trained chemists, and superior technology secured significant economies of scale in rayon production. Courtaulds developed as a leader in the manmade fibres industry. However, this position was protected by the purchase of the patents to produce rayon by the viscose process and strengthened by participation in international cartels.[26] Therefore, the thrust of

---

[23] Chapman (2002).

[24] 'The rationalization movement' in Hannah, *The rise of the corporate economy* (Methuen, London 1976), p. 29.

[25] Quail, 'Debates and Speculations The Proprietorial Theory of the Firm and its Consequences' *Journal of Industrial history* 3(1) (2000).

[26] See 'The new industries' in Wilson, *British business history, 1720–1994* (MUP Manchester & New York 1995), p. 97.

Chandler's tenet that the major firms developed as a result of economies of scale is only partly true in the case of Courtaulds.[27]

Steven Toms and John Wilson[28] challenge Chandler's implied conclusion that success or failure of his three types of capitalism rest on the economies of scale and scope available to entrepreneurs. In Courtaulds' case factors other than economies of scale and scope came into play, notably the 'cash rich' position of the firm following the wartime forced sale of the American Viscose Corporation and later the payment for the sale of Courtaulds' shares in ICI managed British Nylon Spinners. The firm, throughout its history, developed through the purchase of existing patents, technology and buying out its competitors, although it is only fair to note that there was considerable organic development at the same time and that the firm had a very capable research division of its own. However, again Chandler does not rank acquisition with economies of scale as reasons for the development of the large firms of the new industrial era. In practice, the amount of Courtaulds' yarn purchased from the firm's own yarn mills by captive knitting factories eventually became quite minimal, and what remained of any remaining loyalty to the up-stream producers was killed off by the demerger.

The advantage of optimum throughput in the chemicals processing plants, with their high fixed costs and low labour costs was abundantly clear, but this was not so true for the clothing factories in which the unit costs were much more aligned to the cost of labour, which rose and fell somewhat more closely in line with output. Courtaulds soon found that economies of scale in this labour intensive industry were at best very minimal. In general, in the making-up of garments, the ratio of one worker per machine meant the number of workers increased roughly in proportion to output; also on the knitting side, although knitters normally operated several machines at a time, the number of machines per knitter was unaffected by the size of the factory. The opportunity for economies of scale was also severely limited by the number of workers that could be recruited and employed at any site and the labour intensive nature of the plant and equipment used.

Turning to economies of scope, it is vital to consider the clear distinction between survival of the industry and survival of the firm. The industry is limited in its scope to knitting – its defining characteristic basic process – therefore by definition to the type of plant and equipment employed and the merchandise produced. In general, broadening the scope and range into other types of clothing production might improve the viability of a firm but would not improve the production of knitted goods. Unfortunately, in Courtaulds' case, as the downturn came there was nowhere for Courtaulds to go; the firm was already involved in

---

[27] Chandler (1994).
[28] Toms and Wilson, 'Scale, Scope and Accountability: Towards A New Paradigm of Business History' (*Business History October 2003*).

clothing manufacture in many forms, all of which were under price pressure and in decline, although on differing time scales. The hosiery and knitwear industry did have some shared technology with other branches of the clothing trade but Courtaulds could not allow its production sectors to set up in competition and cannibalise each other.

Wholesaling in Courtaulds' supply chain

Wholesalers were offering the clothing manufacturers smaller and smaller orders as time went by and the orders they did place were simply a nuisance and got in the way of the production of large orders for the multiple stores. The traditional supply chain extended from the manufacturers, via wholesalers, to the host of privately owned retailers spread across the towns and villages of the country. From the 1930s, these shops declined in popularity when faced with competition from the multiple retailers, such as M&S and Woolworths and in the next three decades the wholesale traders went into serious decline.

Courtaulds' purchase of much of the wholesaling capacity was made while the wholesalers were still functioning, but this capacity became a misfit in the group. These wholesalers were in competition with each other and the firms 'direct to retail' suppliers such as Wolsey, and therefore tended to drive down prices to the small retailers that they served. On the supply side captive wholesalers were given low priority by Courtaulds' own manufacturing units which were majoring on the multiple outlets. Ultimately, almost all were closed and their high-value sites were sold without serious damage being done to Courtaulds plc.

Globalisation and the supply chain

Around the time of the high point in the industry in the mid-1970s many people in the trade had a false optimism that there would always be a place for 'British goods'. Although Fröbel, Heinrichs and Kreye[29] were writing of the effects of globalisation on the German clothing industries, they provide a clear indication of the impact that low-cost imports were already having at that time. Their work moves the classic division of labour debate from the speeding up of work (by breaking it down into small elements) to moving whole industries to lower-cost emerging industrial nations, forming what they describe as 'the new division of labour'. As the main text has shown, this was not a German phenomenon. British firms and technicians were running factories in low-cost countries as early as 1971[30] using technology that was available on a worldwide market. In practice, British technical skill and management ability was not totally lost in the latter

---

[29] Fröbel, Heinrichs and Kreye (1980), p. 51.
[30] Chapman (2002), p. 276.

part of the twentieth century; rather it was used by UK importers (and the few remaining manufacturers) to exploit opportunities abroad. As a result, there was hope for corporate survival, if not home based manufacturing survival, where this route was taken.

Despite hard lobbying by the Knitting Industries' Federation, trade unions and others, the industry was never able to obtain strong government support in the form of import barriers or tariffs as it had in the interwar years. Had any government allowed unrestricted free trade, the effect would have benefited the purchasing public by reducing retail prices, but the politically unacceptable loss of UK jobs would have been heavy, rapid and localised, affecting especially women in large numbers in the East Midlands and the Borders of Scotland, where there was little alternative employment for the displaced workers. The Multi-Fibre Arrangement was little more than a means of delaying the run down of the industry and furthering the policy of free trade between nations. Successive UK governments were committed to the liberalisation of world trade and the development of export markets, the development of employment, the raising of living standards in third world countries and the lowering of retail prices in the UK. Governments were able to point to a shortage of labour in the industry, rather than the pressure of foreign imports as the main constraint on UK manufacturers.[31] Also, with a more gradual loss of jobs the generally high level of employment could be used to negate the argument that loss of textile jobs was a national tragedy when there was a thriving service industry, both private and state controlled, able to absorb large numbers of displaced workers.[32]

Although globalisation was viewed by many, including a good number of political activists, to be an ogre, there is little to suggest that anyone really objected to lower prices in the shops. Governments faced difficult choices. It would have set awkward precedents had they given anything other than relatively small amounts of financial support to the industry. Singleton,[33] in his study of the Lancashire spinning and weaving industries, takes the view that those industries were supported long after they were useful to the nation. In practice the decline of the hosiery and knitwear industry at the end of the twentieth and commencement of the twenty-first century occurred at a time of generally low unemployment and the benefits of falling prices were passed on to the retail customer. Import tariffs were perceived as raising the retail price of clothing in the UK.[34] Therefore the ability of the industry to fight for the continuation of

---

[31] Letter from The Department of Industry to MP Tom Boardman 28 August 1974, Pick private papers.
[32] Unemployment was generally low in the late 1990s despite a declining manufacturing sector.
[33] Singleton, *Lancashire on the Scrapheap* (OUP Oxford 1991).
[34] Silberston *The Multi-Fibre Arrangement and the UK Economy* HMSO 1984, p. 24.

quota and tariff barriers was weakened, not least because UK manufacturers, and particularly Courtaulds, were less able to lobby against low-cost imports since they had become part of the process about which they had earlier complained. Before 1974 there was little pressure to do anything else and to set up factories in the Far East whilst at the same time pressing for import controls would have been illogical.

In response to price pressures from the non-M&S chain stores, Courtaulds opened manufacturing units in Portugal and Morocco in the 1980s (at that time both relatively low-cost producers). These fuelled the development of competition in the UK high street to the detriment of M&S, its biggest customer.[35] The improving communications, transport and infrastructure in the low-cost economies of the Far East made low-cost sourcing a viable concept. Japan and Hong Kong fell victim to even lower cost competition from countries such as Bangladesh and Sri Lanka and this in turn increased retail price competition between the UK chain stores. But, for any British firm setting up in the Far East, there was no guarantee the Western World would not, under pressure from its own domestic manufacturers, renegotiate the MFA and limit supplies from the developing nations.[36] However, it eventually became more certain that the MFA would run its course and Courtaulds, with the agreement of M&S, made progress in the move off-shore, particularly to Sri Lanka. Within a fairly short time Courtaulds' offshore factories were producing to M&S standards and increasing quantities of this merchandise flowed into M&S stores.

The UK 'industrial cluster' in which Courtaulds operated suffered in line with the industry and its associated apparel industries. The knitting and sewing machine making industries had long been international suppliers and machines were easily available to those with the money to spend. Courtaulds Textiles plc also had few problems obtaining supplies of raw materials, often at falling prices, and the support services continued in business as long as they were viable or until overtaken by competition from foreign specialists.

Changing fashions

It is a popular opinion that the hosiery and knitwear industry declined totally as a result of imports from low-wage countries. Whilst this is undoubtedly largely true, changing fashions also had an impact and as has been noted elsewhere, in

---

[35] Considering the close relationship between Courtaulds and M&S it is inconceivable that M&S was not fully informed at all stages.

[36] Courtaulds could hardly protest because as an international firm it took garments and raw materials from abroad and after setting up factories in developing countries it would have been strange, to say the least, to demand tariff or quota protection for UK factories.

the 1960s the industry suffered from the downturn in demand for fully-fashioned stockings and fully-fashioned knitwear, and forced the subsequent smashing–up of capital equipment that was often still serviceable. Later, the general popularity of women's trousers adversely affected the sales of tights. However, with the exception of tights the UK manufacturing industry declined when the retail market was expanding.

It would also be unfair to attribute the demise of the industry to low-quality production and in the case of Courtaulds it would be manifestly untrue. There was no suggestion that failure was due to poor quality (by international standards), indeed, it fell to the UK firms to upgrade the production of their Far East subsidiaries to the standards required on the British high street. Ultimately, labour costs were the determining factor. Honeyman[37] writes of the Leeds tailoring industry that clung to a declining fashion for its survival with labour costs being the ultimate cause of decline. In contrast, the hosiery and knitwear industry declined while the demand for the product, apart from fine-gauge hosiery, still remained strong, but it did share with the Leeds industry the inability to counter low-cost imports.

The decline of the hosiery and knitwear industry was not a result of individual failings by a few firms. Michael Porter[38] in his 1990 work *The Competitive Advantage of Nations* recognises the role of the individual firm, but at the same time places the firm in a national context and explains the relative advantages and disadvantages faced in global trading. To be realistic, the industry had been uncompetitive in world terms for at least seventy years. The UK hosiery and knitwear industry was insecure and reliant on government support for much of the twentieth century. Heavy tariffs on imports, aimed mainly at the Japanese and German industries, were applied in the mid-1930s. In the late 1930s, the industry had the benefit of large military contacts and this was followed by war time direction of labour that substantially reduced the size of the industry without causing unemployment.

Technology

A salient issue in decline was the British hosiery and knitwear manufacturing industry's lack of any lead in technology. The industry used a wide range of knitting and making-up machinery, most of which was manufactured abroad and as new technology became available it was marketed worldwide.[39] Advanced

---

[37] Honeyman (2000).
[38] Porter (1990).
[39] Channon commenting on the cotton industry writes that… 'Overseas industrialization, especially in Asia, was often initiated by the development of indigenous textile industries ironically built up with Lancashire-made processing machinery. This led to

technology was not exclusive to Courtaulds or even to the UK hosiery and knitwear industry in general, but was available on a worldwide basis. Therefore, it was to the advantage of the UK firms to invest in production units abroad, where the technology was identical or very similar, but the cost of labour was much lower. There were cultural reasons why designers were successful close to the end-users in their home market where 'proximity and cultural similarity make for clearer communications'[40] but the economic advantage was with the low-cost producers.

Courtaulds and Marks & Spencer

Those who controlled the industry were often criticised for concentrating their efforts on the larger customers and were entreated 'not to put all their eggs in one basket'. In Courtaulds' case there was a widespread coverage of the available outlets although in the latter years the wholesale trade was largely abandoned. However, it is impossible to formulate any opinion on the fortunes of Courtaulds without at the same time considering the special relationship with M&S. The UK high street stores were the only sector of the trade that could place the large orders needed to sustain many of Courtaulds' larger clothing plants. M&S had a history of expansion going back to its foundation[41] and had plans to expand on a global scale with little to suggest that it would fail. Consequently, under Christopher Hogg, in an attempt to capitalise on this opportunity, Courtaulds aligned its fortunes with M&S in an unprecedented manner. Later Martin Taylor favoured a move into the designer brand trade but had this been instituted in the larger existing UK manufacturing plants chaos would have reigned.

From the 1980s the chain stores, including M&S, relied more and more on the manufacturers to provide ideas and designs for the merchandise needed in their shops, both in the UK and abroad. The stores' 'selectors' still retained the task of forecasting the colour ranges and themes that would be coordinated across their whole product offer. For the suppliers, design and development was a very expensive service and only the largest, such as Courtaulds, were able to provide this successfully in the manner demanded. Backed by the apparent security provided by the M&S connection and policy of encouraging home trade suppliers, Courtaulds developed its UK supply chain serving M&S and indirectly benefitting the whole range of other multiple suppliers.

---

intense competition, particularly in cotton textiles, which cost the British industry its lucrative overseas markets and caused recession in the domestic market. The more enterprising British companies moved overseas to obtain the cheap labor advantages enjoyed by competitors, ...' Channon (1984), p. 173.

[40] Porter (2000), pp. 86–87. See also 'Cluster groupings' in Chapter 8.
[41] Bevan (2001).

EPILOGUE

Unfortunately for Courtaulds' manufacturing base in the UK, problems at M&S in the late 1990s coincided with this increase in offshore sourcing and it was not possible to organise an orderly reduction in Courtaulds' UK manufacturing, much of which collapsed rather quickly. Plans for the gradual increase in offshore processing were thrown off course by the downturn on the high street and subsequent loss of profits.

Courtaulds Textiles plc had a broad multinational base of manufacturing units serving a wide range of mainly UK outlets. From this base it survived as an M&S supplier longer than most of the other large multi-product textile firms. It is an inescapable fact that the board policy to expand as part of the M&S supply chain had been very successful over a long period. Where there was a conflict of choice over matters such as investment, those parts of the group that supplied M&S were given preference.[42] This could easily be justified because M&S resisted large scale importing far longer than the other large chain stores. Courtaulds Textiles plc was able to benefit in the short term from the close relationship with M&S, which was developed even more after the demise of the competing Corah Ltd.

Ultimately, the bulk of the industry was unable to defend itself from the competition from low-cost countries which were gradually taking an expanding share of the UK market. The downturn in trade during the early 1990s resulted in a period of low profits, and during this time many firms were unable to invest in plant and machinery and this deficit was almost impossible to overcome.

Wells[43] as long ago as 1972 had warned of the dangers of a manufacturer becoming too dependent on one customer and being tied into its supply chain, but Courtaulds had no alternative customer for the volume of orders needed to support its production units.

With the benefit of hindsight, it can be argued that Courtaulds and M&S failed at an early stage to act on the certain knowledge that the UK industry was uncompetitive in world terms. M&S continued for too long to support British industry when an early and orderly transfer of manufacturing capacity to the Far East would still have been a realistic proposition.[44] While competitors failed around them in the 1990s, Courtaulds made a scramble to set up capacity overseas and incurred massive expense in a bid to retain at least some of the business.

---

[42] See 'Overall view of Courtaulds Textiles plc' in Chapter 8.

[43] Wells, *The British Hosiery and Knitwear Industry Its History and Organization* (David & Charles, Newton Abbot 1972), p. 192.

[44] Dr J. B. Smith in personal communication. 'I know from dealing with M&S in Baker Street when I was sales director of Meridian fabrics, that it was around 1988 before they realized the overwhelming price advantage of Far East and other low cost area fabrics, and of equal importance to M&S, that it could be of high quality.' 1 June 2003.

Management Education

Keeble[45] examines the often-presented accusation that Britain's poor economic performance, relative to other major industrial powers, can to some extent be attributed to poor management education. Her general emphasis is that British industry up to the early 1990s had not given enough weight to the recruitment and education of business and commercial general managers, as distinct from specialists; a generalisation that could hardly be applied to Courtaulds. The criticism that education and training within the industry was poor is valid. The training budgets in most firms were low and in many non-existent. The failure of the government sponsored Industrial Training Board highlights this issue. Clutterbuck and Crainer are also critical of educational standards throughout British industry,[46] indicting both management and the education system for this failing. However, taking the hosiery and knitwear industry as a whole there were thousands of workers that were limited by the machinery available, rather than by their lack of skill or education. As a moral issue it can be argued that employers and the state were wrong not to raise the standard of education, but it could equally be argued that better training and education would not have attracted workers into the industry unless accompanied by the possibility of more attractive work and higher wages, particularly during the 1960s when the shortage of workers was acute.

There have always been clever and innovative people in the clothing industries and the hosiery and knitwear trade has certainly had its share of these. But traditionally this was a 'trade' that was learned and followed down in the family. At the time Erickson wrote, no attempt had been made to develop a knitting enterprise vertically integrated into a supply chain running from the cotton field, pulp mill, or chemical plant to the final packaging of the finished product ready for distribution to the UK chain stores in the way Courtaulds attempted. Courtaulds tacked onto the highly technical chemicals industry the small scale garment enterprises typical of the clothing industries. In the process a highly educated supply of managers, mainly transferred from the research departments of the conglomerate, introduced a level of education not previously seen on such a broad scale in these industries.[47] To what purpose is not totally clear: the

---

[45] Keeble, *The ability to manage: A study of British management, 1890–1990* (MUP Manchester 1992).

[46] Clutterbuck and Crainer, *The Decline and Rise of British Industry* (W. H. Allen, London 1988), pp. 66–69.

[47] The technology of the trade was developed by machine builders, yarn suppliers including the chemical engineering firms (such as Courtaulds in the UK and DuPont in USA) and dye manufacturers. The hosiery and knitwear industry depended for its success on direct labour skills and design and marketing flair.

specific skills of scientists in a range of disciplines such as chemistry, chemical engineering, and mechanical and electrical engineering, whilst vital in the broader textile scene[48] were only *desirable* in the hosiery and knitwear industry. Although it must be recognised that intelligence is always necessary in the running of a successful business, flair for fashion, marketing and entrepreneurial skills are vital to success in the fast moving clothing trades.

Although Erickson does not qualify what she means by 'technical leadership', nor does she attempt to lay down the 'best' training for this craft based industry, this does not invalidate her conclusions that higher education did not feature prominently in the industry up to the 1950s. The Courtaulds situation from the 1960s differed enormously from the small-scale proprietorial industry before the 1950s. Its clothing and textile sector was part of a multi-product, international conglomerate that included the science-based chemicals plants, and therefore it is hardly surprising that there was a culture of higher education in the professional, technical and scientific staff at the top, and many people believed that the educated chain-store executives were much more comfortable dealing with people from their own culture than with the tradesmen of the previous eras.

Industrial relations and gender

The notion put forward by Honeyman, that low wages for females in the Leeds clothing industry removed the incentive or need for technical innovation by the management, does not easily equate with the ethos of the UK hosiery and knitwear industry.[49] In reality, there was nothing new in prospect in the form of advanced automation for garment assembly that was not freely available on a worldwide basis.[50] It is inconceivable that with a world market for technology, pressure to innovate would have been held back by the gender differential of wages in the UK East Midlands. It seems more likely that had faster machinery become available in the traditional areas of 'women's work', this would have led to reductions in unit costs with little if anything being passed on to the employees. In general, as new technology did became available its use was insisted upon by the multiple and chain store buyers, but the savings were eventually passed on to the customer in lower prices and were not retained by the manufacturers as profits, or the workers in improved pay.

There was a long history of unequal pay for men and women that persisted until the end of the twentieth century, and for the remnants of the industry

---

[48] Spinning, manmade fibres, dyeing and finishing and the engineering trades such as machine building.

[49] Honeyman (2000).

[50] The basic technology of the sewing machine and other garment assembly machines remained unchanged over many years.

beyond that. This gender divide was unfair and unjustified. However, with the tacit agreement of the union, the industry was able to exploit a supply of female workers that was prepared to work for wages that were low, relative to the earnings of men, and this pool of low-paid workers served to a limited extent to keep down the industry's selling prices, which was vital in international markets.

The priorities of the shop floor workers and the full time union representatives did not always coincide. Courtaulds was a leader in the introduction of improved terms and conditions and fringe benefits. The union fought long and hard on behalf of its members for a pension scheme for the shop floor workers but it was ironic that the long awaited introduction of a subsidised pension scheme, on the same terms as the staff, actually met with an extremely low take-up. The same also applied to the share option scheme.

Relations between Courtaulds and its employees were generally trouble-free. Strike action was rare and agreement was reached on most problems before any threat of strike action was made. KFAT and its predecessors were cooperative over the introduction of new plant and equipment, although there was always some pressure to gain the 'best deal' possible for the employees. Had there been successful resistance to the introduction of new technology the union's members would have become uncompetitive relative to non-union firms and the unions were well aware of that. The hosiery and knitwear union was quite aggressive in the 1960s and 70s but this aggression declined rapidly with the industry's decline after 1974.[51]

The hosiery and knitwear trade was always responsive to the demands of the customers. The workers developed an ability to change styles and to regain production speeds, often within a few hours. Many factories also improved flexibility by employing outworkers, part timers and evening shifts and using small satellite factories on making-up garments, but these employees were very vulnerable to short time working and in slack periods were usually the first to become redundant.

The industry employed a range of people with transferable skills such as accountants, clerical workers, designers, pattern cutters, quality control workers and purchasing staff and considerable numbers were able to gain employment in the new offshore sourcing sector and outside the industry. In decline the main burden fell on those who had industry-related skills such as knitters and the ageing group of female workers, many of whom had come to this country during immigration periods, but many who did find employment were forced to accept lower wages.

---

[51] Chapman (2002), pp. 203–4, appears to attribute this to an enlightened attitude taken by the Union.

Courtaulds Textiles plc loses its corporate identity

In the mid-1980s further strategic change occurred within the firm and in a major restructuring exercise the textiles and garment industries were separated from the chemicals and industrial products for organisational purposes. In 1990 the textiles and garment side was floated as a separate company, Courtaulds Textiles plc. The chemical and industrial side, Courtaulds plc, then sold off major sections of its business to other large firms such as Akzo Nobel and smaller parts to their existing managers, although there is no evidence that the actual motive for the demerger was the breakup of the company.

Following this demerger, the globalisation issue was the continuing problem of the decade for Courtaulds' UK based clothing factories. This resulted from improving productivity in the Far East, the developing transport links and worldwide information technology in an era of favourable exchange rates for UK importers. At the turn of the century Courtaulds Textiles plc, having abandoned most of its UK clothing manufacturing base in favour of overseas production, lost its corporate identity when it was taken over by Sara Lee Corporation, a major player in the consumer goods supply chain.

The fact that Courtaulds Textiles plc did not retain its corporate identity is a separate issue from the shrinkage of its manufacturing base in the UK. At the time that the firm passed into the control of Sara Lee Corporation in 2000, it was still the largest supplier to M&S (through its warehousing and distribution system) for many products from global sources. Market failure could not be cited as a reason for decline – apart from fine-gauge hosiery which had taken a downturn due to the ubiquitous fashion for women to wear trousers, the retail market remained healthy.

Courtaulds' advantage in terms of size and access to capital could not insulate its hosiery and knitwear businesses from the pressures that affected clothing manufacturing in the advanced economies of the Western World, including the members of the European Community. External pressures were the main reason for the overall demise of the industry, but it is within individual firms that reasons for differing rates of corporate decline can be found and Courtaulds Textiles only partly responded in a way that reflected the changed circumstances. Although it was early in supplying low-cost imports to the non-M&S retailers, it was held back by the M&S 'buy British' policy until it was too late to avoid being affected by the sudden downturn in the fortunes of M&S in 1999.

Kearton's acquisition policy almost certainly saved Courtaulds as a major fibres producer in the 1960s, but what had looked to be an inspired strategy turned out to be less successful than might reasonably have been expected. The movement downstream was an attempt to defend Courtaulds' position in the yarn fibres industry but in doing so the firm entered a fragmented set of industries each with its own subsections. Any improvement in the profitability of the hosiery and knitwear factories would have been highly welcome, but the main consideration in the early stages was maintaining the efficiency of the fibre plants. The consequences, had Kearton failed to act with speed, would have been a disaster. In all likelihood the independent spinners, via which the production from Courtaulds' fibre manufacturing units entered the supply chain, would have come under the control of competitors[52] which would have left Courtaulds' manufacturing plants very vulnerable.

By the end of the twentieth century Courtaulds' production in the UK had almost ceased and UK factories had no justifiable claim for capital which could be more usefully employed abroad. Educated staff and skilled workers were freely available in the emerging countries of the Far East. Raw materials were also freely available and the infrastructure, technology and transport facilities were all fully developed. Labour was in full supply, notably in China, and wages and many other costs were vastly cheaper. Finally, access to the coveted UK multiple retail supply chain was available through the importers, including Courtaulds' own warehouses and large former manufacturer Coats Viyella, which was in dire straits and heading for breakup.

It is worth considering what alternatives were available for Courtaulds Textiles plc which was heavily in debt. With the major knitwear competitor Viyella International no longer operating successfully the possibility of a merger within the industry was removed.

Selling the small amount of knitwear manufacturing capacity was an unlikely possibility with the supply chain wide open to foreign competition and Far East merchandise flooding in at alarming rates, whilst believing that failing competitors could be acquired and successfully turned round in double-quick time would have been bordering on the arrogant. Yet investors were always pressing for action and something had to happen and the Sara Lee takeover at least saved something for the Courtaulds Textiles plc shareholders.

The industry survived formidable problems throughout its history but ultimately the retail customers could not resist good quality imports at cheaper prices.

Perspectives

Decline of the UK hosiery and knitwear industry

Throughout its history the UK hosiery and knitwear industry was subject to the normal buffetings of indigenous and exogenous shocks and survived, but after the Second World War, under the General Agreement on Tariffs and Trade,

---

52   Possibly Viyella, ICI or the American firm Chemstrand. Coleman vol. 3, p. 275.

there was pressure to introduce an era of trade liberalisation which would allow developing countries to export their goods to the developed world. Sudden opening up of Western countries to cheap imports would have been disruptive and a series of measures was put in place designed to introduce a planned easing of imports into the developed nations, the most important of these was the Multi-Fibre Arrangement of 1974. After a series of adjustments and revisions to the detail of the agreement, from 1975 onwards the UK hosiery and knitwear industry was in decline. By the time the CTG 2000 report was published in 1986 it was increasingly clear that the MFA was running its course and that there would be no place in the developed world in a decade or so for firms that made non-niche clothing products on a massive scale for the UK chain stores and multiple outlets.[53]

By March 2000 Courtaulds' presence in the UK hosiery and knitwear industry was only a faint shadow of its former self. The Wolsey brand name had been sold in a 1996 management buyout, Rowley and all its branches had been closed and Meridian underwear had closed its remaining Bolsover factory, overwhelmed by cheap imports. The sock division was under intense price pressure and was importing cheap Turkish socks and Aristoc hosiery was importing large quantities of Italian tights.

In 1974 the UK industry had employed around 139,000 people and by 2000 this had shrunk to 24,000, continuing to fall at an alarming rate. Courtaulds' part of the industry suffered in a similar manner: in 1975 employment in the sector was about 18,000; this had reduced to about 400 in 2002 under Sara Lee ownership. A sad but inevitable end to a once important industry.

Corporate decline of Courtaulds Textiles plc

Following the Kearton period there had been a long period of low acquisition activity in UK clothing until the purchase of Corah Sock Division in 1988. Courtaulds was already totally aware of the dire prospects for the UK hosiery and knitwear industry. Not only had the CTG 2000 report set out the policy, the firm had also been active in lobbying for an extension of the MFA. Nevertheless there was an element of sense in acquiring the Corah Sock manufacturing capacity. The deal proved very successful because Courtaulds already had the necessary skills, sales and design organisation and vacant floor space to absorb this extra machinery and trade and there was sufficient time, if given the support of the customers, to introduce offshore produced socks.

However, there was a totally different operating strategy between Courtaulds and M&S and Courtaulds and its other customers. M&S, fearful that lower

---

[53] Under the Uruguay round of GATT negotiations 1991 it was finally agreed that the MFA would be phased out by 2005.

quality goods would slip in, demanded UK clothing on a large scale. BHS, Tesco and others accepted offshore production whilst M&S resisted as long as 1998, but Courtaulds was so committed to M&S that it had invested too heavily to support the retailer's UK supply chain, seriously damaging itself in the process.

The UK hosiery and knitwear industry made only a very small contribution to the demise of Courtaulds Textiles plc. With the ability to source cheap knitted goods on a global scale the firm was well placed to withdraw in an orderly fashion from UK manufacturing even as late as the mid 1990s. However, a series of events impacted about the same time and taken together were too damaging to overcome. The takeover of the Well business cost the firm heavily and the Claremont acquisition was particularly disastrous. Perhaps the firm might even have survived these problems had it not been for two problems outside the firm's control – the suddenness of the downturn in the fortunes of M&S and the depressed state of the stock market – which allowed Sara Lee to bid for the firm at a price that was much lower than its market value only a few months earlier.

APPENDICES

Appendix 1

The Mansfield Hosiery strike

The strike commenced on 3 October 1972. At the subsequent Department of Employment Enquiry,[1] criticism was levelled at all the main parties to the dispute; the workers, management, trade union officials and the company.

The committee of enquiry accepted that the policies of the firm regarding race issues were enlightened:

> Unfortunately the implementation of these policies appears to have been frustrated or at best delayed by what can only be described as a racialist attitude on the part of some of their white employees.[2]

> In the face of this resistance the Company has ... shown insufficient courage in declaring its policy.[3]

The firm's actions did not go unscathed. Referring to the introduction of a major change of working practice in the knitting department during the strike, the Committee wrote:

> Whatever the motives of the Company, this appears to have been a somewhat inept exercise in industrial relations which has occasioned resentment among the Asian workers and further obstructed a settlement.[4]

---

[1] Detail in the Report of a Committee of Inquiry into a dispute between employees of the Mansfield Hosiery Mills Limited and their employer HMSO 1972.
[2] Committee of Inquiry report, p. 14.
[3] Committee of Inquiry report, p. 15.
[4] Committee of Inquiry report, p. 15.

On balance, little criticism was levelled against the striking Asian workers. The chairman of the committee wrote:

> In my view the Asian workers were misguided in failing to pursue their claim through the established procedures within the industry for settling disputes and in spurning the assistance of their Union when it should have become clear to them that this assistance was being sincerely offered. However, it must be acknowledged that their failure to do this stemmed from a lack of understanding of the established procedures, a position which should have been remedied at an earlier stage.[5]

It was clear that the issue was mishandled and that correct procedures were not followed. Union members had made racist comments during the strike, and the Race Relations Board had indicated that the union had been in breach of the Race Relations Act. In addition, the management was unable to negotiate effectively with the union because the union did not represent a cohesive workforce.

---

[5] Committee of Inquiry report, p. 17.

Appendix 2

Trade organisations, Directories etc.

British Hosiery Manufacturers Association
British Textile Confederation
Clothing Export Council
Financial Analysis Group
Knitting Industries Federation
ICC Group
Leicester & County Chamber of Commerce
National Hosiery Manufacturers Federation
National Union of Hosiery and Knitwear Workers
National Hosiery Manufacturers Federation
The Nottingham & District Hosiery Manufacturers Association Ltd
Kellys Directory
Thomas Skinner

Sources and Bibliography

Historical Archives
Akzo Nobel (UK) Ltd Archive Department (private archive). For convenience this archive is referred to in the text as Courtaulds Archives.
Coats Viyella (private archive). These records are in the process of being catalogued. They contain records from Atkins of Hinckley, Byford and Driver, Corah Ltd, NMC (Djanogly Bros) Simpson, Wright & Lowe and Jaeger.
Leicestershire Records Office (public collection).
H.A.T.R.A. (Hosiery and Allied Trades Research Association).
T. W. Kempton.
The National Hosiery Manufacturers' Federation.
Benjamin Russell & Co.
Wolsey Ltd.
Nottinghamshire Records Office (public collection). An important collection of J. B. Lewis (Meridian) papers is held which is not relevant to the period of this thesis other than to place more recent research into context.
Nottingham University Library (public collection). A small collection of Pasold papers is held which is only relevant to the early part of the thesis.
Ruddington Framework Knitters' Museum (available by appointment). The most useful aspect of this specialist collection is its technical content. There is a wide range of official and trade publications.
Sara Lee Courtaulds Archives (private archive). This archive contains the most recent records of the clothing interests of the Courtaulds Group.

Papers in limited circulation
Dyer, C. (1992) *Knitwear's Goliath. Courtaulds Knitwear Business* Conference Notes.
Harte, N. (1973) *A History of George Brettle & Co. Ltd 1801–1964* Uni. College London.
Keast, M. J. (1978) *The History of Kayser Bondor 1928–78* Private publication.
Not Attributed (1947) *Rowley – 80 years* Private Publication.
Not Attributed (1986) *An update of Courtaulds' History from 1962* Private Publication.

Theses and dissertations
Eaglen, R., 'The Economic effects of recent technological change on the Hosiery Industry with special reference to Leicestershire', thesis (Leicester University, 1966).
Thompson, B., 'The Mansfield hosiery strike: a study of industrial relations', thesis (Leicester University 1973).

Rake, D. J., 'The Economic geography of the Multilocational Firm with special reference to the East Midlands', thesis (Nottingham University, 1973).

Video
Courtaulds Demerger Conference, 28 October 1989

Newspaper and journal articles

Business History
Chapman, S. D., 'Mergers and Takeovers in the Post-War textile Industry: The Experience of Hosiery and Knitwear', vols 30–2.
Chapman, S. D. 'International Competition and Strategic Response in the Textile Industries since 1870', vols 32–4.
Toms, S., Wilson, J., 'Scale, Scope and Accountability: Towards A New Paradigm of British Business History', October 2003.

Centre for Business Strategy
Baden-Fuller, C., Stopford, J. M., 'Competitive dynamics in mature industries: The case of the UK Knitwear Industry', 1989.

The Financial Times
Rawsthorne, A., 'Hosiery manufacturers try Europe on for size', 12 January 1990.

Journal of Industrial History
Quail, J., 'The Proprietorial Theory of the firm and its Consequences', vol. 3 (1), 2000.

Knitting International
Chapman, S. D., 'Marketing And Distribution: How Today's System Evolved', February 1989.
Chapman, S. D., 'In Conversation: Donald Anderson of Hoare Govett', July 1989.
Chapman, S. D., 'Whatever happened to the Family Firm', August 1987.
Corah, N., 'Cyril Hurd Lecture: Leadership in Industry', June 1985.
Gibbon, J., 'In conversation: Allan Nightingale', December 1990.
Jeannert, B., 'The presser foot concept', February 1982.
Jervis, N., 'Cyril Hurd Lecture: Textiles into the 21st century', June 1994.
Goadby, D., 'Fully-fashioned to seamless: Productivity and Fashion', February 1989.
Lewis, K., 'On leaving Courtaulds: Mike Batts talks to Kay Lewis', May 1987.
Millington, J., 'Aristoc: Analysis of a Hosiery Company', April 1991.
Millington, J., 'Do we face a labour shortage?', March 1982.
Millington, J., 'How Goliath tries to defeat David and how to avoid becoming a dinosaur', February 1989.
Millington, J., 'Why the current GATT rules must be updated', April 1988.
Millington, J., 'How the West was won – for another 5 years', September 1986.
Noskwith, R., 'Cyril Hurd Lecture: Survival in Hosiery and Knitwear', May 1997.
Taylor, M., 'Large textile companies – utility or futility?', December 1989.
Wallwork, S., 'From Domestic to Factory Industry: Hosiery Statistics and their Interpretation', February 1989.

Not attributed to a specific writer
'De-merged Courtaulds is launched together with new corporate identity', February 1985.
'Silberston: The main Conclusions. Government invites views on MFA Report. Rebuttal of findings by 'Triple Alliance'. Trade Policy Research Centre's MFA Critique Results of EEC Competitive Study', February 1985.
'Coats Viyella: Profile of a World Giant and the man who created this unique textiles and clothing group', February 1988.
'Courtaulds is changing', November 1989.
'How a sleeping Hosiery Beauty awoke to take its place on the high-tech market-led world stage of tomorrow', March 1987.
'NUHKW Conference: Survival problems for the UK tights industry', August 1977.
'The UK case for MFA: A reminder', September 1977.

Textile History
Chapman, S. D., 'I & R Morley: Colossus of the Hosiery Trade and Industry 1799–1965', vol. 28 (1).
Wallwork, S. C., 'A Review of the Statistics of the Growth of the British Hosiery Industry, 1844–1984', vol 22 (1).

Official reports

British Productivity Council
'Report of a visit undertaken to study productivity in the Italian stocking industry by a joint management/trade union team representative of the British hosiery industry, September 13 to 21, 1960' (British Productivity Council, 1961).

Department of Employment
'Report of a Committee of Inquiry Into a Dispute Between Employees of the Mansfield Hosiery Mills Limited, Loughborough and Their Employer' (H.M. Stationery Office, 1972).

Department of Trade and Industry
Silberston, Z. A., *The Multi-Fibre Arrangement and the UK Economy* (H.M. Stationery Office, 1984).
Silberston, Z. A. and Ledić, M., *The Future of the Multi-Fibre Arrangement: Implications for the UK Economy* (H.M. Stationery Office, 1989).

Hansard
House of Commons Multi-Fibre Arrangement Debate (1988).

HATRA
European knitting industries; their size, trade organisations and research facilities (1972).

Knitting Industries Federation
The British Industry; to live or let die? a programme of action (1980).

Leicestershire County Council
Directory of Asian and Afro-Caribbean Businesses (1990).
Ethnic Business Directory (1994).

Mailleurop
The European knitting industry and the M.F.A. ... beyond (1981).
The M.F.A. – vital necessity for the European Knitting Industry (1985).

Manpower Services Commission
The hosiery and knitwear industries in Leicestershire; Recruitment difficulties and skill shortages (1985).

Monopolies and Mergers Commission
Coats Viyella plc. and Tootal Group plc. Parliamentary papers (1989).
A report on the supply of man made cellulosic fibres (1968).

National Economic Development Office – Knitting sector
Financial league table and companies in order of ranking within industry sector (1967).
Progress report on manpower (1967).
Exports are booming (1969).
Exporting for profit; a guide to financial evaluation of exporting opportunities (1970).
Hosiery and Knitwear in the 1970s; a study of the industry's future prospects (1970).
Attainable production times in the making up of ladies' cardigans and jumpers (1971).
A Study of profitability in the hosiery and knitwear industry (1971).
Industrial report ... on the economic assessment to 1972 (1970).
NEDC industry strategy; knitting (1976).
Industrial strategy; Progress report (1978).
Industrial strategy; Progress report (1979).
Growth through exports (Export sub-group) (1979).
Progress report (1980).
Progress report (1981).
Opportunities in knitwear (1982).
The British Knitting Industry; prospects and profits in the 1980s (1983).
Proposals for Government assistance to the knitting industry (1983).
Higher productivity from existing resources (Johnson Hill) (1983).
Improving performance in the manufacture of F. F. Outerwear a HATRA survey of companies (1984).
Exporting knitted goods to the U. S. market (1984).
Spearhead USA; a practical guide to the US market for knitted goods (1984).
Selling knitted apparel to France and West Germany (1985).
Planning a profitable future; knitting sector map (1987).
Dynamic response; how retailers, manufacturers, spinners & dyers can improve their response to consumer demand (1987).
Export Target – Spain: Information and Strategic Framework for UK Clothing, Knitwear and Home Textile Companies Who Want to Develop an Export Market in Spain (1987).
The cost of Quality; a report on quality associated costs (1988).

SOURCES AND BIBLIOGRAPHY

Opportunities in boy's and men's knitwear. Manufacturer – Retailer panels (1988).
Spearhead Germany: Increasing Exports of UK Knitted Goods to the Federal Republic of Germany (1989).
Spearhead France; Exports of knitted goods (1990).
Opportunities in ladies knitwear, tops and blouses (1990).
A Study of profitability in the Hosiery and Knitwear Industry (1971).

Bibliography

Allen, E. P., *Background to Aristoc: an essay on the fine gauge full fashioned hosiery industry* (Aristoc, 1957).
Beaver, P., *Readson Limited 1932–82* (Melland: London, 1983).
Bevan, J., *The Rise and fall of Marks & Spencer* (Profile: London 2001).
Birley, S. (ed.), *European Entrepreneurship: Emerging Growth Companies* (EFER: Cranfield, 1989).
Boswell, J., *The Rise and Decline of Small Firms* (George Allen & Unwin: London, 1973).
Broadway, F., *State intervention in British Industry* (Kaye & Ward: London, 1969).
Buck, D., *More Ups than Downs* (Memoir Club: Spennymoor, 2001).
Cairncross, F., *Changing perceptions of Economic Policy* (Methuen: London, 1981).
Chandler, A. D., *Scale and Scope: the Dynamics of Industrial Capitalism* (Harvard, 1994).
Channon, D., *The Strategy and Structure of British Enterprise* (Harvard, 1973).
Chapman, S. D., *Hosiery and Knitwear: Four Centuries of Small-scale Industry in Britain c1589–2000* (Oxford UP, 2002).
Charkham, J., *Keeping Good Company* (Oxford UP, 1994).
Clutterbuck, D. and Crainer, S., *The Decline and Rise of British Industry* (W. H. Allen: London, 1988).
Coleman, D. C., *Courtaulds: An Economic and Social History; Vol. 1 The Nineteenth Century – Silk and Crape* (Clarendon Press: Oxford, 1969).
Coleman, D. C., *Courtaulds: An Economic and Social History; Vol. 2 Rayon* (Clarendon Press: Oxford, 1969).
Coleman, D. C., *Courtaulds: An Economic and Social History; Vol. 3 Crisis and Change 1940–1965* (Clarendon Press: Oxford, 1980).
Davis, W., *Merger Mania* (Constable: London, 1970).
Erickson, C., *British Industrialists: Steel and Hosiery 1850–1950* (CUP, 1959).
Felkin, W., *A History of the Machine-Wrought Hosiery and Lace Manufacturers* (Burt Franklin: New York, 1967).
Fröbel, F., Heinrichs, J., Kreye, O., *The new international division of labour* (CUP, 1980).
Gulvin, C., *The Scottish Hosiery and Knitwear Industry 1680–1980* (John Donald: Edinburgh, 1984).
Gurnham, R., *A History of the Trade Union Movement in the Hosiery and Knitwear Industry 1776–1976* (NUHKW, 1976).
Hague, D. and Wilkinson, G., *The IRC – An Experiment in Industrial Intervention* (George Allen & Unwin: London, 1983).
Hannah, L., *The Rise of the Corporate Economy* (Methuen: London 1976).
Honeyman, K., *Well Suited: A History of the Leeds Clothing Industry 1850–1990* (OUP: Oxford, 2000).
Jeremy, D., *A Business History of Britain 1900–1990s* (OUP, 1998).
Jones, G., *Renewing Unilever: Transformation and Tradition* (OUP: New York, 2005).
Jopp, K., *Corah of Leicester 1815–1965* (Newman Neame (Northern), 1965).

Keeble, S., *The Ability to Manage: A Study of British Management, 1890–1990* (Manchester UP, 1992).

Keesing, D. B., and Wolf, M., *Textile Quotas against Developing Countries* (Trade Policy Research Centre: London, 1980).

Knight, A., *Private Enterprise and Public Intervention: The Courtaulds Experience* (George Allen & Unwin: London, 1974).

Moore, J., *Rich and Rare: the story of Dawson International* (Henry Melland: London, 1986).

Morton, J., *Three generations in a Family Textile Firm* (Routledge: London, 1967).

Owen, G., *From Empire to Europe* (Harper Collins, 1999).

Owen, G., *The rise and fall of great companies: Courtaulds and the reshaping of the man-made fibres industry* (Oxford UP, 2010).

Pasold, E., *Ladybird Ladybird: A Story of Private Enterprise* (MUP, 1977).

Pickering, A. J., *The Cradle & Home of the Hosiery Trade* (Pickering: Hinckley, 1940).

Pool, A. and Llewellyn, G., *British Hosiery Industry: A Study in Competition: First Report* (Leicester UP, 1955).

Pool, A. and Llewellyn, G., *British Hosiery Industry: A Study in Competition: Second Report* (Leicester UP, 1957).

Pool, A. and Llewellyn, G., *British Hosiery Industry: A Study in Competition: Third Report* (Leicester UP, 1958).

Porter, M., *The Competitive Advantage of Nations* (The Free Press: New York, 1990).

Pick, J. B., *The Pick Knitwear Story 1856–1956* (J. Pick: Leicester, 1956).

Pick, J. B., *The Pick Knitwear Story: Book Two 1956–1991* (J. Pick: Leicester 1991).

Rees, G., *St Michael: A history of Marks & Spencer* (Weidenfeld & Nicolson: London, 1969).

Reichman, C., *Principles of Knitting Outerwear fabrics and Garments* (NKOA: New York, 1962).

Rose, S. A., *Limited livelihoods: Gender and class in Nineteenth Century Britain* (Routledge, 1992).

Sampson, A., *Company Man: Rise and Fall of Corporate Life* (Harper Collins, 1995).

Sanderson, M., *The Universities and British Industry, 1850–1970* (Routledge, 1972).

Singleton, J., *Lancashire on the Scrapheap* (OUP: Oxford, 1991).

Stanworth, P. and Giddens, A., *Elites and Power in British Society* (CUP, 1974).

Thomas, F. M., *I. & R. Morley: A record of a hundred years* (Chiswick Press: London, 1900).

Tse, K. K., *Marks & Spencer: the Anatomy of Britain's Most efficiently Managed Company* (Pergamon, 1985).

Ward-Jackson, C., *A History of Courtaulds* (Curwen: London, 1941).

Wells, F. A., *The British Hosiery Trade: Its History and Organization* (George Allen & Unwin: London, 1935).

Wells, F. A., *The British Hosiery and Knitwear Industry: Its History and Organisation* (Curwen: London, 1972).

Wells, F. A., *Hollins and Viyella: A Study in Business History* (David & Charles: Newton Abbot, 1968).

Westwood, S., *All Day, Every Day: Factory and Family in the Making of Women's Lives* (Pluto Press: London, 1984).

Wignall, H., *Knitting Technology* (NKOA: New York, 1968).

Wilson, J. F., *British business history, 1720–1994* (MUP: Manchester, 1995).

Wolf, M., Glismann, H., Pelzman, J. and Spinager, D., *Costs of Protecting Jobs in Textiles and Clothing* (Trade Policy Research Centre: London, 1984).

Wrigley, C., *British trade unions, 1945–1995* (MUP: Manchester, 1997).

Index

SUBJECTS

Advertising 46, 52, 86, 105, 146, 152, 222–224, 228, 249, 270

Capital intensive 30, 36, 116, 170, 238–239, 276, 283
Competitive advantage 161, 242, 244, 246, 252, 287
Consolidation 108, 126, 135, 149, 152–153, 223
Courtaulds Textile Group 2000 (CTG 2000) report 67, 169–170, 258, 264–265, 268
Culture 114–115, 117–118, 144, 151, 153, 167, 210, 225, 253, 268, 276–277, 280, 291

Decline (HK industry) 40–41, 176– 177, 179, 225–235, 241, 266, 286–287, 294–295
Demerger 168, 171, 257, 260–263, 266, 293
Development areas, special and assisted 22, 53, 123, 237–240
Devolution of authority 113,160, 163, 166–167, 263, 281
Direct to Retail 35, 49, 50, 65, 69, 93, 96, 104–105, 146, 150, 220, 222–223, 234, 247–249, 284
Diversification 12, 15, 25–26, 37, 112, 162, 277
Division of Labour 204, 244–245, 284

Economies of scale and scope 36–38, 160–162, 227, 241, 282–283
Education (General) 13, 204, 290–291
Education (Technical) 214–215, 290–291
Education (Operative training) 203–204, 245, 290
Education (Management) 209–216, 276–277, 290–291
EEC (Common Market) 30, 253
Employers' associations 184, 201–202, 207
Employment (Courtaulds) 179, 218–219, 295
Employment (Industry) 22, 40–41, 179–180, 242, 295
Ethnic minorities 178, 205, 297–298
Exports/Imports/markets (UK) 226–227, 230, 232–235
European expansion 267–268

Financial accounts 29, 31, 172, 264

Gender and differentials 11, 21–22, 112, 182–185, 188, 191–193, 207, 291–292
General Agreement on Tariffs & Trade (GATT) and MFA 24, 170, 243–244, 258, 275, 285–286, 294– 295
Geography 110, 162, 202, 237–238, 240–241, 250
Globalisation and offshore manufacturing 169–171, 176, 243, 246, 250, 253, 255, 284, 293

Human Resources 112, 167, 197, 201–202, 215–216

Industrial Reorganization Corporation (IRC) 30, 37–38, 164
Industrial Training Board (ITB) 204

Labour intensive 161, 171, 193, 241, 261, 283

Monopolies & Mergers 37, 106

Networks and clusters 250, 251, 255, 286
Northern Plan 30–31, 37

Payment by results (PBR) 184– 185, 188–196
Price comparison (including imports) 8, 143, 145, 155, 170, 220, 243–244, 246–247, 249, 285–286
Production (HK industry) 226–227, 229–230, 232–235

Salaries 202, 216, 222
Sewing machines 145, 193, 251, 286, 291
Strategy
 see Diversification
 see also High risk strategy in Tetley 12–15
Structure of Courtaulds (Corporate and organisation) 7, 33, 38–39, 108–109, 111–116, 156–157, 163, 165–168, 263, 277–280, 282
Structure of HK industry (Corporate and organisation) 24, 35, 39, 110, 174, 208, 241, 257, 276–277, 280
Supervision (Factory) 184, 202–203
Supply Chain 30–31, 34, 37, 65, 90, 116–117, 144, 162, 220–222, 247–248, 251–253, 255, 257, 267, 270, 273, 278–279, 284, 289–290, 294, 296

Takeover bid ICI 18, 25, 28– 29, 117, 159, 277–278
Takeover bid Sara Lee 271–272, 274, 294
Tariffs 13, 22–24, 176, 243, 275, 286
Technology 12, 19, 132, 144–145, 175, 193, 229, 251, 256, 258, 261, 270, 287–288
Trade Unions 174–182, 188–192, 195–197, 199–202, 205, 207, 216, 268, 285, 292

Vertical integration strategy 19, 32–33, 38, 112, 160, 163, 165, 167, 169, 210, 222, 255, 257–258, 275, 278, 290

Wage bargaining 196, 200, 202
Working benefits 10–11, 197, 292
Working conditions
 physical 177, 198–200, 205,
 outwork 177, 206–207
World War I 21, 57, 65
World War II 17, 23, 46, 52, 66, 69, 82, 184, 203, 287

PRODUCTS, PROCESSES, YARN & FIBRES

Acetate Filter Tips 26, 27, 36
Acrilan 2
Acrylic Fibre 6, 15, 19, 25, 26, 30, 165, 168
Alginate 15
Artificial Silk see Rayon 13, 22

Cashmere 96, 104, 135
Celon see nylon 33, 34, 48, 63, 70, 71, 82, 101, 117, 118, 123, 160, 210, 240, 279
Cotton 13, 17, 24, 30, 47, 279, 290
Courtelle 26–27, 29–31, 34, 51, 78, 83, 118, 134, 160
Courtolon 72
Crape 10, 12–13, 25

Dicel 26–27, 34
Dyeing & Finishing 14, 26, 68, 87, 93, 107, 140, 152, 163, 238, 242, 251, 254–255, 291

Enkalon 48

Fibro 34
Fibrolane 26–27
Filament 13, 30, 165

Leacryl 160
Lirelle 34
Lycra 118

Nylon 15, 17–19, 25–26, 28, 33, 47–48, 61–62, 71–72, 80, 82, 99, 117–118, 160, 165, 167, 276

Orlon 34, 78

INDEX

Packaging/Paper/Film/Cellophane/ Plastics 15, 25–26, 165, 168, 251, 254
Paint & Coatings 15, 26, 110, 165, 168–169, 171

Rayon 13–19, 22–23, 25–26, 28, 30–31, 33, 47, 78, 110, 156, 282
Silk 9–11, 13–15, 22–23, 46, 52, 78, 104, 260, 282
Specialist supplies etc 254
Staple 15, 17, 25, 27, 31, 165, 168

Terylene 28
Tricel 26–27, 34, 77
Tyre Cord/Yarn 15, 17, 25, 33

Vincel 34

PLACES & DISTRICTS

America (USA) 14, 16, 17, 25, 31, 46, 79, 81, 103, 112, 243, 246, 251, 257, 265, 268, 273, 275, 277, 280, 283, 290, 294
Australia 17, 25, 168, 215

Bangladesh 215, 247, 286
Bedfordshire 44, 53, 55, 119–121, 131
Belgium 81
Birmingham 64, 66, 238

Cambridgeshire 96
Canada 25, 107, 239
China (PRC) 170, 245–246, 253, 267–268, 294
Co. Durham 91
Coventry 13, 17, 32, 36, 201, 209–210

Czech Republic 251

Derby 68–69, 73, 93, 137–138, 140–141, 147–148, 151–153, 156
Derbyshire 2, 11, 18, 26–27, 33, 36, 44, 46–48, 53, 55–57, 59–60, 70–71, 79, 84, 87–88, 91, 94–96, 107, 120–128, 131–133, 139, 142, 144, 146–148, 150–152, 194, 198–199, 240, 251, 295

East Anglia 10–11, 242
East Midlands 19, 88, 135, 174, 242, 285, 291
Essex 9–13

Far East 164, 170, 192, 220, 243, 254–255, 258, 286–287, 289, 293–294
France 2, 9, 25, 257, 265, 267–268

Germany 25, 69, 81, 107, 176, 244, 251, 284, 287
Greece 170

Hertfordshire 4, 53, 55, 68, 78, 123, 198
Hong Kong 170, 215, 221, 243, 245, 247, 258, 286
Humberside 242

India 215, 267
Indonesia 170, 246
Isle of Man 44, 47–48, 119, 121, 137, 139
Italy 48, 119, 123, 125, 176, 227, 251, 254, 267, 295

Japan 22, 135, 176, 245, 251, 254, 286–287

Korea 170, 174, 243

Lancashire 11, 24, 30–31, 44, 53, 66, 110, 120–123, 142, 160, 176, 182, 196, 209, 238, 279, 285, 287
Leicester 19, 22, 45, 47, 51, 60–61, 64–68, 71–72, 84, 91, 93–94, 96–97, 99–100, 104–106, 127, 129, 132–134, 137, 142–143, 145–152, 154–156, 160, 174, 184, 187, 196, 198, 203, 205, 207–208, 214, 237–238, 242, 245, 251, 274
Leicestershire 44–45, 60, 62, 64, 68, 72, 88, 93–94, 100–101, 106, 121, 127, 130–132, 134–137, 141–142, 146–148, 188–189, 191, 206, 214, 238
Lincolnshire 17, 66, 93, 106, 137, 142–143, 238–239, 242
London 9, 12, 16, 19 55–57, 87, 91, 100, 104, 167, 210

Malaysia 170
Middle East 146
Morocco 143–144, 265, 270, 286

309

New Zealand 265
Norfolk 11
North Africa 220
Northern Ireland 17, 44, 50–51, 121, 123, 127, 131, 237, 239–242
Nottingham 19, 46, 49, 51, 61–62, 68, 75–76, 84, 86–88, 93–94, 121, 127, 131–132, 136–137, 140, 142, 145, 147, 150–152, 163, 174, 196, 198, 203, 208, 214–215, 225, 230, 238, 279
Nottinghamshire 19, 44–46, 49–51, 61–62, 68, 71, 73, 75–76, 86–88, 91, 93, 106, 117–118, 121–122, 127, 129–134, 136–138, 140, 150, 198, 238, 240, 267

Pakistan 215, 246
Philippines 136, 170, 265
Portugal 143–144, 170, 233, 242, 265, 286

Rutland 66, 238

Scandinavia 146
Scotland 19, 22, 68, 74–78, 82, 93, 98–99, 102–103, 106–107, 127, 129, 134–137, 141–142, 176, 232, 240, 242, 285
South Africa 25, 33
Spain 25, 170, 225, 267
Sri Lanka 143–146, 234, 246, 270, 274, 286
Suffolk 11
Sussex 56, 242
Sweden 244
Switzerland 244, 251

Taiwan 170, 243
Thailand 170, 246, 268
Turkey 144, 156, 170, 270, 295
Tyne & Wear 93, 107, 141, 144, 146

Wales 22, 66, 68, 78, 93, 107, 123, 141–142, 238, 240

Yorkshire 45, 47, 63, 66, 68, 71, 73, 124, 126–127, 131, 137–138, 141, 177, 192–193, 221, 238, 242, 287, 291

PEOPLE

Allen, A. E. 46
Allen, Ken 139
Anderson, Betty 189, 258
Archer, W. T. 37
Aspinall, Percy 46
Ault, F. V. 54

Barnes, Brenda, C. 274
Bernard, Dallas 29
Bignall, George 87
Blount, Freddy 69
Boyes-Watson, John 34, 75
Brettle (Family) 55–57
Brian, J. H. 274
Broughton, Royden 152
Browne, D. H. 12
Bywater, John 81, 82

Chambers, Paul, 28
Churchill, Winston 17
Cleland (Family) A. E., J. H., J. 82
Coast, H. J. 213
Colefax, Michael 80–82
Corah, Nathaniel 64
Courtauld (Family) 9–13, 15

Dale, Bill 213
Deacon, M. 248
Dyer, Colin
  and CTG 2000 report 169
  and trading conditions 269, 271

Eccles, John
  and management continuity 211–212
  and personal background 265

Foister, Charles, Maurice 71
Fry, John 190–191

Goodenday, David, John 78–82
Green, Martin 21
Greenbury, Richard 224, 270
Grew, John 117, 125, 210

Hanbury-Williams, John 17, 25, 28–29, 210
Hardwick, Benjamin 56
Harrison, Ian 167–168, 171
Harrison, John 200–201, 243, 247
Harvey, T. W. 100, 151–152, 154

310

Hayes, John 152, 154
Hogg, Christopher
  and corporate governance 168, 262
  and demerger 171, 260–262
  and M&S relationship 255, 288
  and management continuity 165
  and management structure 112, 165–166, 169, 257, 280
  and personal background 164, 211–212
Holbrooke, Bill 152
Hollenden, Lord 89
Hope Morley, G. 91
Hughes, Glyn 51

Jervis, Noel
  and CTG 2000 report 169
  and demerger 266
  and management strategy 160, 264–265

Jones, Roy 145

Kearton, Frank
  and in retrospect 156, 275–276
  and personal background 30, 276
  and personal control 115
Knight, Arthur
  and management strategy 281
  and personal background 159, 164, 276
  and vertical integration 38, 163, 165, 167, 278

Latham, Thomas 12
Lazell, H. G. 115
Lee, William 19, 21
Lewis, J. B. 84
Lissaman, Colin 149, 151
Lyle, W. 102

Mason, David 151–152
Matlock, J. 183, 188, 190–191, 195, 197
McIntyre, E. 176
McMeekin, B. 227–228
Michael, Nigel 153
Morley, (Family) John, Richard, Samuel 88–89
Morris, J. R. S. 130, 139

Nash-Smith, R. 197–198
Nettlefold, Frederick 12

Palfreyman, R. A. 61, 63, 149
Pasold, Eric 50–51
Perridge, Denis 149, 151
Prevezer (Family), Samuel, Sydney 69–70
Prew-Smith, Harry 95

Quail, John 278, 280, 282

Robertson, Leslie C. 98
Rowley, Robert, Thomas 96–98

Scott, W. 102
Scrimshaw, A. G. 105–106
Sharp, James 55
Sheppard, Mrs, Sidney 49
Sieff, Israel 80, 106, 224
Sieff, Marcus 258
Silberston, Z. A. 22, 243, 258, 285
Skinner, John 149
Slater, 115
Smart, J. N. 82
Smith, Oliver 116
Stern, C. H. 13
Stevenson, G. 221–222
Suddens, David 169
Swirles, D. 151–152

Taylor, J. E. 77
Taylor, Martin
  and international expansion 257
  and M&S relationship 257
  and management continuity 211
Tetley, Henry
  and high risk strategy 12–15
Thomas, E. B. 213
Toms, S. 283
Townsend, Matthew 19
Turton, M. R. 77
Twyford (Family), Harry, Helen, Henry, Lionel 56–58

Victoria, Queen 10, 13
Vincent, P. A. C. 74

Walker, Robert 96, 104
Ward, John, William (Family) 12, 55
Weinstock, A. 115
Wessel, R. L. 106
White, Keith 125

Williams, H. E. 47
Williams, J. H. 46
Willock, J. 213
Wilson, Alan Harries 25, 29
Wilson, Harold 37
Wilson, J. 282–283

BUSINESSES (EXTERNAL)

Adria 124, 228
Akzo-Nobel 16, 260, 293
Aldi 155
Alexander 135
Arcadia 271
Asda 124, 141, 255
Atkins 124

Baird 225
Barber & Nicholls 124
Bear Brand 124, 265, 267
Bellmans 102, 279
Bentley 48, 58, 70, 101, 252
Bentley Smith 265
Berkshire 124
Berlei 273
Blackburn 58
Boots 122, 125
Braemar 102
British Home Stores (BHS) 90–91, 141, 150, 155, 220, 258, 271, 296
British Nylon Spinners (BNS) 17–18, 26–29, 48, 71, 117, 283
Burberry 135
Burton, Montague 250, 271
Burton by Post 102
Byford 47, 97, 107, 150, 224, 235, 238

C&A 130, 258
Carrington & Dewhirst 31
Chamberlain-Nettlefold 12
Chambers, Wilson & Morley 87
Chanel 136
Charles Creed 102
Chilprufe 51
Christian Salveson 250
Coats Viyella 24, 67, 133, 181, 197, 200, 204, 206, 208, 214, 216, 225, 236, 241–242, 247, 250, 253, 279, 294

Combined English Mills 31
Cooper inc. 103–104
Corah N. 20, 40, 64–67, 71, 105–106, 155, 181, 190–191, 197–198, 202, 204, 214, 230, 236–238, 241–242, 289
Couture 124

Dawson 225
Debenhams 135, 271
Dewhirst 225, 253
Dim 267, 272
DMF 265
Driver H. L. 99–100
Dunnes 135, 141, 150
DuPont 2–3, 16–17, 28, 34, 118, 290

Elbeo 124
Empire Stores 102
English Sewing 31
Exel Logistics 250

Fine Fare 150
Fuller & Hambley 91

Gall & Co 150
Galeries Lafayette 274
Greenhalgh & Shaw 31

Hall & Sons 150
Harrods 104, 135, 274
Hartstone 267
Hayes J. J. 31
Haynes 273
Home Bros. 102
House of Fraser 134

ICI 15, 17–18, 26, 28–31, 33, 36, 117, 159, 276–277, 283, 294

Jenners 104
Jennings Hosiery 124

K Leigh 124
Kempton 128, 198, 204
Kingsley Forrester 151

L'Eggs 273
Ladybird 22, 50
Lancashire Cotton Corporation 110, 209

INDEX

Lewis J. B. 20, 71, 84, 86
Lewis's 130, 134–135
Littlewoods 58, 77, 122, 130, 134, 141, 150, 152, 155, 220
Lonati 48
Lucian 60–61
Luvisca 36

Mackinnon, S. 99
Mansfield Hosiery Mills 178, 297
Marks & Spencer (M&S)
  and confidence 75–76, 279
  and downturn 224–225, 269–271, 273, 289, 293
  and ethos 66, 140, 199, 220
  and pricing 155–156, 220
  and quality 71, 77, 155, 286, 295
  and relationships 61, 65–66, 70, 74–75, 95, 106, 128, 130, 132, 139–141, 154, 224–225, 253, 258–259, 270, 279, 286, 288–289
  and supply chain 34, 80, 143–144, 194, 230, 234, 267, 286, 296
  and yarn intake 33
Matalan 154, 270, 273
Melas 124
Mellor Bromley 58
Mensley 133
Mothercare 100, 130, 132, 135, 140, 142–143, 150–152, 154, 233, 271

Nottingham Manufacturing Co. (NMC) 36, 100, 124, 132, 192, 208, 225, 230, 256

Pasold 22, 42, 50–51
Penn Nyla 274
Peter Scott 102
Pex 97
Pick 23, 97, 285
Pinchin Johnson 110
Playtex 273
Pretty Polly 48, 124–125, 227–228, 256, 267, 274
Pringle 102

Sainsbury 125, 154, 159
Sara Lee 24, 146, 149, 156, 227, 253, 267, 271–274, 293–296

Scottish CWS 102
Shima 132
Simpson, Wright & Lowe 67, 236
Slane 265
Slater Walker 115
Smith W. H. 263

Taylor Woods 64, 107
Tesco 124, 141, 150, 155, 250, 255, 296
Texplant Corporation 102
Thiollier 265
Tibbett & Britten 250
Tootal 31
Treforest 265
Tudsbury 124

UDS 130

Vas Ferreira 143
Viyella 31, 224, 235, 294

Wildt Mellor Bromley 251, 254
Woolworths 62–63, 122, 130, 154, 284

Zodiac 64, 70

BUSINESSES (COURTAULDS)

Aristoc 33, 41, 44, 46–48, 63, 86, 110, 118–119, 121–123, 126, 137, 139, 198, 213, 220, 228, 240, 273, 295
American Viscose 14, 17, 283
Arber W. L. 46

Bairnswear 35–36, 41, 44, 49–51, 77, 83, 110, 126, 128–135, 157, 198, 213, 215, 217–218, 220, 229, 238
Ballito 33, 36, 41, 44, 46, 48, 52–55, 64, 119–122, 126–127, 130–131, 157, 210, 223, 229
Beasley 93, 100–101, 119, 121, 158
Beauvale 44, 48, 63, 111
Bell Nicholson & Lunt 63, 223
Berlei 273
Blount 33, 68–71, 119, 121, 123, 137, 139, 158, 213
Booton 45, 61–63, 111, 123, 152, 227
Boswell Brown 104–105

313

Bradbury Greatorex 63, 223, 248
Brettle 39, 42, 44, 55–59, 63, 69–71, 119–123, 137, 139, 147–150, 158, 210, 222, 240
British Celanese 17–18, 26, 36, 110, 117, 281
British Lego 26, 139
Broughton A. H. 45, 61–62
Buswell 61

Carnall J. F. 45, 61–62, 147–149, 152–153, 198
Christie 272, 274
Claremont Textiles 225, 270, 272, 296
Clarkes of Arnold 94
College Hosiery 44, 60–61, 67, 107, 147, 155, 158
Contour 33, 45, 48, 61–63, 119, 121, 147–149, 157, 211, 216, 227
Cook & Watts 45, 63–64, 121, 222–223, 248
Corah Sock Division 40, 45, 64, 66–67, 107, 110, 147–149, 155, 157, 219, 236, 257, 265, 270, 295

Derby & Midland Warp Knitting Co. 33, 68–71, 119, 209

Fine Spinners & Doublers 31, 110, 209
Foister, Clay & Ward (F,C&W) 34–35, 37, 41, 68, 71–75, 78, 102, 108, 110, 118–119, 126–129, 132, 134, 137–139, 147–150, 157, 210, 220, 232, 238
Full Fashioned Hosiery Co. Ltd. 78
Furzebrook Knitting 17, 117

Georges Rech 257, 265, 272, 274
Ginns, G. 45, 61–62, 147–149, 152–153, 198
Gossard 36, 273
Granby Garments 141

Hartwood Hosiery 44, 53, 121
Hendry & Spiers 68, 75–76, 95, 137, 158
Highfield Productions 68, 76–77, 126, 128, 134, 136, 158
Holt & Co. 63–64
Hosiery Services 45, 61–62

International Paint 110, 165, 168, 209
Irvine Knitters 68, 77–78, 126–128, 134–135, 158

John Hampden Press 92, 111

Kayser Bondor (KB) 4, 22, 33, 35, 41, 48, 68–69, 78–82, 110, 118–119, 121–123, 157, 198, 210, 215, 220, 223, 228, 240
Kilsyth Hosiery 68, 82–83, 126, 128, 158, 218–219

Lancashire Cotton Company 31
Lockley & Garner 45, 61–62, 101, 119
Luvisca 36
Lyle & Scott 41, 93, 102–107, 127,130, 134–137, 146, 158, 213, 217–219, 220, 229, 232, 240, 272, 274

Meridian 20, 35–36, 41, 48, 68, 71, 84–87, 121, 126–128, 130–145, 147–148, 150, 152–153, 157, 198, 213, 215, 217–218, 229, 231–232, 238, 240, 289, 295
Morley 20, 39, 41–42, 56, 58, 68, 71, 87–92, 119, 126–131, 137–138, 146, 158, 210, 229, 231–232, 240

Percy Taylor 93–94, 101, 119, 121, 158
Pinchin Johnson 110
Prew-Smith 75–76, 93–96, 137, 139–140, 144–145, 158, 213, 232

Queen of Scots 68, 74, 78, 102, 127–130, 134–135, 240

Reliance Hosiery 45, 66, 147–148, 154–155, 238
Rowley R. 20, 36, 46, 67, 71, 93, 96–100, 110, 127–128, 130–132, 134–135, 137, 139–140, 142–143, 145, 147, 157, 198, 204, 213, 217–218, 233, 239, 242, 248–249, 295

Samuel Courtauld & Co. 10–11, 265
Sellors 61–62, 119, 121
Skolnick 93, 100–101
Stewarton 93, 101–102, 127–128, 158

Theta Dyeworks 92, 146
Tor 44, 53

Walker R. 20, 96, 104,
Ward & Son 55
Well 265, 267–268, 272–273, 296
West Riding Hosiery 45, 63–64, 122
Wilkinson & Riddell 63, 223, 248
Wolsey 20, 37, 41, 61, 67, 71, 84, 93, 96–97, 102–107, 119, 127, 130–131, 134–140, 145–148, 150–157, 185, 204, 213, 215, 217–220, 223–224, 229, 231–232, 234–235, 240, 265, 273, 284, 295
Wovenair Ltd. 81

Yates A. S. 68, 72, 108, 127, 129, 133

Zorbit 272, 274